NORTH KOREA
AFTER KIM IL SUNG

NORTH KOREA AFTER KIM IL SUNG

Continuity or Change?

Edited by
THOMAS H. HENRIKSEN
and
JONGRYN MO

HOOVER INSTITUTION PRESS
Stanford University
Stanford, California

The Hoover Institution on War, Revolution and Peace, founded
at Stanford University in 1919 by President Herbert Hoover,
is an interdisciplinary research center for advanced study on
domestic and international affairs in the twentieth century.
The views expressed in its publications are entirely those of
the authors and do not necessarily reflect the views of the staff,
officers, or Board of Overseers of the Hoover Institution.

Hoover Institution Press Publication No. 438

Copyright © 1997 by the Board of Trustees of the
    Leland Stanford Junior University

First printing, 1997
04   03   02   01   00   99   98   9   8   7   6   5   4   3   2

Manufactured in the United States of America

The paper used in this publication meets the minimum requirements
of American National Standard for Information Sciences—Permanence
of Paper for Printed Library Materials, ANSI Z39.48–1984. ⊗

Library of Congress Cataloging-in-Publication Data

North Korea after Kim Il Sung : continuity or change? / edited by
Thomas H. Henriksen and Jongryn Mo.
        p.   cm.
  Includes bibliographical references and index.
  ISBN 0-8179-9462-9
  1. Korea (North)—Politics and government.   2. Korea (North)—
Economic conditions.   3. Korea (North)—Foreign relations.
I. Henriksen, Thomas H.   II. Mo, Jongryn, 1961–   .
DS935.5.N66   1997
951.9304'3—dc20   96-35055
                                                      CIP

Contents

Acknowledgments

This volume resulted from the conference "North Korea after Kim Il Sung," held at the Hoover Institution February 27–28, 1996. The conference was organized by Thomas H. Henriksen and Jongryn Mo as part of the Hoover Institution's Korean studies program. This program supports research, publications, conferences, and workshops, all of which aim to enhance exchanges of information and viewpoints about the Korean peninsula and its economic, political, and security relations to the Pacific region and the United States.

The Hoover Institution is appreciative of the generous financial support from the Korea Foundation for the Korean studies program. The conference and this volume represent a portion of the program's activities.

The editors wish to express their gratitude and thanks to Hoover Institution director John Raisian for his personal encouragement and administrative support for the Korean studies program and its activities. We also wish to express our thanks to Wendy Minkin and Charlene Moran for their assistance in coordinating the conference. For preparing the manuscript for publication, we are grateful to Kristin Gustavson and Charlene Moran.

Contributors

BYEONGGIL AHN is an assistant professor of political science at Michigan State University. His research interests include international conflicts, Korean politics, and formal modeling. He was a contributor to the recently published book *Rationality and Politics on the Korean Peninsula.* Ahn received a Ph.D. from the University of Rochester in 1994; his thesis was "Domestic Politics, Rational Actors, and Foreign Conflicts."

BRUCE BUENO DE MESQUITA is a senior fellow at the Hoover Institution. He specializes in international conflict and the study of policy decision making. He earned his Ph.D. in political science at the University of Michigan in 1971 and his bachelor's degree from Queens College of the City University of New York in 1967. He has been the recipient of the Karl Deutsch Award in International Relations and Peace Research, and he was elected to the American Academy of Arts and Sciences in 1992. Bueno de Mesquita is the author of *The War Trap, War and Reason* (with David Lalman), *European Community Decision Making* (with Frans Stokman), *Strategy and Personality in Coalition Politics,* and, most recently, *Red Flag over Hong Kong* (with David Newman and Alvin Rabushka).

HONG-TACK CHUN is a fellow with the Korea Development Institute in Seoul, Korea. He graduated from Seoul National University (B.A. in economics) and received his Ph.D. in economics at Cornell University (1985). Chun has written numerous articles and books on the North Korean economy. His books include *Foreign Direct Investment Laws of North Korea* (1995) and *Transformation of North Korean Economic System* (1996).

KRISTIN R. GUSTAVSON is a research assistant to Thomas Henriksen at the Hoover Institution. She received her B.A. in international relations and her M.A. in Russian and East European studies from Stanford University. She continues to pursue her studies in international affairs.

THOMAS H. HENRIKSEN is a senior fellow and associate director of the Hoover Institution. He has written and edited several books and numerous articles on revolution, international politics, and U.S. foreign policy. His most recent book, *One Korea? Challenges and Prospects for Reunification*, was edited with Kyongsoo Lho. His administrative responsibilities include developing Hoover's Korean studies program.

B. C. KOH is a professor of political science at the University of Illinois at Chicago. He has also taught at Louisiana State University–Baton Rouge, at Temple University in Japan, and at Seoul National University in Korea. He has written numerous articles and several books on East Asian affairs including, most recently, *Japan's Administrative Elite*. Koh holds an LL.B. degree from Seoul National University and M.P.A. and Ph.D. degrees from Cornell University.

JONGRYN MO is an assistant professor of international relations at Yonsei University in Seoul, Korea. He received his Ph.D. in political economics from Stanford University in 1992 and was a national fellow for 1995–96 at the Hoover Institution after leaving the University of Texas at Austin. Professor Mo is currently conducting research in the areas of international bargaining theory and the political economy of the Asia-Pacific region. His articles have appeared in *American Political Science Review*, *Journal of Conflict Resolution*, and *Comparative Political Studies*.

CHUNG-IN MOON is a professor of political science at Yonsei University. He has published seven books and more than eighty articles in scholarly journals and edited volumes. His most recent book is *Arms Control on the Korean Peninsula: International Penetrations, Regional Dynamics and Domestic Structure* (Yonsei University Press, 1996).

MARCUS NOLAND was educated at Swarthmore College (B.A.) and the Johns Hopkins University (Ph.D.). He is currently a senior fellow at the Institute for International Economics and a visiting associate professor at the Johns Hopkins University. Noland is the coauthor (with Bela Belassa) of *Japan in the World Economy*, the author of *Pacific Basin Developing Countries: Prospects for the Future*, coeditor (with C. Fred Bergsten) of *Pacific Dynamism and the International Economic System*, and coauthor (with Bergsten) of *Reconcilable Differences? Resolving United States-Japan Economic Conflict*. He has served as a consultant to the World Bank, the New York Stock Exchange, and the Advisory Committee on Trade Policy and Negotiations.

JINMIN LEE-RUDOLPH graduated from the Massachusetts Institute of Technology with a bachelor's degree in economics and a minor in political science. She holds a juris doctorate from Northwestern University School of Law.

HENRY SOKOLSKI is the executive director of the Nonproliferation Policy Education Center. He also teaches graduate school courses on strategic weapons proliferation at Boston University's Institute of World Politics in Washington, D.C., and is currently completing a book on proliferation, *Armageddon's Shadow*. His work has appeared in the *Wall Street Journal*, the *Christian Science Monitor*, the *Washington Post*, *Orbis*, *Comparative Strategy*, the *Washington Quarterly*, *International Defense Review*, and the *Annals of the Academy of Political and Social Science*.

HIDESHI TAKESADA received his degree from Keio University Graduate School (Tokyo). He entered the National Defense College (the National Institute for Defense Studies) in 1975 and completed a Korean-language program at Yonsei University (Seoul). He has been a visiting scholar at Stanford University and George Washington University and a visiting professor at Chung-Ang University (Seoul). He was coauthor of *International Politics in the Cold War Era* (Tokyo, 1987). He has also contributed many articles to the *Journal of National Defense* (Tokyo), *Revue Diplomatique* (Tokyo), and the *Korean Journal of Defense Analysis* (Seoul).

Introduction

THOMAS H. HENRIKSEN and JONGRYN MO

Ever since the partition of the Korean peninsula following World War II, the Democratic People's Republic of Korea (DPRK) has been a country sealed off from the rest of the world. Its totalitarian regime continues to prevent communication and access north of the demilitarized zone (DMZ). North Korea still considers South Korea the main enemy of its orthodox socialism; even in the face of its economic decline and current food crisis, Pyongyang remains reluctant to accept economic assistance from Seoul.

So far North Korea has escaped a host of calamities that have engulfed similar regimes. At home, the government survived the death of Kim Il Sung, the Great Leader, whose mythical figure still pervades every corner of the society. In his place stands Kim Jong Il, who lacks his father's charismatic presence and solid standing in the military and Korean Workers' Party (KWP). Abroad, the DPRK suffered even more momentous buffetings.

Having survived the breakdown of communist regimes and the formation of new democracies in Eastern Europe in the early 1990s, the DPRK has remained largely immune from the economic reforms taking place in Russia, Eastern Europe, and nearby China. Yet the post-Soviet world imposes severe strains on the Stalinesque regime in Pyongyang. Without the Soviet Union, North Korea is virtually isolated in its international relations. The economic liberalization among North Korea's former communist trading partners has exacerbated the North's existing economic crisis because those countries now demand hard currency in exchange for their exports to the DPRK.

Pyongyang has several options for reforming and/or opening the North Korean economy to prolong the regime's existence while avoiding popular unrest over a threatened famine. Still, it will be difficult for the regime to resolve its catch-22 predicament: economic reform is necessary to avoid potential collapse, but the political and ideological concessions necessary for economic reform are likely to threaten the regime's internal security as well as its ideological and political hold over the people. The events in Eastern Europe and Gorbachev's Soviet Union constitute graphic examples of the consequence of relaxing political control—an end to Leninist rule.

South Korea, predictably nervous about a potential collapse in Pyongyang, is considering policy options that will protect itself from, or at least lessen the effects of, the volatile situation developing in the North. The South is also concerned with maintaining security on the peninsula in view of the North's continuing military buildup, warlike statements, and reported nuclear weapons capability.

The North's nuclear capacity compounds the stability problem and greatly strengthens Pyongyang's bargaining position with South Korea and the United States. Seoul, in turn, fears that the gradually improving relations between Pyongyang and Washington may cause its own exclusive relationship with the United States to decline in importance. Washington's relations with North and South must take into account both the residue of the cold war in the peninsula's division and the post–cold war realities. Among these new developments are the burgeoning economic and military power of China, the growing ambivalence of Japan in its relations with the United States versus those with Asia, and the possible reunification of North and South Korea.

These issues and policy considerations were discussed at the Hoover Institution's February 27–28, 1996, conference entitled "North Korea after Kim Il Sung: Continuity or Change?" which was built around papers prepared by South Korean, American, and Japanese scholars. Addressing the question posed by the conference, experts debated the state of change or continuity in the post–Kim Il Sung regime north of the DMZ. They discussed North Korean politics, economic issues, trade, military affairs, and inter-Korean relations, as well as Washington's options for dealing with the two Koreas.

University of Illinois professor B. C. Koh began the discussion with his paper, "Recent Political Developments in North Korea." He noted that Kim Jong Il is the de facto leader of the regime but his positions remain the same as when Kim Il Sung's health was declining. That Kim Jong Il still has not formally assumed the top two posts (president and general secretary) held by his late father may be explained by the symbolic role Kim Il Sung continues to play in the regime. The small number of Kim Jong Il's public appearances does not necessarily indicate that his power base is fragile; he may dislike or lack talent for public speaking.

Koh maintains that although Kim Jong Il is in charge, the military may now have greater influence in policy making than during the leadership of Kim Il Sung. Military power may thus be increasing at the expense of political power, at least in the cases of the KWP Central Committee and the DPRK Supreme People's Assembly, which have not met formally since the death of Kim Il Sung in July 1994.

The North Korean leadership is aware that its citizens are becoming increasingly alienated, according to Koh. The regime continues to exhort its people through propaganda and coercion in an attempt to increase productivity. Because Pyongyang is economically and politically unable to offer the people material incentives for greater efforts, its only recourse seems to be an "intensification of ideological indoctrination." This policy, however, will become less and less effective, or even counterproductive, as the economic situation worsens.

Hoover Institution senior fellow Bruce Bueno de Mesquita and national fellow Jongryn Mo offer another view in their paper, "North Korea under Kim Jong Il: Prospects for Economic Reform and Political Stability." They suggest that Pyongyang may be able to improve its economy with low-scale reforms, such as relaxing central planning in order to offer more incentives for competition and increased production.

Policy preferences differ among North Korean political actors due to their conflicting organizational interests and varying capacities of leverage. Bueno de Mesquita and Mo use a model to predict North Korean economic reform and trade liberalization policy outcomes based on the potential power and policy preferences of each actor in the North Korean leadership (Kim Jong Il, his family and second-generation leadership, the military, the partisans, ideologues, and heavy industry) as well as the importance of each issue to each actor. The model predicts a lengthy debate over reform, resulting in wide policy swings and political instability. The policy outcome will likely involve no economic restructuring because the military, partisans, ideologues, and heavy industry have the leverage to prevent it. The North Korean economy will open slightly but not enough to permit normal trade with the South.

Bureaucratic conflict apparently exists even within the North Korean military, making it difficult to guess what the military's role would be in a regime crisis; Mo and Bueno de Mesquita predict that such a crisis in Pyongyang would lead to a struggle between the army and the security apparatus, similar to the conflict that ensued in Bulgaria.

Marcus Noland, a scholar from the Institute for International Economics, presented a paper, "Implications of North Korean External Economic Reform," that provides a great deal of useful background information about North Korean trade patterns.

According to Noland, North Korea's attempts to apply bandages to its economy since the mid-1980s have had little if any success. The joint venture law of

1984, probably inspired by China's similar law, did not result in greater foreign investment. The 1991 creation of a special economic zone (SEZ), which legalized foreign business in North Korea, has helped increase Pyongyang's supply of foreign exchange but has produced little additional foreign investment. As Noland points out, SEZs have failed in most countries to integrate imported technology into an economy, especially in countries such as North Korea, where the regime prefers that the SEZ remain isolated.

Noland argues that North Korea cannot follow the example of the gradual, agricultural-led reforms that took place in China and Vietnam because those countries were less industrialized and more agriculture based than North Korea. Noland's suggestions for improving the North Korean economy are similar to those of Mo and Bueno de Mesquita; they include price reforms, debureaucratization of agriculture, reform of the planning mechanism to rely more on the market for decision making and competition, and the development of functioning capital markets.

External support will be needed for the reforms to succeed. Noland suggests encouraging South Korean investment, pressing Japan to send North Korea its payment of postcolonial compensation similar to the funds South Korea received in 1965, and approaching international development banks. With this assistance and North Korea's considerable inherent potential for growth, Noland predicts that Pyongyang's national income could increase by as much as 40 to 50 percent.

Noland sees several steep obstacles to reform, however. The first obstacle is the sheer magnitude of change needed to reform the North Korean economy, one of the most distorted in the world. Next is the need for resources to ease the transition in the heavy industrial sector. Third, South Korea represents a huge ideological challenge for the North. Thus, reform could undermine Pyongyang's raison d'être. Finally, the military may oppose reforms, which could complicate North Korea's external security.

The first section of Hong-Tack Chun's paper, "Economic Conditions in North Korea and Prospects for Reform," examines the structural nature of the food, energy, and foreign exchange shortages in North Korea. To solve the food problem, Chun, an expert from the Korea Development Institute, suggests normalizing the supply of fertilizer and other agricultural inputs and transitioning from collective farming to family farming. In the short run, however, Pyongyang will be forced to continue importing grain to offset the annual shortages. Chun indicates that the energy shortage has resulted from decreased production of coal, North Korea's most important energy source, due to obsolete coal-mining technology. This is a typical problem of centrally planned economies in which "bottlenecks in coal mining, transportation and steel production interact to form vicious cycles." Pyongyang faces another vicious cycle due to its foreign exchange shortage: exports must be increased to obtain more foreign exchange for external trade, but North Korea has only a limited capacity to manufacture goods that can compete in the international market.

Chun suggests that agricultural reforms will build a foundation for economic recovery in North Korea. Further reforms should include the promotion of exports and foreign investment, liberalization of the distribution and service sectors, small-scale privatization, onetime price and gradual trade reforms, and gradual state enterprise reform.

According to Chun, North Korea's economy is ahead of the prereform Chinese economy in terms of industrialization but is not as advanced as the prereform East European economies. Because of its foreign currency shortage, North Korea faces a much worse macroeconomic situation than did prereform China and Eastern Europe. Chun believes that Pyongyang is stable at present but that economic reform will not be as successful in North Korea as it was in China because Pyongyang is less willing to open its economy and accept foreign assistance. Moreover, major reforms in North Korea would mean criticizing or rejecting the ideology and personality cult of Kim Il Sung, on which the regime's legitimacy is based. Thus, reform is likely to lead to instability for North Korea.

Byeonggil Ahn's paper, "Constraints and Objectives of North Korean Foreign Policy: A Rational Actor Analysis," sets up a theoretical foreign policy framework for North Korea with economic and security concerns as constraints on and determinants of North Korea's "consistent and goal-oriented" foreign policy. A Michigan State University professor, Ahn agrees with Mo and Bueno de Mesquita that there are at least two factions in North Korean domestic politics: the hard-liners and the reformers. This view is demonstrated by the fact that North Korea received food assistance despite the military's hard-line view that food aid would have dubious positive effects and might adversely affect domestic politics in North Korea by invalidating its ideology. In this case, economic concerns proved to be more important to the regime than ideological considerations. Other similar departures from the regime's traditional policy of *juche*, or self-reliance, include the encouragement of foreign investment and the creation of the SEZ, which resulted from the downgraded role of ideology in North Korean foreign policy since the end of the cold war.

According to Ahn, hard-liners in North Korea must continue to allow the reformers to influence external negotiations toward making security concessions in exchange for economic aid, so that the regime may continue to avoid collapse. Ahn believes that the reformers will eventually win their struggle, especially if the economy continues to disintegrate.

In his paper, "The North Korean Military Threat under Kim Jong Il," Hideshi Takesada discusses the North Korean military buildup and its implications for Japan. Despite the improvement in U.S.-DPRK relations, Kim Jong Il strengthened the military in 1995 by increasing its personnel and weapons arsenal and reinforcing the DMZ. According to Takesada, a scholar from the National Institute of Defense Studies in Tokyo, nuclear weapons and missiles are attractive to North Korea for the following reasons: they can be exported to the Middle East in exchange for hard currency, they will contribute both to North Korea's ability to compete militarily with the South and to the North's military independence from China and Russia, they will enable North Korea to cut military expenditures, they will strengthen the regime's power base and credibility, and they will strengthen Pyongyang's bargaining position vis-à-vis Washington, Tokyo, and Seoul.

Japan is concerned about the possibility of military confrontation in the Korean peninsula in view of North Korea's growing military posture. Takesada believes that, at present, Japan cannot count on receiving the same military support from the United States that it did during the cold war. In fact, Washington now seems more concerned about China and Russia than North Korea. Japan, in contrast, feels a greater threat from Pyongyang than from Beijing or Moscow because North Korea seems more likely than China or Russia to attack Japan.

The next three papers discuss Korean-U.S. relations, possible resolutions of the North Korean problem, and South Korea's policy options for dealing with the North. Jongryn Mo, in his paper, "Security and Economic Linkages in the Inter-Korean Relationship," uses a two-level game model from international bargaining theory to explain how security concerns affect trade negotiations and which conditions are necessary for one side to get concessions from the other. Assuming that North Korea does open its economy to trade with South Korea, there are four possible combinations of economic and security conditions on the Korean peninsula: (1) economic advantage for the South and security advantage for the North, (2) no economic advantage for the South and security advantage for the North, (3) economic advantage for the South and no security advantage for the North, and (4) no economic advantage for the South and no security advantage for the North. In turn, in each of those four scenarios three outcomes are possible: economic warfare, permissive trade, and linkage between economic aid and security.

In the first scenario, according to Mo, linkage is possible because the South Korean military, with its security disadvantage, will be less compromising than the North Korean military. Permissive trade is the most likely outcome for scenarios two and four; in the third scenario, deadlock will result in continued economic warfare. For South Korea the most favorable outcome is linkage, represented by the first scenario; therefore, the South needs to maintain its economic advantage and emphasize its security disadvantage. One way to do this might be to reduce Pyongyang's outside trade options by discouraging the United States and Japan from increasing their trade with the North. South Korea can also encourage its businesses to favor trade with China and Vietnam over North Korea. Mo suggests that the model of linkage used by East and West Germany could be used successfully in inter-Korean relations.

Henry Sokolski's paper, "The Korean Nuclear Understanding: Three Alternative Futures," analyzes policy options for the United States and South Korea for negotiating nuclear issues with the North. Representing the Non-Proliferation Policy Education Center, Sokolski sees the Agreed Framework as a vague document whose terms are neither defined nor legally binding. Seoul and Washington, depending on their overall strategic aims with regard to Pyongyang, may choose between three policy options for implementation of the Agreed Framework (AF): (1) supporting the regime in Pyongyang by assisting with gradual reform and implementing the AF as is currently being done, (2) buying time by not helping North Korea but also acting to avoid its collapse, using the time to prepare the South for peaceful reunification, or (3) isolating and punishing the North in order to precipitate its decline.

According to Sokolski, AF supporters see no need for change in the Agreed Framework and thus prefer the first policy option because they believe North Korean nuclear activity and lack of dialogue with the South are temporary problems. They feel that more can be learned about North Korea's activities with the framework agreement in place than without it. The AF requirement for the United States to reach a nuclear agreement with North Korea will prevent Washington from losing the billions of dollars it has invested in the North Korean reactor project and will keep Pyongyang from resuming nuclear production.

So far the United States and South Korea have only considered the first option, but Sokolski indicates that the second and third options are also worth investigating because their outcomes are at least as likely. He sees the third option as reasonable because the North is unlikely to reform itself, and Washington and Seoul can always terminate the AF if Pyongyang violates its terms. For the second policy option to be successful, South Korea must prevent the North from manipulating the AF to its advantage; to do this, Seoul must make sure that Washington declines to offer goods of any kind to Pyongyang. Also, the South should offer to complete the North Korean reactor project in place of the United States in view of the legal obstacles to U.S. cooperation. The bilateral agreement for U.S.–North Korean nuclear cooperation required by the Agreed Framework must be in place before the United States can export nuclear power reactor parts. But it is impossible to complete such an agreement without the approval of the U.S. president and Congress, which is unlikely because of North Korea's refusal to allow inspections by the International Atomic Energy Agency (IAEA). In turn, Pyongyang's violation of IAEA standards, according to the U.S. Atomic Energy Act, prohibits the United States from exporting nuclear materials or technology to North Korea. Furthermore, nuclear cooperative agreements so far have only been achieved with governments formally recognized by the United States, and it seems unlikely that North Korea could receive full diplomatic recognition in view of its violations of IAEA standards.

According to Professor Chung-in Moon of Yonsei University in his paper, "The North Korean Problem and the Role of South Korea," there is little South Korea can do to prevent a possible "big bang" or sudden internal collapse and chaos from occurring in North Korea, other than to attempt to alleviate conditions in the North that could lead to such an outbreak. In Moon's view, South Korea sees reunification as inevitable, and to that end it must prepare for the high economic costs of accommodating refugees and integrating them into the South Korean sociopolitical entity. In the interim, continual free riding and spoilership behavior by Pyongyang could result in negative domestic political consequences for South Korea, as well as increased mutual distrust between the two Koreas.

Seoul is afraid that it will be isolated as a result of the improving relationship between Pyongyang and Washington and that it will be left in a vulnerable position if the armistice is replaced by a new peace treaty that brings about the withdrawal of U.S. military forces from South Korea. Such a departure would leave a power vacuum on the Korean peninsula and leave Pyongyang free to attack without fear of U.S. reprisals. Moon lists three options for South Korea for dealing with the North: accommodation of the eventual peace treaty between the United States and North Korea, linkage of such a peace treaty to inter-Korean conflict management, and continuation of the status quo strategy. According to Moon, accommodation is unacceptable to South Korea because the North cannot be trusted. A linkage policy would be ideal, but it would be difficult to satisfy the minimal conditions for its success, including Pyongyang's willingness to participate, continued security on the peninsula despite the probable withdrawal of U.S. forces from South Korea, and broad South Korean support for a linkage policy. Seoul has always favored maintaining the status quo, insisting that inter-Korean relations must improve before any negotiations can take place regarding withdrawal of the U.S. military. Moon argues, however, that the status quo strategy will only lead to a stalemate and later to a probable big bang scenario that will entail huge costs and consequences for the South.

Moon suggests a more desirable fourth option for South Korea, which he calls a "strategic offensive initiative," a departure from its previous policy. This endeavor calls, first, for Seoul to prevent Pyongyang from linking a U.S.-DPRK peace treaty with diplomatic normalization. Then, with the cooperation of the United States and the United Nations, Moon envisions an end to the problematic armistice. The armistice has led to a stalemate between the two Koreas because the South was not a signatory to the armistice and the North treats it merely as an armed truce. For the strategic offensive to work, several conditions must be satisfied. Article V of the Basic Agreement (which states that the armistice treaty will stand until there is peace on the peninsula) needs to be amended in order to resolve its conflict with the strategic offensive. Pyongyang also must be willing to participate in negotiations despite the continued presence of the U.S. military. Finally, South Korea needs to convince its own domestic political opposition (likely to be high, according to Moon) that a strategic offensive policy will neither accommodate the North nor perpetuate the division between North and South.

The final two papers were added after the conference. Kristin R. Gustavson, a graduate of Stanford University's master's program in Russian and East European studies, and Jinmin Lee-Rudolph, a graduate of Northwestern University Law School, submitted a paper, "Political and Economic Human Rights Violations in North Korea." Their paper lays out a theoretical framework to define human rights as the rights necessary for human dignity and then applies this framework to the United Nations Universal Declaration of Human Rights to present a modern world view of human rights.

According to Gustavson and Lee-Rudolph, North Korea has long been recognized as one of the world's primary human rights violators. The North Korean government claims that its constitutional provisions protect its citizens' legal, civil, political, and economic rights, but these laws are rarely observed in practice. The regime apparently sees human rights not as fundamental universal rights but as "citizen's rights" that apply only to the regime's loyal followers. Thus, people in the "wavering" and "hostile" classes in North Korea have virtually no rights at all. Pyongyang, in fact, claims it has no human rights problem because the Great Leader's actions, by definition, are always in the people's best interests.

Although all human rights violations in North Korea remain a serious issue, the economic human rights situation is currently the greatest threat to the people and the regime. Food rations fell to extremely low levels following the summer 1995 floods, and, as a result, many people are now suffering from malnutrition and other health problems. For the first time in its history, Pyongyang was forced to appeal to the outside world for emergency aid. Response was slow at first, however, because other countries doubted the seriousness of the food shortage and believed the aid would be diverted to North Korea's imposing military. In June 1996, the United States, Japan, and South Korea pledged to give a significant amount of aid without strings attached but with the hope that the North will agree to participate in the proposed four-nation talks between the United States, South and North Korea, and China. Gustavson and Lee-Rudolph suggest, however, that North Korea is likely to avoid any negotiations if it is not given meaningful incentives. Pyongyang will simply continue to ask for help until it realizes that its problems cannot be solved without fundamental economic changes.

Thomas Henriksen, senior fellow and associate director of the Hoover Institution, traced U.S.–North Korean relations since the collapse of the Soviet Union. Henriksen noted that changes in the international landscape wrought by the demise of the Soviet empire profoundly affected North Korea. Kim Il Sung, realizing that he must adapt because his regime no longer had a Soviet patron to provide security and aid, cleverly engaged the United States with a mixture of bluff, concessions, and adroit diplomacy. This effort culminated when the Clinton administration and the new Kim Jong Il government signed the Agreed Framework in Geneva in October 1994.

According to Henriksen, this agreement gained North Korea not only material benefits but also direct contact with Washington, a goal requiring a lapse in Kim's declared goal of *juche*, or self-reliance. By negotiating the Geneva accord, Washington set a bad international precedent that would allow other nuclear states to sell sensitive technology or build reactors in rogue states.

Kim Jong Il has continued the policy of engagement with Washington along the lines established by Kim Il Sung. Both Kims, employing provocative actions for prestige and economic rewards, have practiced a version of Mao Zedong's "limited belligerency" to enhance North Korea's international status.

Henriksen suggests, however, that Kim Jong Il cannot fully exploit this blackmail policy for conventional economic benefits, for if it is carried further, then the self-contained North Korean society would be breached by an openness to outside trade, communications, and contact. The North Koreans have every incentive to sell missiles and even to develop nuclear weapons and export fissile material, and thereby cheat on the Agreed Framework.

Concluding Thoughts

The DPRK's totalitarian features have limited the availability of data and analysis so beloved by social scientists. Despite these handicaps, however, conference participants were able to shed light on one of the world's most closed societies. Although commentators noted North Korea's terrible economic plight, they also called attention to the regime's capacity for survival. Therefore, predictions of North Korea's imminent collapse could be premature. Because of its regimented controls, North Korea may be able to postpone disintegration for some time, particularly if the regime continues to adhere to rigid authoritarianism.

Yet the seeds of change were also detected by conference scholars, who underscored generational shifts in the military, party, and bureaucracy. The need for food imports and currency inflows to modernize industry also places constraints on a regime bent on preserving the status quo. More than one scholar mentioned Pyongyang's astute handling of its nuclear capability to win concessions and recognition. This nuclear diplomacy was seen as evidence of a regime determined to negotiate successfully with the outside world. Contrasting North Korea's handling of nuclear technology with Libya's behavior gives an observer an insight into the negotiating skills of the DPRK. Moreover, it demonstrates that Pyongyang seeks not to be isolated.

Dangers lie ahead for the North Korean regime. It has become a rusting relic in a world adapting to high technology and instant communications. Change is natural to all societies, and damming off adaptation is not a long-term solution for a hard-pressed and out-of-date regime. As such, Pyongyang could be tempted to strike across the DMZ into the wealthy but less warlike South. The threat of conflict challenges both Seoul and Washington to stay engaged and strive for creative means while not diminishing their defense.

The North Korean conundrum is one of East Asia's major flashpoints. Its peaceful and constructive resolution will engage American and South Korean attention for the foreseeable future. Working together, as most conference participants agreed, offers the best hope for a peaceful and stable Korean peninsula.

.... 1 ....

Recent Political Developments in North Korea

B. C. KOH

Introduction

Emblematic of the paucity of reliable information about North Korea is the mystery surrounding the most rudimentary question: who is in charge in Pyongyang? Few outside observers can answer that question with a high degree of confidence.

Developments in North Korea and actions taken by the government of the Democratic People's Republic of Korea (DPRK) vary widely in the degree of their relative transparency. Most tend to be opaque; many are simply invisible. To cite those that are transparent first, the best known and perhaps the most puzzling of all is not a development but a nondevelopment—the failure of formal succession to materialize. As of late 1996, more than two years after the death of Kim Il Sung, the top two posts he held remain vacant. His eldest son and heir apparent, Kim Jong Il, has yet to assume either the general secretaryship (*ch'ong-bisŏ*) of the Workers' Party of Korea (WPK) or the presidency (*chusŏk*) of the DPRK.

Other transparent developments include the growing prominence of the military, the continuing salience of ideological indoctrination, the worsening of the food situation, and the blending of a hard line and pragmatism in external policy.

To the opaque or invisible column, in contrast, belong a host of questions concerning the causes and implications of the preceding phenomena. What accounts for Kim Jong Il's failure to fill the top party and state posts? Does the marked increase in the visibility of the military signal its ascendancy in the inner sanctums of power? What does the escalation of indoctrination suggest about its efficacy? How serious is the food shortage? What helps explain the hard line as well as the occasional surge of pragmatism in Pyongyang's external policy?

Needless to say, trying to explore some, let alone all, of these questions would require a large measure of imagination. But given the pressing need to decipher the riddle of North Korea, a regime that is widely perceived as capable of behaving in a way that is not only unpredictable but also inimical to Seoul, Washington, Tokyo, and beyond, the kind of speculative excursion that I propose to embark on may not be an entirely futile exercise.

Power Structure

During the Kim Il Sung era North Korea's power structure was marked by the prepotent position of the WPK and its overarching presence on the political landscape. Despite a wide array of institutions both within and without the party, a high degree of overlap in their upper echelons ensured a concentration of power in the hands of a few dozen people.[1]

The extraordinary intensity of the cult of personality centered on the Great Leader, however, did not necessarily mean that he was the supreme ruler of his domain in a functional sense. In the last few years of his life, poor eyesight prevented Kim Il Sung from reading, forcing him to depend on tape-recorded reports prepared by Kim Jong Il.[2] Kim Jong Il thus controlled a significant portion of information on which his father's decisions rested. As Kim Il Sung put it in January 1994, moreover, "in our country Comrade Kim Jong Il has been wisely leading all the work of the party, the state, and the armed forces; thus the problem of succession has been brilliantly solved."[3] Given all this, one may surmise that Kim Il Sung reigned while Kim Jong Il ruled.

Strange as it may seem, Kim Il Sung's death on July 8, 1994, did not put an end to his reign. For all practical purposes, Kim Il Sung continues to reign in the North; his portraits are still "respectfully carried" on the breasts of North Korean citizens during their waking hours—in the form of obligatory buttons—and they are constantly exhorted to carry out the "teachings bequeathed by the Great Leader" (*widaehan suryŏng ŭi yuhun*). The ubiquitous slogan "The Great Leader President Kim Il Sung Shall Be with Us Forever" (*Widaehan suryŏng Kim Il Sung chusŏgŭn yŏngwonhi uriwa hamkke kyesinda*) is a virtual reality. His embalmed body lies in Kumsusan Memorial Palace, the same building in which he used to conduct his presidential business and to which hundreds of visitors, both domestic and foreign, flock or are steered every day to pay their respects.

What needs stressing is that it is not simply the laudatory title *suryŏng* (Great

Leader) but also the official title *chusŏk* (president) that are reserved exclusively for the late Kim Il Sung. Kim Jong Il, meanwhile, is referred to either as *ch'oego yŏngdoja* (supreme leader) of the party and the people or, more frequently, as *widaehan yŏngdoja*. Although the latter can be translated as the "great leader," there is in fact a significant difference between the Korean words *suryŏng* and *yŏngdoja*.

Kim Jong Il, of course, is unsurpassed among his living compatriots in terms of official ranking. With the death of O Jin U in February 1995, Kim Jong Il became the sole member of the Presidium of the Political Bureau of the WPK Central Committee. His father's death made him the ranking party secretary, albeit not yet the general secretary. His most visible titles are chairman of the DPRK National Defense Commission and supreme commander of the Korean People's Army (KPA). These two positions place him at the pinnacle of North Korea's armed forces; it is this aspect of his leadership role that has become most visible since the death of his father.

From December 24, 1991, when Kim Jong Il was "elevated" to the supreme commandership of the KPA, to July 8, 1994, when Kim Il Sung died, Kim Jong Il appeared in public seventy-three times — that is to say, his reported activities totaled seventy-three. Of these, nineteen (26 percent) were related to the military. In the latter half of 1994, eleven of the fifteen reported activities of Kim Jong Il were connected with the death of his father. In 1995, however, seventeen of the twenty-eight reported activities (61 percent) were related to the military. In a symbolically significant move, he began the new year with a visit to a military unit.[4]

In lieu of the customary New Year's message (*sinnyŏnsa*) from the Great Leader, the North Korean people were presented with joint editorials by the daily organs of the three pivotal institutions in their country in both in 1995 and 1996 — *Nodong Sinmun* (Labor news), *Chosŏn inmin'gun* (The Korean People's Army) and *Nodong ch'ŏngnyŏn* (The working youth). The last-named paper is the organ of the League of Socialist Working Youth (*Chosŏn sahoejuŭi nodong ch'ŏngnyŏn tongmaeng* or *Saroch'ŏng*).[5]

Perhaps the single most important change in post–Kim Il Sung North Korea has been the marked increase in the visibility of the military. Given the frequency with which Kim Jong Il engages in KPA-related activities, one should not be surprised to see top military leaders occupying prominent spots in the vicinity of Kim Jong Il on many public occasions. The celebration of the fiftieth anniversary of the WPK's founding on October 10, 1995, is a case in point. For the first time in the annals of the DPRK, the centerpiece of the celebration was a military parade showcasing not only tens of thousands of military personnel but also an array of heavy equipment and weapons. In the photograph of Kim Jong Il waving to the parade participants from a reviewing stand that appeared in the North's printed media, *all* the people standing next to him, of whom seven or eight are visible either fully or partially, are wearing military uniforms heavily adorned with medals.[6]

Also notable is the North's practice of placing the *ch'asu* (vice marshal; equivalent to a five-star general) immediately below the alternate members of the Central Committee Politburo but ahead of Central Committee secretaries in listings of participants in ceremonial events. (In the North the order in which a person's name is listed is scrupulously controlled and reflects his or her ranking in the power hierarchy.) On October 8, 1995, two vice marshals, Choi Gwang and Li Ul Sol, were promoted to the rank of marshal (*wonsu*), creating an unprecedented situation in which Kim Jong Il, who nominally heads the military, shares the rank of marshal with *two* others. Until his death, O Jin U had been the only other person sharing the same rank with Kim Jong Il. Kim Il Sung's military rank was grand marshal (*tae wonsu*), a rank that is theoretically available to Kim Jong Il. Concurrently with his promotion, Choi, who had served two stints as the KPA's chief of the general staff (1963–1968, 1988–1995), was appointed as the minister of the People's Armed Forces, a post that had become vacant due to the death of O Jin U eight months earlier.[7]

Both Choi and Li Ul Sol, who heads the KPA unit that guards top leaders (*Howi ch'ongguk*), are in their seventies. Three KPA generals were promoted to vice marshal in October 1995, bringing the total number of vice marshals to eight. All three of the new vice marshals are in their sixties.

The increase in the visibility of the military in post–Kim Il Sung North Korea is in contrast to the near banishment of other institutions from the public view. Neither the WPK Central Committee nor the DPRK Supreme People's Assembly (SPA) has met (or they have met in secret since the death of Kim Il Sung). An indirect sign that the Central Committee may have held an unannounced plenum appeared in May 1995, when the party newspaper published slogans chosen by the committee to commemorate the party's fiftieth anniversary on October 10.[8] The possibility cannot be ruled out, however, that the slogans may have been drafted and adopted by the WPK secretariat.

The failure of the SPA to convene at all in 1995, in contrast, is mystifying, for it is the nominal legislature that approves the DPRK's annual budget and settles the preceding fiscal year's account. What is more, the five-year term of the ninth SPA officially expired on April 22, 1995. Because there is no precedent for unannounced SPA elections, one must assume that none has been held. Nor is there any evidence that secret SPA sessions have ever been convened. Hence one must assume that someone other than the SPA has approved the new fiscal year's budget.

Another key institution that has been all but invisible since July 1994 is the DPRK Central People's Committee (CPC), the "supercabinet" that was created in 1972. One of the few signs that the CPC had not been dismantled appeared in September 1995, when it added its name to an obituary of a top leader of a pro-DPRK Korean residents' federation in Japan.[9]

If there is a top policy-making structure, as there must be, then it may be an ad hoc structure consisting of all or selected members of the WPK Central Committee Politburo and those military leaders who belong to either or both the WPK Central Military Affairs Committee and the DPRK National Defense Commission. Although the National Defense Commission, of which Kim Jong Il is the chairman, was elevated to a status equal to that of the DPRK CPC in the April 1992 revision of the DPRK Socialist Constitution, the WPK Central Military Affairs Committee is believed to be a pivotal institution as well. A striking overlap in their membership, however, makes the question of which is more powerful moot.[10]

It remains to dwell briefly on the puzzling question of why Kim Jong Il has not assumed one or both of the top two positions in the party and the state. Although no official explanation has been forthcoming, at least one high-ranking official — Foreign Minister and full Politburo member Kim Yong Nam — reportedly told the German daily *Frankfurter Allgemeine Zeitung* in December 1994 that Kim Jong Il's wish to observe the traditional three-year mourning period is the reason for the delay in his assuming formal titles.[11]

If this is the reason, then the mourning period would come to an end on July 8, 1996, with the "three" years actually equaling two years because the counting begins on the day of death. In July 1996, however, it was reported that the North would observe a three-year mourning period in a literal sense, thus postponing Kim Jong Il's possible formal succession until after July 1997. Even if Kim Jong Il does formally succeed to one or both of his late father's titles after that date, the mourning period would not necessarily have been the cause of the delay. Equally plausible reasons may be found in the serious economic difficulties in which the North finds itself, Kim Jong Il's health or related factors, or the fragility of his power base.

Regarding Kim Jong Il's health, even if one were to discount all the rumors, none of which is verifiable, one would still be left with the fleeting image of his haggard appearance in the days following his father's death. Not to be overlooked, moreover, is the absence of any credible proof of his public-speaking ability. His longest public utterance recorded and videotaped for the outside world is the single sentence "Glory to the officers and soldiers of the heroic Korean People's Army" (*Yŏng'ungjŏk Chosŏn inmin'gun changbyŏng ege yŏnggwang'i issŭra*), which he shouted from the reviewing stand of Kim Il Sung Square on April 25, 1992, during the celebration of the KPA's sixtieth anniversary.[12]

In none of the functions related to his father's death did Kim Jong Il utter a word. Nor did he attend, let alone make any speeches in, a number of important functions held in 1995 such as the April 9 ceremony marking the second anniversary of his election as chairman of the National Defense Commission, the April 25 celebration of the KPA's sixty-third anniversary, and the August 15 ceremony marking the fiftieth anniversary of Korea's liberation from Japanese colonial rule. Although, as noted, he did attend the celebration of the WPK's fiftieth anniversary on October 10, he did not utter a word; it was Choi Gwang, the newly promoted marshal and the minister of the People's Armed Forces, who made the main speech.

If all this suggests that Kim Jong Il either dislikes making speeches or suffers from speech impediments of some kind, it could explain his reluctance to assume official titles. As the general secretary of the WPK, for example, he would be expected to deliver a long speech, typically lasting three to four hours, to a party congress that must be convened sooner or later. The last congress—the sixth—was held in October 1980, and the sixteen-year hiatus is more than three times as long as what the party constitution decrees.

Finally, what can one say about the fragility or, for that matter, solidity of Kim Jong Il's power base? Kim Jong Il was carefully groomed as his father's successor over two decades. He had ample opportunity to learn the ins and outs of running the party and the state and to place persons deemed loyal to him in strategic positions in key institutions in the North. Aware of the pivotal importance of the military in ensuring his succession plan, the late Kim Il Sung took pains to forge links between his son and the KPA as well. By the time Kim Il Sung died, Kim Jong Il had successively acquired such key military posts or titles as first deputy chairman of the NDC (May 1990), the supreme commander of the KPA (December 1991), the marshal of the republic (April 1992), and the chairman of the NDC (April 1993).[13]

Kim Jong Il's power base, then, may not be fragile at all. One cannot, however, preclude the possibility that his style of leadership may be somewhat more consensual than his father's. Lacking Kim Il Sung's charisma, Kim Jong Il may not be as intimidating to those in the top echelons of power, particularly those in the military. Power may very well be shared, albeit not equally, among a few dozen leaders, many of them military, who make up an ad hoc policy-making council.

Under these circumstances the ubiquitous phenomenon of bureaucratic politics—the rivalry for incremental advantages and the jockying for greater influence and a larger share of the limited resources—may have become more salient than ever before. This line of reasoning is buttressed by the signs of discord that have surfaced in recent months between the military and the foreign policy bureaucracy.[14]

Internal Policy Outputs

Internally, the challenge facing the regime in Pyongyang is two-fold: (1) how to cope with the crisis precipitated by the flagging economy and (2) how to maintain political control over an increasingly alienated populace. These two are obviously interrelated. The inability to contain deteriorating economic conditions would seriously erode the regime's grip on the populace. Fears of adverse political side effects, in contrast, seriously constrain the regime's ability to take bold measures to turn the economy around.

The signals emanating from Pyongyang strongly suggest that the imperative of political control has eclipsed all other considerations. State control of the economy does not appear to have diminished; mobilization and exhortations remain the preferred means of raising productivity. With economic resources on the verge of depletion, utilitarian control (i.e., control based on material inducements) has become elusive. That leaves normative and coercive control as the only real options.

Coercive control encompasses not only the pervasive surveillance over the citizenry by formal and informal security apparatuses but also the regulation of potentially subversive activities. Citizens, for example, are required to report any material, especially publications, obtained from outside sources such as relatives visiting from other countries. In hotels catering to foreigners, non-Caucasian guests, primarily those whose appearances are not clearly distinguishable from North Koreans, are occasionally asked to identify themselves. Taxi drivers routinely request the affiliation and mission of their would-be fares.

The food shortage, however, has led to some loosening of controls over citizens' movements. Trips aimed at finding food are said to be permitted, either explicitly or tacitly. Black markets apparently flourish where the scarce rice can be bought at prices that are beyond the reach of most citizens.[15]

There has been an unmistakable escalation of ideological indoctrination. In 1995 alone the regime published some 240 slogans in commemoration of the fiftieth anniversary of the WPK's founding and three long articles, one of which is called *tamhwa* (talk), by Kim Jong Il. The title of his June 19 article sums up the regime's overall strategy: "To Put Ideological Work ahead of Everything Else Is a Prerequisite to the Fulfillment of the Great Socialist Tasks."[16]

In that article, Kim Jong Il reiterates his earlier argument that the collapse of socialism in Central Europe and the former Soviet Union stemmed primarily from "revisionist policies" followed by "traitors to socialism" in those countries. By adopting "the capitalist relations of ownership and capitalist methods of economic management" and by introducing "'pluralism' on the pretext of 'reforming' and 'restructuring,'" they helped bring about socialism's demise. Ideological contamination—the "penetration of imperialist ideology and culture"—and "right-leaning opportunism," coupled with "collusion between the imperialists and counterrevolutionary forces," helped seal socialism's fate.[17]

Given this analysis, the only logical option is to adhere to the orthodox path to socialism, shunning reform, restructuring, and opening; tighten up controls; and step up indoctrination. Kim Jong Il's stern warning that "the act of insulting the Great Leader [*suryŏng*] and forerunners of the revolution [*hyŏngmyŏng ŭi sŏnbae*] is tantamount to treason" may indicate the regime's recognition of and apprehensions about the spread of discontent among the masses. His devoting a separate paper (called a talk) to this very topic in December 1995 suggests the gravity of the regime's concern.

The intensification of ideological indoctrination, then, may bespeak not its efficacy but the reverse. It is because indoctrination has passed the point of diminishing returns that the regime is redoubling its efforts in that domain. Unless the economic situation improves markedly, however, the efficacy of indoctrination is likely to remain low; it may even become counterproductive. The stark contrast between the rhetoric of "our-style socialism" (*urisik sahoejuŭi*) and the reality of chronic hunger is bound to create cognitive dissonance, if not outright resentment, on the part of the vast majority of the North Korean people. Foreign countries have posted a rash of defections by North Koreans, a growing number of whom belong to the North's elite in terms of political background and current status, which suggests that such alienation may not be confined to the lower strata of North Korean society.

External Policy Outputs

Because inter-Korean relations and foreign policy are beyond the scope of my chapter, I shall only touch in a cursory fashion on the probable linkage between the domestic political situation and external policy outputs. The most notable development in the post–Kim Il Sung period is the sharp deterioration of inter-Korean relations. In one sense, however, the landscape is not as desolate as it may first appear.

For the first time since the emergence of two separate states on the Korean peninsula, one of them has requested and received assistance from the other. Unofficial economic relations, moreover, continue to grow by leaps and bounds.

Meanwhile, intergovernmental relations are all but suspended. Even the rice negotiations in Beijing in the summer of 1995 were only quasi-governmental, with only the South dispatching a real vice minister; the North sent a "vice minister–level" negotiator who tried hard to dilute his links with the government in Pyongyang. Despite Seoul's providing 150,000 tons of rice at no charge,

Pyongyang's response was to forcibly hoist a DPRK flag on the first ROK ship bringing rice to Chongjin harbor and to detain the entire crew of another ROK ship that had just delivered rice, on the grounds that one crew member had engaged in espionage by taking unauthorized pictures of the harbor.

If the unprecedented request for Seoul's aid reflected how dangerous the food shortage had become, Pyongyang's hostile posture toward Seoul bespoke the depth of the North's anger at the inhumane behavior (*pan illyunjŏk haengwi*), in Pyongyang's words, displayed by the Kim Young Sam government toward Kim Il Sung in the wake of his death. The rice negotiations showed, nonetheless, that dire necessity can compel the North to set aside politics and grudgingly choose pragmatic approaches.

Nowhere was Pyongyang's capacity for pragmatic adaptation more visible than in its relations with Washington. This may have been due to Pyongyang's realization that the United States could no longer be viewed as its enemy and principal obstacle to reunification on its own terms and that the United States could serve as its lifeline—the main guarantor of its security broadly defined. Given such a transformation in the role of the United States in its strategic calculus, Pyongyang could not allow the death of Kim Il Sung to get in the way of negotiations with Washington. Having played a pivotal role in the resuscitation of the U.S.-DPRK talks, the late Great Leader, in fact, had shown the way; to deviate from it would be to dishonor his memory and legacy.

The convergence of interests on all sides produced a compromise. Subsequent developments—notably Pyongyang's grudging acceptance of both the South Korean model light water reactors (LWRs) and South Korea's "central role" in the LWR project—showed, nonetheless, that the post–Kim Il Sung regime is capable of optimizing its interests in difficult diplomatic negotiations. This serves to undercut the view, enunciated by some observers, that no one is in charge in Pyongyang.

Change or Continuity?

Insofar as domestic political developments are concerned, the death of Kim Il Sung triggered a series of changes. The single most important change is the marked increase in the visibility of the military and, by implication, in the power and influence of top military leaders. Owing to a combination of health problems and a carefully crafted succession plan, the general pattern of leadership during the twilight years of the Kim Il Sung regime could best be described as one of coleadership—Kim Il Sung reigning and Kim Jong Il actually doing the ruling.

This basic pattern may not have changed radically in the post–Kim Il Sung period. Kim Il Sung's death has not removed him from the center stage of North Korean society, for it is not only his embalmed body that is being preserved in Kumsusan Memorial Palace, his erstwhile place of work, but his teachings— known as *yuhun*—which continue to guide the North Korean people and help shape internal and external policies of the DPRK as well. To a striking extent and at least in the short run, Kim Il Sung seems to have attained a goal he had so assiduously sought: immortality.[18]

The failure of formal succession to materialize thus far—in the sense of Kim Jong Il's assuming the two top party and state posts vacated by his father—may not necessarily signify that Kim Jong Il's power base remains fragile or yet to be consolidated. Whether or when formal succession will occur, however, is shrouded in mystery. One thing is reasonably certain: the viability of the North Korean political system, regardless of who is pulling its levers of power, is inextricably bound up with the amelioration of the economic conditions in the North. No system that is incapable of feeding its people can survive for long. Pyongyang's ability to avert famine in the short run and to reinvigorate its long-moribund economy in the medium to long run hinges on whether it can fend off both internal and external challenges. Such ability in turn is contingent to a significant extent on the policies of Washington, Seoul, Tokyo, and Beijing.

Notes

1. At the policy-making level, the top elite consisted of members, both full and alternate, of the Political Bureau (PB) of the WPK Central Committee (CC); members of the CC Secretariat; members of the WPK Central Military Affairs Committee; members of the DPRK Central People's Committee (CPC); and members of the DPRK National Defense Commission. For a list of these people, see *Chōsen Minshushugi Jinminkyōwakoku soshikibetsu jinmeibō* (North Korea directory), 1994 (Tokyo: Radiopress, Inc., 1994). The translation of the title, which is not a literal translation, is Radiopress's.

2. In an interview with the *Washington Times* in Pyongyang in April 1994, three months before his death, Kim Il Sung said: "Because I have some eye problems, [Jong Il] has arranged for all reports to be recorded to save me from having to spend hours reading them. I am very proud to have such a good son. He is so concerned about my health. If I don't go to the countryside, he gives instructions for me to do so through my secretary." *Washington Times*, April 19, 1994.

3. *Nodong sinmun* (Labor news) (Pyongyang), January 5, 1994. This is the daily organ of the WPK.

4. For the 1992–1994 period, see *Kita Chōsen no genkyō* (The present condition of North Korea), 1995 (Tokyo: Radiopress, Inc., 1995), pp. 50–54; for 1995, see *Vantage*

Point (Seoul) 18, no. 12 (December 1995): 51–53. For purposes of counting Kim Jong Il's activities, sending messages was excluded.

5. At its "representatives' meeting" (*taep'yoja hoeŭi*), held in Pyongyang on January 19, 1996, *Saroch'ŏng* adopted a resolution renaming it *Kim Il Sung sahoejuŭi ch'ŏngnyŏn tongmaeng* (Kim Il Sung League of Socialist Youth). *Nodong sinmun*, January 20, 1996.

6. See the front pages of *Nodong sinmun*, October 11, 1995, and *T'ong'il sinbo* (Reunification news) (Pyongyang), October 14, 1995. See also *Kŭmsu kangsan* (Land of beautiful rivers and mountains) (Pyongyang), November 1995, p. 9.

7. For Choi's career path, see *Chōsen Minshushugi Jinminkyōwakoku soshikibetsu jinmeibō, 1994*, p. 249 (in Japanese) and p. 266 (in English).

8. *Nodong sinmun*, May 1, 1995, p. 1.

9. Ibid., September 22, 1995.

10. Whereas the National Defense Commission (NDC) was one of the constituent units of the CPC under the 1972 constitution, the 1992 revision makes the two coequal, placing the six articles delineating its functions ahead of the seven that pertain to the CPC. See the text of the revised constitution (in Japanese) in *Kita Chōsen no genkyō, 1995*, pp. 501–20.

11. *North Korea News* (Seoul), no. 767 (December 16, 1994): 1–5.

12. The videotape of Kim Jong Il's utterance can be found in *Kim Hyon Hui: watashi to Kita Chōsen* (Kim Hyon Hui: I and North Korea), Bunshun Nonfiction Video (Tokyo: Bungei Shunju, 1994).

13. For an insightful analysis of the process by which Kim Jong Il's power base was forged, see Takashi Sakai, "The Power Base of Kim Jong Il: Focusing on Its Formation Process," in Han S. Park, ed., *North Korea: Ideology, Politics, Economy* (Englewood Cliffs, N.J.: Prentice-Hall, 1996), pp. 105–22.

14. In announcing a decision to discourage foreign relief agencies from organizing aid programs for its flood victims, North Korea's foreign ministry officials "blamed army leaders in part for the change in policy." See Nicholas D. Kristoff, "North Korea Tells Groups to Halt Drive for Flood Aid," *New York Times*, February 8, 1996.

15. According to a letter that was smuggled out of North Korea recently, one *mal* (about 7.5 kilograms) of rice costs between 1,200 won and 1,300 won on the black market. The author of the letter writes that her husband's monthly income is 195 won. She adds that she was forced to sell all her clothing except what she was wearing. If she had some capital (*mitchŏn*), she writes, she would like to engage in commercial activity (*changsa*). She also reveals that even though medical care is free, anyone who needs penicillin must purchase it for 25 won. The letter is addressed to her relatives in the United States, from whom she hopes to get some help. Although she asks them never to mention anything about her letter in their future correspondence, saying that the consequences would be enormous (*hukwaga maktae haljul saenggak hamnida*), she nonetheless takes the precautionary step of quoting from the Great Leader and noting that no one in the North blames the state for their plight.

16. Kim Jong Il, "Sasang saŏp ŭl apseunŭn kŏsŭn sahoejuŭi wiwŏp suhaeng ŭi p'ilsujŏk yogu ida," *Nodong sinmun*, June 20, 1995.

17. For an earlier exposition of these views, see Kim Jong Il, *Inmin taejung chungsim ŭi urisik sahoejuŭi nŭn p'ilsŭng pulp'ae ida* (Our kind of socialism that is centered on the masses is ever-victorious and invincible) (Pyongyang: Choson Nodongdang Ch'ulp'ansa, 1991); idem, *Sahoejuŭi kŏnsŏl ŭi yŏksajŏk kyohun kwa uri tang ŭi ch'ong nosŏn* (The historical lesson of socialist construction and the general line of our party) (Pyongyang: Choson Nodongdang Ch'ulp'ansa, 1992); and idem, "Sahoejuŭi e taehan hwebang ŭn hŏyong doelsu ŏpda" (Obstructive manuevers against socialism must not be allowed) *Nodong sinmun*, March 4, 1993, pp. 1–2.

18. For a discussion of "symbolic immortality," see Robert J. Lifton, *Revolutionary Immortality: Mao Tse-tung and the Chinese Cultural Revolution* (New York: Random House, 1968), p. 7 and passim.

2

Prospects for Economic Reform and Political Stability

BRUCE BUENO DE MESQUITA and
JONGRYN MO

Introduction

Since the collapse of the communist regimes in Eastern Europe, North Korea watchers have been looking for signs of a regime crisis. Although the North Korean communist regime has been more resilient than initially believed (it has survived the 1994 death of Kim Il Sung and an extremely hostile international environment), it may face the same fate as the Eastern European regimes unless it addresses its deteriorating economic conditions. But will the leadership undertake necessary economic reforms or might it see such reforms as a threat to its hold on power? To answer this question, we conduct a rigorous analysis of policy choice in North Korea. We focus on two issues, namely, (1) what kinds of domestic economic reforms are likely to be adopted? and (2) how open will the North Korean economy be in the next few years?[1] Based on this analysis, we also assess the probability of a "regime crisis" emerging in North Korea. Finally, we describe a likely scenario of regime change in North Korea in case of a regime crisis. There were several patterns of regime change in Eastern Europe and the former Soviet republics. We argue that the conditions in North Korea point to a repetition of the Bulgarian experience.

Competing Groups in North Korea

Although the structure of authority is centralized and Kim Jong Il appears to have total control in North Korea, there is evidence that policy differences exist among North Korean leaders. The South Korean media and policy makers commonly use the terms *hawks* and *doves* to describe internal politics in North Korea. There have also been reports about riots and coup attempts. Thus, North Korea is hardly the monolithic and homogenous society that many scholars portray. Nor does North Korea seem driven entirely by ideological purity. Time and again, North Korea has taken actions inconsistent with its *juche* ideology, which emphasizes self-reliance (e.g., the joint North and South Korean admission to the United Nations and efforts to open its economy).

If North Korean policies change over time and there are policy disagreements among political leaders, there appears to be room for applying models of interest group politics. There are of course many difficulties. Although there are reports that some individuals (e.g., Vice Premier Kim Dal-hyon) espoused views that were later discredited, we do not know which interests they represented because North Korean leaders do not speak for any group or interest in public. They all speak in the name of Kim Il Sung, the party, or *juche* ideology. Nevertheless, we see groups operating in North Korea along the following cleavages in view of the experiences of other communist countries:[2]

First, we must distinguish the interests of the ruling class from those of its agents, who have a far smaller stake in regime maintenance. In North Korea, the ruling class consists of Kim Jong Il, members of Kim Jong Il's extended family (the Kim family), Kim Il Sung's partisan comrades in arms (partisans), and their children (second-generation leaders). Members of this class are the founders of the North Korean regime and their family members. The agents of North Korea's ruling class are the administrative elites, who consist of ideologues, security forces, the military, economic technocrats, managers of state-owned enterprises, and foreign service officers.

Second, the monopoly of power by revolutionary leaders is coming to an end in North Korea. This "routinization," or "normalization," process has been accompanied by the rise of technocrats in the hierarchy of power. The administrative elites and the second-generation leaders of the ruling class are expected to be less rigid about ideology and change and less willing to use force (or terror) than revolutionaries.

Third, institutional and functional conflicts are expected to exist among administrative elites despite efforts by the Korean Workers' Party to penetrate all government institutions. The experiences of Eastern Europe and the former Soviet Union show that members of the communist party had different attitudes, depending on their institutional affiliation, toward protecting the communist regime. The security forces and party leaders fought to protect the system, but the military and, to a lesser extent, state institutions (e.g., the Supreme Soviet) were not as supportive of the communist party.

In this study, the ideologues are defined as officials in the party, military, and government who engage in activities relating to organization, education and culture, propaganda, or ideology. The North Korean security establishment consists of the Secret Service, the Ministry of Public Security, the State Inspection Commission, the party militia, and Kim Jong Il's personal security guards. (We also include those engaging in intelligence operations against South Korea as part of the security establishment.) Members of the military are the field officer corps in the People's Armed Forces and those managing industrial enterprises controlled by the military. (Military officers in the security forces are assumed to have separate organizational interests and are thus excluded.)

The interests of economic technocrats as to policy outcomes are likely to diverge according to their current position.[3] The planners responsible for overall planning and economic policy include the premier, the chairman of the State Planning Commission, the chairman of the Economic Policy Commission, and the party secretary for economic affairs. The heavy industry sector is represented by officials in the Ministries of Metal, Machine, Chemical, Shipbuilding, Nuclear Power, and Electronics and Automation. Those bureaucrats in light industry, agriculture, and the external economy sector (broadly called light industry in this chapter) represent interests that will benefit from economic reform. The other technocrats are (1) those charged with the supply of energy and natural resources such as coal, electric power, and mining, (2) officials working in construction, post and communications, and building materials industries, and (3) managers of state-owned enterprises who have been formidable opponents to economic reform policy in Eastern Europe and Russia.

It is a basic perspective of interest group politics that policy outcomes are obtained as a result of competition among groups. Interest groups with conflicting preferences over policy outcomes compete to have their preferred policies adopted. To predict policy outcomes, then, our first task should be to identify what the issues are and what the positions of various groups are on those issues.

Future Domestic Economic Policies

To avert a regime crisis, North Korean leaders must improve economic conditions in their country. With an improved economy, Kim Jong Il may be able to maintain power for the foreseeable future. Still, economic reform also carries risks. Changed economic arrangements are likely to shift the balance of political interests in North Korea, benefiting some at the expense of others.

The range of policy options currently under consideration by North Korean policy makers is unclear. Because the most immediate cause of the current economic crisis in North Korea was the collapse of its export markets in Eastern Europe and the former Soviet Union, the loss of export earnings to buy key imports such as energy and intermediate goods (parts and components) is the most urgent problem. Several years of bad harvests have also caused severe food shortages.[4] In response, North Korean policy makers have experimented with a more open economic policy to earn foreign exchange and reform agricultural production.

In the medium term, North Korean policy makers must address the problem of consumer goods to prevent social instability. This requires the reallocation of resources from heavy industry to the consumer goods sector. North Korea has tried various policies to accelerate industrial restructuring, but these policies do not seem to have been effective (Jeong 1995). The main obstacle to industrial restructuring is the military-industrial complex. Given the size of the military economy, industrial restructuring in North Korea means military conversion, and it is highly unlikely that North Korean leaders are prepared to embark on such a plan.

In the long run, North Korea must upgrade its technological capabilities and reverse the falling standards of living in order to survive. More than any other communist regime, North Korea's competition with capitalism is direct and intense owing to the presence of South Korea.

North Korea might earn foreign exchange in the short run by attracting foreign investors. But its medium- and long-term problems cannot be solved without serious domestic economic reform. The experience of other transition economies shows that top-down reforms that preserve the structure of a command economy do not work.[5] Still, North Korean leaders may not have to adopt radical reform, or "shock therapy." In view of developments in China and Eastern Europe, many argue that North Korea can achieve significant reform "without abandoning socialism, without privatizing state-owned enterprises, and without permitting widespread FDI [foreign direct investment]." North Korea may need to relax central planning only enough to permit the managers of state-owned enterprises to compete against one another. The managers, workers or farmers would then be provided with incentives to compete.[6]

In terms of the degree of market reform, we place the various policy options on a scale ranging from 0 to 100:[7]

   0   Reversion—North Korea can revert to the pre-1984 economic policy
       where the basic structures of a closed command economy were in place.

  10   Planning Improvement—Policy makers attempt to improve central
       planning to increase the production of consumer and agricultural
       goods.

  20   Organizational Reform (status quo)—Organizational and managerial
       reforms such as decentralization and incentives are introduced; but
       resources are not taken away from the "favored" sectors, and the basic
       planning structure is not altered.

  40   Direct Restructuring—North Korean policy makers may take a "direct"
       approach to industrial restructuring by promoting light industry and
       reducing subsidies to the heavy and military industries at the same time.

  60   Military Diversion—Industrial restructuring deepens with cutbacks in
       the military budget and reduction of troops.

  80   Chinese-Style Reform—Economic decision makers rely more on mar-
       ket forces than on planning to allocate resources. This stage is charac-
       terized by more autonomy to the managers of state-owned enterprises,
       reduced subsidies, and competition between state-owned enterprises.
       The decontrol of prices begins.

 100   Privatization—Private enterprises are allowed and state-owned enter-
       prises are privatized.

What is the attitude of competing groups toward domestic economic reform?
In what follows we examine each group's position in detail: Kim Jong Il, the Kim
family, and the second generation would be about 80 on the scale, and the
partisans, 10. The ruling class will benefit most from successful reform, which
will enhance the support of the general population for the regime. Private benefits to the ruling elites will also be sizable because, like their Chinese counterparts, they are in the best position to take advantage of new economic opportunities. But ideology will exert more influence on Kim Il Sung's partisan
comrades, so their interests will diverge from those of second-generation leaders
like Kim Jong Il. The partisans will insist on "planning improvement," whereas
Kim Jong Il, the Kim family, and the second-generation leaders will be willing to
go as far as "Chinese-style reform."

Ideologues with no direct ties to the losing sectors of the reformed economy
do not have much material incentive to oppose reform and would thus be at
about 20 on the scale. In fact, like the ruling families, the ideologues with powerful positions in the party and government will be in a good position to benefit
from new economic opportunities. But, given the nature of their jobs, they will

be ideologically rigid, albeit not as rigid as the founders of the North Korean state, the partisans. So the ideologues' position will coalesce around "organizational reform."

The security forces enjoy a privileged position under the current system, but do not have a direct stake in reform as long as their benefits are maintained; thus they would be about 40 on the scale. Ideologically, they are not as rigid as the ideologues and partisans and conceivably support the position of Kim Jong Il, whose regime they are supposed to protect. Given their fear of popular unrest as a result of economic reform and their military backgrounds, however, the attitude of the security forces toward economic reform will not be as liberal as Kim Jong Il's, so their favored policy is direct restructuring.

The interests of the military over economic reform are not uniform but overall are about 10 on the scale. The basic concern of the officer corps will be total military spending, especially on items that affect their benefits. Thus, the officer corps will support economic reform as long as its budget is not seriously affected. Consequently it may prefer direct restructuring. Those working in enterprises owned by the military, however, care more about the subsidies to the military industries in general, so they are likely to support reforms that do not reduce subsidies to military industry (i.e., organizational reform). Because the military runs the arms industry in North Korea, the division between the officer corps and the military industry is unlikely to become a factor. Thus, the military will follow the interests of its arms industry and oppose industrial restructuring.

Economic reforms such as industrial restructuring will produce losers even among economic technocrats. Sectors likely to suffer are the heavy industry and the military sectors because they have been heavily subsidized, so they will only support minimal reform (i.e., planning improvement, 10 on the scale). Light industries and agriculture as well as the external sector will benefit most from economic reform. The advocates of those interests will hold liberal attitudes toward economic reform (i.e., Chinese-style reform, 80 on the scale). Planners whose positions are not tied to any specific industry will have liberal attitudes toward economic reform. But their position will not be as liberal as Kim Jong Il's because they still support planning and oppose movement to a market economy. After all, many North Korean planners have careers centered on heavy industry; thus their assumed current position is 50, that is, between direct restructuring and military diversion.

In principle, managers should welcome some economic reform measures such as decentralization. In reality, they resist those measures that are accompanied by more responsibilities. Their preferred position would be planning improvement (10 on the scale).

Diplomats have less at stake in economic reforms and their foreign experience makes them more reform-minded. Unlike economic technocrats, central planning is not important to them, so their favored policy position is assumed to be on the liberal side, favoring Chinese-style reform (80 on the scale).

The Direction of North Korea's Economic Opening Policy

The second issue is opening the economy. North Korea has always traded with other countries, even, since 1987, with South Korea. In fact, it has depended on imports as a key source of energy and civilian and military technologies. When the command economies in Eastern Europe and the former Soviet Union collapsed, however, North Korea's export markets, which had already been shrinking, disappeared altogether. In the face of foreign exchange shortages, North Korea has actively sought foreign investment (e.g., joint ventures).

To date, however, North Korea's opening policy has not succeeded. North Korea cannot compete with China and Vietnam without substantial domestic reforms. But more important has been North Korea's policy toward South Korea. From 1992 to 1994, the dispute over North Korea's nuclear program kept everyone away from the North Korean market. In December 1994, South Korea formally broke the link between economic exchange and the North Korean nuclear program, but North Korea has refused to formalize its trade and investment relationship with South Korea. North Korea can accept indirect trade with South Korea and investment from South Korean firms but opposes direct trade and is unwilling to negotiate with the South Korean government to establish a legal framework for trade and investment (e.g., protection of investment, direct shipping routes, a clearing system, etc.). Apparently, the current North Korean position is "opening with informal and unofficial status for South Korea." North Korean leaders fear that open economic exchanges with South Korea may lead to a regime crisis, as the people of North Korea may demand comparable standards of living or threaten to "vote with their feet."

The problem is that, without South Korean cooperation, investment from Japan and the United States will not come. Moreover, South Korean firms seem interested in investing in North Korea despite the adverse conditions. Thus, the success or permissiveness of North Korea's opening policy depends on what kinds of policy it adopts toward South Korea; the more liberal its policy, the more "opened" its economy will be. The current North Korean policy is still more liberal than autarky or than a policy of opening with the complete exclusion of South Korea. Still, it is a less liberal economic policy than would be one involving nondiscriminatory opening or opening with preferences for South Korea (e.g., a free trade area between North and South Korea). We place these policy choices on a scale indicating their permissiveness:

    0   Autarky
   30   Opening excluding South Korea
   50   Opening with informal South Korean trade (status quo)
   80   Opening without discrimination
  100   Opening with South Korean preferences

North Korean elites have shown more flexibility in opening their country's economy than in introducing a market economy, and this is not because the *juche* ideology lacks as strong a hold on economic opening as it has on domestic reform. Rather, most elites seem to agree on the need for limited opening. In other words, the distributive consequences of opening may be less polarizing; as long as opening would be limited to special economic zones, most elites seem to see its benefits.

Although many groups in North Korea are concerned about public unrest following economic opening, Kim Jong Il and other members of the ruling class have the most to lose. The administrative elites, however, who may survive under a new regime, would be more willing to take the risk and support significant opening.

Thus, Kim Jong Il, his family, and the second generation will take a moderate position, equivalent to opening with informal South Korean trade; although an opening policy brings material benefits to them and their supporters, it may also be destabilizing. The partisans, who will favor autarky, are an exception; they may not even believe that opening is necessary.

Given North Korea's comparative advantage in labor-intensive industries, opening will result in some reallocation of resources from heavy to light industries. Thus, technocrats associated with external economic affairs and light industry will favor opening without discrimination. The heavy industry interests and the military would be adversely affected, but their opposition to opening will be less intense than to domestic reform. Energy and new technologies, which are vital to them, cannot be secured without opening. The planners will align with heavy industry and the military in opposing opening the economy because such an opening would diminish their ability to control the economy. Thus, the preferred position of heavy industry, the planners, and the military—hoping to generate the necessary foreign exchange—would be opening excluding South Korea.

The party ideologues and the security forces will oppose any opening (autarky is their favored position). Opening is not consistent with the *juche* ideology, and the security forces would fear the inevitable easing of control. Diplomats will favor opening without discrimination, which will end North Korea's isolation in the international community.

METHODOLOGY

Once we identify the policy positions of competing groups, we need to develop a model of how they resolve their differences and agree on a policy outcome. The analysis of the issues we have raised is carried out through the use of a model whose details are reported elsewhere (Bueno de Mesquita and Stokman 1994; Bueno de Mesquita, Newman, and Rabushka 1996, 1985; Bueno de Mesquita 1984, 1985). "The model is a game in which actors simultaneously make proposals and exert influence on one another. They then evaluate options and build coalitions by shifting positions on the issue in question. The above steps are repeated sequentially until the issue is resolved" (Bueno de Mesquita 1994, 74). This model predicts policy outcomes based on three variables: the *potential power* and *policy position* of each actor on each issue examined and the *salience* each actor associates with those issues. An independent U.S. government audit has placed the accuracy of the model at better than 90 percent (Feder 1987). A sample of real-time published predictions can be found in Bueno de Mesquita (1984, 1990), Bueno de Mesquita and Kim (1991), and Kugler and Feng (forthcoming).

POLITICAL POWER

Table 2.1 indicates the position of each group in the hierarchy of power in North Korea. Kim Jong Il, who is expected to exert the most influence of any stakeholder in North Korean policy debates, is not only the official leader but also has effectively ruled the country for the last twenty years. We assign the number 100 as a benchmark measure of his capabilities. The capabilities of other groups in North Korea have been measured against Kim Jong Il. We calculate a group's capabilities based on how many of its members were represented among the top forty-two leaders on the list of leaders who attended the ceremonies marking the fiftieth anniversary of the founding of the Korean Workers' Party, October 10, 1995 (the latest leadership list).[8] B. C. Koh (1996) writes, "In the North the order in which a person's name is listed is scrupulously controlled and reflects his or her ranking in the power hierarchy."

ISSUE SALIENCE

In analyzing the policy debate over domestic economic reform, note that the importance of this issue is not uniform across all groups. Certainly, the issues of domestic reform and opening policy are likely to draw the attention of most elites in North Korea, but they are not the only pressing issues. For example, the international dispute over North Korea's nuclear program may be a higher priority issue for Kim Jong Il. The economic issues are most salient to those

Table 2.1   Approaches to Domestic Economic Reform

Groups	Capabilities	Policy Preferences	Salience
Kim Jong Il	100	80	70
Kim family	80	80	50
Partisans	80	10	50
Second generation	70	80	50
Ideologues	70	10	80
Security forces	60	40	50
Military	80	10	80
Heavy industry	40	10	90
Planners	60	50	90
Light industry	40	80	90
Infrastructure	10	10	50
Managers	0	10	90
Diplomats	30	80	50

responsible for managing the economy and those significantly affected by them—heavy industry, light industry, planners, managers, and the military. Given the ideologically charged atmosphere in North Korea, the ideologues will take great interest in reform issues, but other groups will be less active. The Kim family, the partisans, and the second generation may not participate in policy debate as separate groups, leaving policy making to the relevant officials, unless there is an imminent regime crisis. Economic reform per se does not directly affect the interests of the security interests and diplomats. Kim Jong Il as chief executive will be more active than other members of the ruling class. The salience figures in table 2.1 are constructed accordingly.

Unlike domestic economic reform, opening policy has more direct security consequences, so it has high salience to the security forces. Diplomats will be more active because opening is a foreign policy issue. Heavy industry and its managers will be less active because opening without substantial reform is unlikely to affect their position significantly. The salience of this issue to the other groups is assumed to be the same as that of domestic economic reform. The results are summarized in table 2.2.

Predicting Policy Choices

Our analysis of the prospects for North Korean economic reform begins with an evaluation of the most likely policy choice. As figure 2.1 makes clear, this is a highly volatile issue. The front bar, denoting the predicted outcome

Table 2.2   Approaches to Economic Opening

Groups	Capabilities	Policy Preferences	Salience
Kim Jong Il	100	50	70
Kim family	80	50	50
Partisans	80	0	50
Second generation	70	50	50
Ideologues	70	0	80
Security forces	60	0	80
Military	80	30	80
Heavy industry	40	30	60
Planners	60	50	90
Light industry	40	80	90
Infrastructure	10	80	50
Managers	0	30	60
Diplomats	30	80	80

based on the model we are using, shows that debate over the question of economic reform is likely to be prolonged and lead to big swings in policy. First, considerable support surrounds Kim Jong Il's preference to move North Korea's economy in a direction similar to the reforms put in place in the People's Republic of China over the past fifteen or so years. Forces opposed to such reform, however, can quickly reassert themselves, reversing the process. Chinese-style reforms are then abandoned in favor of direct restructuring to promote light industry and to reduce subsidies to heavy industry and the military. Although this still represents reform relative to the status quo, it is a far cry from the fundamental changes that occurred in Deng's China and may not be sustainable. The model-based analysis supports the contention that the military, partisans, ideologues, and representatives of heavy industry will ultimately exert enough leverage to prevent almost any economic restructuring. They, not Kim Jong Il and his followers, are the true powers behind North Korean economic policy making.

It is instructive to examine the predicted shifts in position of the competing power centers in North Korea. Although we assume that Kim Jong Il favors marked economic change, it is evident in figure 2.1 that political pressure (especially from the security forces and the hard-liners) would force him to retreat from his preferred position. The security interests, recognizing the threat to their own interests from the military and its backers, persuade Kim Jong Il to back them, thus forestalling, for the time being, the rising influence of the hard-liners and shoring up a power center sympathetic to their interests. Kim Jong Il's concessions, however, will pave the way for deeper conflicts among competing power interests.

Figure 2.1   North Korean Economic Reform

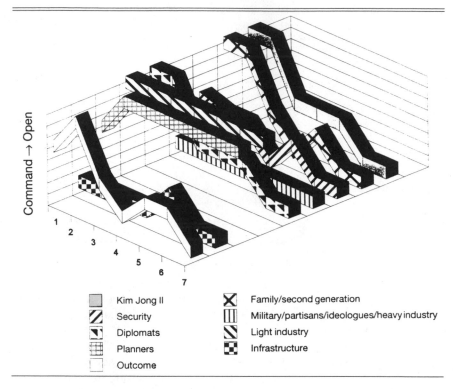

▢ Kim Jong Il		☒	Family/second generation
▨ Security		⦀	Military/partisans/ideologues/heavy industry
◣ Diplomats		◩	Light industry
▦ Planners		▚	Infrastructure
▯ Outcome			

   The Kim family and the second-generation leaders will initially endorse
Chinese-style reforms along the lines favored by Kim Jong Il. It will not take them
long, however, to recognize Kim's political vulnerability and to distance themselves from him. The family and second generation will break with Kim Jong Il
just as he builds stronger ties to the security interests.

   The family and the second generation will throw their weight behind the
hard-liners in heavy industry and the military in an effort to stifle economic
reform. They will vacillate momentarily, retreating to Kim's position, but then
place themselves solidly behind the hard-liners. Ultimately, this combination of
interests will be irresistible as even Kim aligns himself with their antireform point
of view. At this juncture, facing a choice between political isolation and defeat or
holding onto at least titular power, he chooses the latter, while real authority
probably passes to the military and, through it, to the family and the second
generation. It is important to note that the military and heavy industry interests
have the leverage to attract strong support, but, by themselves, they do not have
the power to defeat Kim Jong Il's reform program. To do that, these hard-liners

must garner the support of Kim's family and the second generation. It appears that this combination of interests represents the pivotal powers behind the throne in present-day North Korea.

Given the volatility of policy stances and the eagerness of so many factions to hold onto power—the North Korean factions generally want to enhance their political clout and see policy primarily as an instrument for achieving this end— it is not surprising that North Korea appears rife with internal political conflict. Indeed, we estimate that about 87 percent of stakeholder interactions that do not start out in complete agreement are conflictual or coercive at the outset, with fewer than 1 percent of such interactions leading to compromise. This extraordinarily high initial level of conflict strongly suggests that North Korea is entering a period of significant political instability. In particular, we find that for Kim Jong Il all initial relationships that do not represent complete policy agreement represent conflict. Those conflicts taper off as he accommodates the will of others, but the initial circumstance highlights the volatility and vulnerability of his situation. Disagreements pertaining to the method and extent of economic reform in North Korea will, we believe, precipitate a fundamental shake-up wherein Kim Jong Il may be reduced to little more than a titular leader. Political relations are likely to produce instability as the military, Kim Jong Il, his family, and the second generation all vie for political control and political survival.

The picture could not be more different when we turn to the issue of economic openness. For instance, although initial conflict is still high on this issue, it is not nearly as high (60 percent). Of the remaining 40 percent of interactions, three-quarters (30 percent of all interactions) reflect compromises. What is more, the issue is, according to our model, quickly resolved, albeit not to the satisfaction of many interests on both sides of the question. Figure 2.2 shows our predicted evolution of this issue over the next few years. As the outcome line (the overall prediction) makes clear, the issue quickly moves to a seemingly stable resolution at 30 on the scale. A score of 30, of course, reflects a shift away from the status quo and is not encouraging for North Korea's economic development, for it means that the North Koreans are prepared to open their economy but are not prepared to include South Korea in that opening (beyond current levels) even on an informal basis. Because the South Koreans are the ones most likely to be inclined to invest in the North, and because others are likely to look (correctly) at their exclusion with some nervousness, it seems unlikely that North Korea's anticipated economic program will move the country away from its collision course with bankruptcy and poverty.

Figure 2.2 highlights additional underlying political tensions within the North Korean leadership, including the fact that the issue is resolved without a consensus forming. Rather, Kim Jong Il moves quickly to endorse the policy preference of the military (which appears to exert the greatest influence on him). At the same time, the security forces and the party ideologues steadfastly oppose

Figure 2.2   North Korean Economic Openness

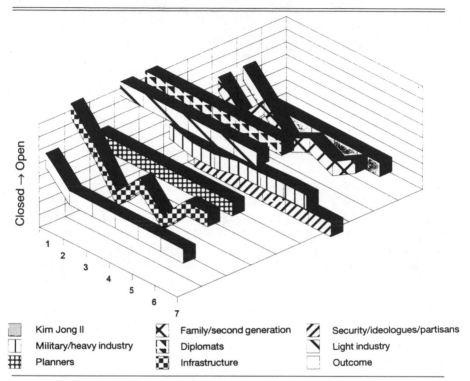

	Kim Jong Il		Family/second generation		Security/ideologues/partisans
	Military/heavy industry		Diplomats		Light industry
	Planners		Infrastructure		Outcome

any opening of the economy, sticking to their hard-line position from start to finish. Similarly, and not surprisingly, those with a stake in light industry and in foreign cooperation (i.e., the diplomats) support the most open policy. Neither they nor the antiopenness forces ever shift away from their initial point of view, meaning that the military/Kim Jong Il compromise reflects a tenuous centrist coalition, not a broad consensus. Obviously, North Korean decision making on this issue does not appear to be monolithic.

As in the economic reform issue, we again see signs that Kim Jong Il's hold on power is tenuous, with significant prospects of political instability. On both issues he is compelled by political realities to abandon his initial policy preference. His family and the second-generation interests, who split with him after initially backing the policy he prefers, seem to shop around for a political position that will differentiate them and enhance their political importance. This leads them, in a transparently opportunistic manner, to endorse a policy of greater openness than that supported by Kim Jong Il and then to endorse a policy less sympathetic to openness. In the end, however, they do not win. The true winner on this issue is the military. Indeed, on both issues the military's wishes are ultimately identical to the long-term predicted outcome. Winning coalitions move to what they want; they never shift to accommodate anyone else's wishes, which may be the most important lesson to take from this exercise. The military, more so than Kim Jong Il or anyone else, is in a position of political preeminence in North Korea and is likely to remain so for the next few years. In the political tug-of-war that we believe is taking shape in North Korea, the military is best positioned to be the winner. But even it represents the core of a fragmented coalition that has only a tenuous hold on power over the longer term.

The model also suggests that there are strategies available to various North Korean interest groups whereby they could alter the predicted outcomes and stabilize the situation. Such strategies, however, involve actions the protagonists are not likely to take because they overestimate the adverse consequences. For instance, the partisans have leverage that they do not recognize according to the model. This leverage would allow them to persuade Kim Jong Il, the planners, the Kim family, light industry, the second generation, and the diplomats to accept a compromise at around 45 to 50 on the economic reform scale. (Such an outcome is equivalent to North Korean policy makers promoting light industry, reducing subsidies to the heavy and military industries and moving toward deeper cutbacks in military spending.) The partisans' reticence to press their case leads Kim Jong Il and others to look elsewhere for a political coalition that can shore up their hold over the perquisites of power. If the partisans were to recognize how ready others are to follow their example, they might forge the compromise coalition described above, thereby diminishing the influence of North Korea's military and helping to promote meaningful economic change.

Conclusion

We have examined two important issues regarding North Korean economic policy. Using a model with a strong track record of predictive accuracy, we have specified how Kim Jong Il's hold over power in North Korea might unravel. The analysis presented here suggests that the military and heavy industry interests are pivotal powers in North Korea and that Kim Jong Il's family and the second generation are opportunists who are likely to break with Kim Jong Il to secure their own political well-being. Such a breach is likely to result in a slowing of economic reform and a decline in economic openings to South Korea. North Korea is then expected to enter a period of political instability that would render Kim Jong Il little more than a figurehead. Barring strategic efforts by the partisans or others with credible leverage, North Korea is unlikely to improve its economy or stabilize its government in the next two or three years.

How will a regime crisis play out in North Korea? Some observers see the emergence of black markets as signaling an imminent regime collapse because they create a new class of resource holders that can challenge the current structure of power (Collins 1996). Because civil society has been almost nonexistent in North Korea, however, discontented North Koreans may not start to protest until they see signs of the elites' unwillingness to use violence. Di Palma (1991) argues that it was the leaders' loss of faith that caused the collapse of the communist regimes. How rulers lose the will to fight can be explained by a contingency model of transition (Przeworski 1991) whereby regime crises split the ruling class into hard-liners and soft-liners. Democratic transition begins "by mistake," as soft-liners or reformers tend to overestimate their popular support or underestimate the potential for mass mobilization and thus lose control of the process. But this scenario leaves several questions unanswered. First, who are the hard-liners in communist regimes? Second, if the hard-liners can intervene any time, did they try to reverse the process in Eastern Europe? Third, when reformers do not have any one to negotiate with, as was the case in the Soviet Union and is likely to be true in North Korea, what are the forces that drive the dynamics of transition?

When communist regimes faced mounting crises (i.e., when the reformers could not control the transition process), the role of the armed forces became critical. If the military cooperates with the hard-liners (and it is often made up of hard-liners), it can have the means to maintain the regime. But none of the Eastern European militaries fought to the end. In Hungary, Poland, and Czechoslovakia, the military did not repress the demonstrations. In Bulgaria, the military turned against the party and led the transition itself. The Romanian army initially carried out orders to shoot but soon changed sides. The communist leaders had more confidence in the loyalty of their security forces and party militia, but only the Czech and Romanian security forces mounted any resistance. Barany (1993) argues that this pattern reflects the varying party-military relations that exist during communist rule: When authoritarian leaders consider using force, their ability to do so hinges on how loyal and unified their armed forces are. The military will not intervene if it has serious misgivings about the regime, such as the privileges enjoyed by the party technocrats and the security forces. Thus, we need to explore party-military relations in North Korea. How centralized and unified is the Korean People's Army (KPA)? Has the military been co-opted (e.g., is there significant military representation in party leadership and protection of the military economy in North Korea)? How are KPA officers treated relative to their counterparts in the security forces?

The Korean People's Army has a centralized command structure organized by the Communist Party. But there are numerous potential cleavages that may undermine the support of the military for Kim Jong Il (Koh 1991). As noted, there is a generational division. Most top leaders have partisan backgrounds (i.e., they fought with Kim Il Sung before 1945). But second-generation leaders may now control positions of power within the KPA. Furthermore, the KPA has several overlapping command structures. Like other communist armies, the party has its own line of command within the KPA through party committees and political officers. On top of that, members of the Three Revolution Movement Squad (which is organized down to the company level) allegedly have an independent line of communication with Kim Jong Il. Thus, professional officers are burdened with multiple channels of command.

Apparently, the military has priority in food rationing and officers earn relatively high salaries. But the officers in the party militia and the security forces are much better treated than those in the regular army.[9] Although there are no reliable data, these security forces are known to be sizable (including the Secret Police, Ministry of Public Safety, State Inspection Commission, the militia belonging to the Operations Department of the Central Committee, and armed divisions protecting Kim Jong Il).

In short, the large North Korean military contains multiple sources of internal conflict. Thus, if the Kim Jong Il regime faces a crisis, an open conflict may flare up between regular armies and security forces and the winner of this conflict may dictate the transition process.

Notes

The authors would like to thank Chae-Jin Lee, Marcus Noland, Han S. Park, and Robert Warne for their helpful comments.

1. For a comprehensive survey of the North Korean economy, see Noland (1996).

2. We consider only elites in North Korea, ignoring associations and other organized groups. There is little evidence that organized groups outside the institutions of government have any impact on government policy. Although some scholars describe certain "groups" (such as intellectuals and former residents of Japan) as potential dissidents, they do not yet pose any threat to the regime.

3. North Korean technocrats tend to stay in one ministry or policy area for their entire career, so it is reasonable to expect them to look after their institutional interests.

4. Chun (1996) describes the problems of food, energy, and foreign exchange shortages in North Korea.

5. Susan Gates (1995) distinguishes between administrative and economic conversion and between direct and indirect conversion.

6. Based on the Chinese experience, McMillan (1995) argues that successful reform does not have to involve privatization as long as the market remains competitive.

7. Here we treat industrial restructuring as the central problem in domestic economic reform. Because of uncertainty over the outcome of policy, the debate over industrial restructuring is assumed to be over policy mechanisms rather than the numerical targets for industry share. Chun (1996), however, argues that the North Korean economy, al-

though industrialized, is more dependent on agriculture than the prereform Eastern European economies, so the reform of agricultural production may also be important for the success of North Korean economic reform.

8. A group with x number of representatives on the list is assigned the score equal to "x times 10."

9. Kim (1994) describes press accounts (*Naewoe Tongsin*, November 18, 1993, and Foreign Broadcast Information Service, *Daily Report*, March 3, 1994) of the special treatment accorded the officers in the Party Operations Department and the General Guard Bureau. They not only draw higher salaries but also receive a level of rice allowance that is three times higher than the regular military officers of the same rank.

References

Barany, Zoltan. 1993. "Civil-Military Relations in Comparative Perspective: East-Central and Southeastern Europe." *Political Studies* 41 (December): 594–610.

Bueno de Mesquita, Bruce. 1984. "Forecasting Policy Decisions: An Expected Utility Approach to Post-Khomeini Iran." *PS*, spring, pp. 226–36.

Bueno de Mesquita, Bruce. 1985. "The War Trap Revisited." *American Political Science Review*, March, pp. 157–76.

Bueno de Mesquita, Bruce. 1990. "Multilateral Negotiations: A Spatial Analysis of the Arab-Israeli Dispute." *International Organization*, summer, pp. 317–40.

Bueno de Mesquita, Bruce, and Chae-Han Kim. 1991. "Prospects for a New Regional Order in Northeast Asia." *Korean Journal of Defense Analysis*, winter, pp. 65–82.

Bueno de Mesquita, Bruce, David Newman, and Alvin Rabushka. 1985. *Forecasting Political Events*. New Haven: Yale University Press.

Bueno de Mesquita, Bruce, David Newman, and Alvin Rabushka. 1996. *Red Flag over Hong Kong*. Chatham, N.J.: Chatham House.

Bueno de Mesquita, Bruce, and Frans Stokman. 1994. *European Community Decision Making*. New Haven: Yale University Press.

Chun, Hong-Tack. 1996. "Economic Conditions in North Korea and Prospects for Reform." This volume.

Collins, Robert. 1996. "Pattern of Collapse in North Korea." *Wolgan Chosun*, May, pp. 369–81.

Di Palma, Giuseppe. 1991. "Legitimation from the Top to Civil Society: Politico-Cultural Change in Eastern Europe." *World Politics* 44 (October): 49–80.

Feder, Stanley. 1987. "Factions and Policon: New Ways to Analyze Politics." *Studies in Intelligence*, spring.

Gates, Susan. 1995. "Defense Conversion and Economic Reform in Russia." In *Economic Transition in Eastern Europe and Russia*, ed. Edward P. Lazear. Stanford: Hoover Institution Press.

Jeong, Kap-Young. 1995. "The North Korean Economy in Transition." Paper presented at the International Conference on Northeast Asia, Otaru University of Commerce, July 23–26.

Kim, Pan Suk. 1994. "Prospects for Political and Administrative Development in North Korea." *In Depth* 4: 157–86.

Koh, B. C. 1991. "Political Change in North Korea." In *North Korea in Transition*, ed. Chong-Sik Lee and Se-Hee Yoo. Berkeley: Institute of East Asian Studies, University of California at Berkeley.

Koh, B. C. 1996. "Recent Political Developments in North Korea." This volume.

Kugler, Jacek, and Yi Feng. Forthcoming. "Applications of the Expected Utility Model" (tentative title). *International Interactions*, special issue.

McMillan, John. 1995. "China's Nonconformist Reforms." In *Economic Transition in Eastern Europe and Russia*, ed. Edward P. Lazear. Stanford: Hoover Institution Press.

Noland, Marcus. 1996. "The North Korean Economy." *Joint U.S.-Korea Academic Studies* 6:127–78 (Washington, D.C., the Korea Economic Institute of America).

Przeworski, Adam. 1991. *Democracy and the Market*. Cambridge, Eng.: Cambridge University Press.

·············· **3** ··

Economic Conditions in North Korea and Prospects for Reform

HONG-TACK CHUN

Introduction

The North Korean economy is in a deep crisis. Output has declined for six consecutive years since 1990. On top of this, floods in 1995 caused extensive damage to agriculture, the infrastructure, and industrial facilities. Various independent assessments of the food supply problem in North Korea conducted by such institutions as the Department of Humanitarian Affairs of the United Nations, the World Food Programme, and the Food and Agriculture Organization of the United Nations indicate that, unless substantial food aid is provided, malnutrition and possible starvation will affect millions of people. Some analysts even argue that North Korea may collapse in three to five years because of the crisis caused by food shortages and economic decline.

If economic conditions do indeed threaten the collapse of the state, North Korea will surely undertake full-scale reforms. With regard to such a possibility, the following questions need to be asked.

How serious are the economic difficulties in North Korea? What are the most pressing problems? How does the reform experience differ between China and Eastern Europe? What are the similarities and disparities between the North Korean economy and the prereform economies of China and Eastern Europe? What are the implications of comparative analyses of the economies of North Korea and prereform socialist countries on prospects for reform in North Korea? What model will North Korea choose if it does undertake reform?

This chapter is organized as follows. In the first section, I analyze North Korea's long-run growth trends to discover whether its current economic difficulties are temporary or structural. In addition, three serious problems of the North Korean economy are investigated: food problems, energy shortages, and foreign exchange constraints.

In the second section, I draw lessons from the reform experiences of China and Eastern Europe and compare their prereform economies with the North Korean economy. On the basis of that analysis, I derive some implications for North Korea's future reform.

The third section discusses prospects for reform in North Korea with an emphasis on the political economy of reform.

Economic Problems

North Korea is probably the most secretive country in the world even by communist standards. Furthermore, the reliability of the scanty available information provided by North Korea or estimated by outside researchers is often disputed. Any study of the North Korean economy is constrained by the dearth of information, and thus the results of the quantitative analyses in this chapter should be considered accordingly.

GROWTH TRENDS BEFORE 1990

Figure 3.1 shows the growth trends of gross national product (GNP), primary energy supply, and electricity generation in the period 1960–1990. The North Korean economy grew fairly rapidly in the period 1960–1975; however, in the second half of the 1970s the growth rate of GNP declined sharply, to 4 percent, less than half that of the period 1960–1975. Growth rates dropped further, to 1 percent, in the second half of the 1980s (see figure 3.1).

The growth of the primary energy supply and electricity generation, both closely related with output, shows exactly the same trend as that of GNP. It is apparent that a period of deep stagnation had begun by the mid-1980s. The growth path of North Korea is similar to that of the former USSR and Eastern Europe, in which the growth rate of GNP per manhour plummeted from 3.5 percent in the period 1950–1975 to 1 percent in the period 1975–1990.[1]

It is not a coincidence that all these centrally planned economies began to stagnate at about the same time as if inflicted by a common disease. For the purpose of this chapter, however, it is sufficient to point out that structural problems of centrally planned economies lie at the heart of the sudden collapse of growth in the economies of the USSR, Eastern Europe, and North Korea.[2]

Figure 3.1   Growth Trends of the North Korean Economy

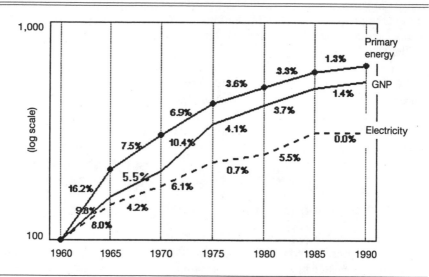

NOTES: 1. Growth rates of primary energy supply between 1961 and 1970 were estimated by the Central Intelligence Agency (CIA) and thereafter by the International Energy Agency (IEA).

2. Gross national product (GNP) growth rates through 1985 were estimated by the CIA and thereafter by the National Unification Board (NUB) of South Korea.

3. Growth rates of electricity generation were estimated by the CIA.

SOURCES: IEA, *Energy Statistics Yearbook 1992*; NUB, *Overview of North Korea 1991*; CIA, *Handbook of Economic Statistics, 1980, 1990*.

FOOD PROBLEMS

Except for occasional announcements of doubtful grain production figures, North Korea does not publish agricultural statistics. The most recent announcement was in 1984, reporting that it had achieved a grain production target of ten million tons.

South Korea's Rural Development Administration (RDA), in collaboration with the National Unification Board (NUB) of the Republic of Korea, independently estimates North Korea's grain production by cultivating North Korea's grain seeds in a farm near North Korea and considering total acreage under cultivation, irrigation facilities, weather conditions, quantity of fertilizer applied, and so on. According to the RDA and the NUB, North Korea's agriculture began to face problems in the second half of the 1980s as productivity stagnated due to the inherent deficiencies of collective farming.

Furthermore, the supply of agricultural inputs such as fertilizer began to shrink, and farm machinery began sitting idle due to a fuel shortage that began in 1990. At first North Korea appeared to meet food shortages by adjusting downward the proportion of rice in the grain rationing and by increasing grain imports. In 1992, however, grain demand began exceeding supply by more than one million tons, and it seems that North Korea began reducing grain rationing for food, feed, and other uses. To determine exactly by how much grain consumption was reduced is difficult. An educated guess for the maximum quantity of grain consumption that can be reduced through food rationing is 500,000 to one million tons, assuming that a minimum caloric intake was provided and that grain consumption for feed and other uses can be cut in half (see table 3.1).[3] Shortages of grain in 1992 (1.15 million tons) and 1993 (1.22 million tons) were well below the maximum quantity of grain consumption that can be reduced through food rationing and cutting down on other uses.

In 1994, however, the demand for grain based on rationing norms exceeded the available supply by 2.19 million tons; in 1995 it exceeded 1.7 million tons, which is greater than 1.5 million tons, the maximum quantity of grain consumption that can be reduced.[4] North Korea appears to have drawn on grain stock to make up the shortfalls in 1994 and 1995.

Food problems will become even more serious in 1996 because of the previous year's floods. Table 3.2 shows estimates of food supply and demand for 1996: figures in the first column were reported to the United Nations by North Korea, numbers in the second column are estimates by the Food and Agriculture Organization (FAO) and the World Food Programme (WFP), and those in the last column are estimates by the NUB of the Republic of Korea.

According to the North Korean reports, demand (630 grams a day of food per person) exceeds production by 3.88 million tons. The consensus among a wide range of observers is that grain demand reported by North Korea, which was obtained by assuming normal food rationing, is far greater than actual consumption under the reduced food rationing system. In addition, the loss of grain due to floods seems overestimated. A recent joint FAO/WFP report came to a similar conclusion. It estimates that demand (450 grams a day of food per person) exceeds production by 1.91 million tons. Estimates by the NUB of the Republic of Korea are in line with the FAO/WFP assessment.

The quantity of grain produced in 1995 will meet demand for eight months according to the FAO/WFP estimate and more than seven months according to the South Korean authority's estimate. Therefore, North Korea appears to have enough grain to last at least until May or June of 1996. Some regions may experience severe food shortages before that time, however, because of regional differences in food production, transportation, and rationing systems. It is difficult to judge how serious food problems will be in the second half of 1996, for assessment differs over the quantity of reserved grain in stock and North Korea's capability to import food.

Assuming that no grain stock exists, grain import requirements (1.9–2.3

Table 3.1   Grain Demand and Supply (1989–95) (in thousands of tons)

	1989	1990	1991	1992	1993	1994	1995
Total Demand (A) [a]	6,000	6,200	6,400	6,500	6,580	6,670	6,720
Principally for food [b]	4,219	4,359	4,500	4,570	4,627	4,690	4,725
For other uses [b]	1,781	1,841	1,900	1,930	1,953	1,980	1,995
Total Supply (B)	5,901	6,343	6,081	5,347	5,358	4,484	5,018
Production [c]	5,210	5,482	4,812	4,427	4,268	3,884	4,125 [d]
Net imports [e]	691	861	1,269	920	1,090	600	893 [f]
Shortage (A−B)	99	−143	319	1,153	1,222	2,186	1,702

NOTES:

[a] Estimates by the Rural Development Administration.

[b] Distinction between grain demand for food and for other uses is available only for 1991. Proportion of food in 1991 is thus applied to all years.

[c] Previous year.

[d] Loss of grain stock due to floods is not considered.

[e] Un-Kun Kim, "North Korea's Food Problem," *The Reunified Korean Economy*, November 1995.

[f] United Nations, Department of Humanitarian Affairs, Preliminary Findings of United Nations Assessment Mission, 12 September 1992.

million tons), consisting of half rice and half maize, will cost between $390 and $472 million. Considering North Korea's recent grain imports (0.6–1 million tons), export volume ($1 billion including exports to the South), and foreign exchange shortage, this is a heavy burden. North Korea, however, may have a substantial grain reserve in stock. In addition, it may be capable—in view of the military expenditure of more than $5 billion and the $100–$800 million reportedly remitted by pro–North Korean residents in Japan—of importing enough grain to make up for the shortfall.

In any case, North Korea's food problem is apparently structural[5] and needs outside assistance. Rehabilitating North Korea's agriculture by normalizing the supply of fertilizer and other inputs is urgent. Ultimately North Korea will have to make the transition away from collective farming to family farming, as China and Vietnam have done.

ENERGY

The energy sector is one of the most serious bottlenecks in the North Korean economy. Energy supply indexes in 1994 by energy source, of which the base year is 1989, are as follows: coal production 58.7, petroleum imports 35.0, and electricity generation 79.1 (see table 3.3). Coal is the most important source of energy in North Korea, accounting for 82 percent of primary energy and 75 percent of final consumption. Coal consumption is broken down as follows:

Table 3.2   Demand for and Supply of Grain, 1996 (in thousands of tons)

	North Korea [a]	FAO/WEP [b]	NUB [c]	
Total Demand (A)	7,639	5,988 [d]	5,780 [d]	(6,730) [e]
Principally for food	4,869	3,688	—	
For other uses	2,770	2,330	—	
Actual Production (B)	3,764	4,077	3,450	
Original forecast	5,665	4,967	—	
Losses due to floods	1,901	890	—	
Production Shortfall (A−B)	3,875	1,911	2,330	

NOTES:

[a] United Nations, Department of Humanitarian Affairs, "Assessment of Damage and Immediate Relief Requirements Following Floods," 12 September 1995.

[b] Food and Agriculture Organization (FAO) and the World Food Programme (WFP), "Crop and Food Supply Assessment," December 1995.

[c] Appeared in *Seoul Shinmun*, 2 February 1996.

[d] Based on actual food rationing.

[e] Based on food rationing norms.

industry and other sectors (final demand) 72.6 percent, electricity generation 21.1 percent, and other uses (coking, liquefaction, etc.) 2.7 percent.[6] A decrease in coal production is the cause of economic stagnation as well as its effect.

The major cause of the coal shortage is underdeveloped mining technology. North Korea lacks the technology to mine coal at more than moderate depths, whereas coal pits have become deeper as a result of long and continuous mining.[7]

In addition, although North Korea has substantial coal reserves, the varying quality of its coals and the location of some of its better coal reserves have set limits on their utilization. Some of the coals mined in North Korea have ash contents as high as 65 percent and heating values as low as 1,000 kilocalories per kilogram (roughly one-sixth the energy content of high-quality coals).

Approximately half of the coal reserves in the Anju area, which is northwest of Pyongyang and the largest coal mining region in North Korea, are under the seabed. Thus the mines are close to the sea, and miners have to pump out six tons of seawater per ton of coal mined because of saltwater infiltrating into the low-lying coal seams. North Korea currently lacks the technology to effectively and safely extract this coal, some of which is high quality.

There are also reports that bottlenecks in coal mining, transportation, and steel production interact to further constrict the North Korean economy. This is the classic command economy problem of a shortage of coal for steel and power production on the one hand and constraints on transporting coal to end users owing to the lack of iron and steel to maintain the rail system on the other.

Table 3.3   Energy Supply, 1989–94

	1989	1990	1991	1992	1993	1994
Coal production						
Million tons	43.3	33.1	31.1	29.2	27.1	25.4
Index	100.0	76.4	71.8	67.4	62.6	58.7
Crude oil imports						
Thousand tons	2,600	2,520	1,890	1,520	1,360	910
Index	100.0	96.9	72.7	58.5	52.3	35.0
Electricity generation						
Billion kilowatt-hours	29.2	27.7	26.3	24.7	22.1	23.1
Index	100.0	94.9	90.1	84.6	75.7	79.1

SOURCE: Bank of Korea, "Estimation Results of North Korea's GNP," various years.

Next, a decrease in petroleum imports caused critical problems in transportation and agriculture. Because the petrochemical industry, which requires imported oil, is underdeveloped in North Korea as a result of the self-reliance principle (relying on domestically produced coal for energy and minimizing oil imports), most refined petroleum is used as fuel for transportation and agricultural machinery. Therefore, when petroleum imports declined by 65 percent, from 2.6 million tons in 1989 to 0.9 million tons in 1994, transportation and agriculture were hit hard.

Approximately 50 percent of electricity generation is hydroelectric and 50 percent thermal, mostly coal fired.[8] Electricity generation declined by 21 percent from 1989 to 1994, largely as a result of the decrease in coal production. North Korea will be provided with heavy oil under the U.S.–North Korea Agreed Framework: 300,000 tons in 1996 and 500,000 tons thereafter annually until the construction of light water reactors is completed. The Ung-gi Power Plant can operate at 100 percent capacity with 500,000 tons of heavy oil. When fully operational, the plant will generate 1.6 billion kilowatt-hours, which equal 7 percent of the electricity generated in 1994.

Because electricity generation should increase by 26 percent just to return to the 1990 level of generation, however, the electricity shortage will continue unless coal production increases substantially.[9] Therefore, energy sector reforms such as price reform, diversification of energy sources, and improvement of energy efficiency are necessary to solve the energy problem.

FOREIGN EXCHANGE CONSTRAINTS

Although North Korea is one of the most closed economies in the world, trade with socialist countries was important to sustain its economy because it acquired petroleum, grain, and equipment and parts from those countries at low prices. North Korea's gains from trade with socialist countries are summarized as follows.

First, trading among socialist countries did not require foreign exchange because they were essentially barter deals. Second, North Korea imported petroleum from the USSR and China at roughly half the international price (see table 3.4). Third, the USSR and China did not press North Korea for political considerations to fulfill export obligations under the bilateral trade agreement, although their trade balance with North Korea recorded persistent deficits, implying de facto assistance. Fourth, North Korea obtained petroleum and grain in exchange for soft goods because trade among socialist countries is based on agreements between governments in consideration not only of economic interests but also of international politics.

It was, therefore, a devastating blow to North Korea's economy when the former USSR and China undertook trade reform and requested North Korea to pay international prices in hard currency for their exports to North Korea. North Korea's external trade declined by over 40 percent in 1991 as its trade with the former USSR contracted to one-sixth the previous year's volume (see figure 3.2). North Korea's international trade has stagnated since then, remaining at its 1991 level.

North Korea's demand for hard currency shot up dramatically because of the above-mentioned trade reforms in the former USSR and China, whereas its supply of hard currency increased but little owing to its limited capacity to produce hard goods. A foreign exchange shortage is one of the biggest constraints to economic activity, for it limits a country's ability to import capital goods, petroleum, and grain. For that reason, North Korea must promote export industries to increase foreign exchange earnings.

Lessons from the Reform Experiences of Socialist Countries and Their Implications for North Korea

CHINA AND EASTERN EUROPE

China has grown rapidly since economic reforms began in 1978, whereas Eastern Europe and the former Soviet Union have faced economic turmoil and significant declines in output. This has resulted in debates over shock versus gradualism approaches to reform. In this section, I attempt to draw three lessons from the experiences of China and Eastern Europe and their implications for North Korea.[10] First, the economic structure helps determine the reform strategy and the performance after reform.

Table 3.4   China's Oil Export Prices (in U.S. dollars per ton)

	1988	1989	1990	1991
To North Korea	$63	60	58	126
To world	$98	113	142	131

SOURCE: Japan External Trade Organization, *Prospects for Economy and Foreign Trade of North Korea*, 1992, p. 59.

In prereform China, agriculture accounted for 72 percent of total employment; industrial state enterprises accounted for less than 8 percent. Thus agriculture was first to undergo reform and was a leading sector in the early stage of postreform economic development in China. Because state enterprises were of limited importance, China was gradually able to move away from a planned economy to a market economy. This is the essence of the two-track approach: continuing control of state enterprises while a new nonstate sector grows largely outside state control. The Chinese economy has grown rapidly without declines in output or additions to mass unemployment because the Chinese transferred labor from low-productivity agriculture to high-productivity industry.

In Eastern Europe, the aim of reform was structural: cutting employment in inefficient and subsidized industrial state enterprises to allow new jobs in efficient industries and services. Large declines in output and unemployment were necessary, at least temporarily, to expedite structural adjustments.

Second, macroeconomic stability also determines the speed and scope of reform and affects the postreform performance of the economy. At the outset of reform in China, stabilization policies were not required, for prices were stable and external debts were negligible. In contrast, Poland faced inflation rates of more than 100 percent and a heavy foreign debt burden. Therefore, the big bang style of price and trade liberalization was chosen together with tight fiscal and monetary policies in Poland because macroeconomic stabilization was a prerequisite for successful reform. Because stabilization policy has a contractionary effect, some stagnation was unavoidable.[11]

The third, and probably the most important, lesson is that political conditions largely determine the process of reform.[12] If a noncommunist, democratic government is elected after the collapse of a communist government, as in Eastern Europe, the big bang style of reform is likely to be chosen because the transition to a market economy would be the mandate of the new government. In contrast, a gradual strategy requires an effectively managed reform. Therefore, whether the state retains the capacity to control will affect many aspects of the reform process. In addition, political stability encourages both the domestic and the foreign investment essential for a smooth transition.

Figure 3.2   The External Trade of North Korea

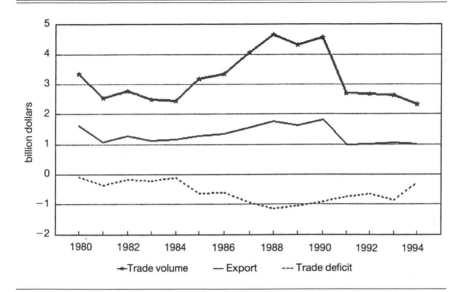

NORTH KOREA

Economic structure. When we look at production structure in terms of GDP distribution by sector, North Korea is closer to prereform China than to pre-reform Eastern Europe (see table 3.5). Because of large declines in industrial output, North Korea's production structure in 1994 almost matches China's production structure in 1979. However, the agricultural proportion of North Korea's economically active population is less than half that of prereform China, though it is significantly greater than that of prereform Eastern Europe.[13] This suggests that North Korea is more industrialized than prereform China though not quite as industrialized as prereform Eastern Europe.

Table 3.6 shows some socioeconomic indicators of North Korea, prereform China, and Eastern Europe. North Korea appears to be at a level of social development, measured by life expectancy and infant mortality statistics, similar to that of China. In contrast, North Korea and prereform Eastern Europe are comparable on urbanization.[14] But the urbanization data are unreliable because the definition of an urban area in North Korea is unknown, and thus the data likely overstate the relative urbanization of North Korea.

A comparison of the degree of openness (measured by the ratio of exports to GNP) shows that North Korea is less open than Eastern Europe as well as

Table 3.5   Structure of Production in North Korea and
               Prereform Socialist Countries (in %)

	DISTRIBUTION OF GROSS DOMESTIC PRODUCT			*Economically active population in agriculture*
	Agriculture	*Industry* [a]	*Services*	
North Korea (1990)	27%	56%	17%	33.5%
North Korea (1994)	29	43	28	30.1
China (1979)	31	48	21	74.2 [b]
China (1990)	27	42	31	67.5
Bulgaria (1989)	11	59	29	12.2 [c]
Czechoslovakia (1989)	6	57	36	9.3 [c]
Hungary (1989)	14	36	50	11.5 [c]
Romania (1989)	18	48	34	20.2 [c]
Poland (1989)	14	36	50	20.8 [c]

NOTES:

[a] Mining, manufacturing, construction, electricity, gas, and water

[b] 1980

[c] 1990

SOURCES: Bank of Korea, *Estimation Results of North Korea's GNP, 1990, 1994*; *China Statistical Yearbook 1990*; Food and Agriculture Organization of the United Nations, *Yearbook Production 1994*; World Bank, *World Development Report 1991*.

Colombia, the Philippines, and Thailand, all of which are lower-middle-income countries like North Korea with a comparable population size (see table 3.7). In fact, North Korea is almost as closed as prereform China.

Macroeconomic stability.   Prereform China's economy was relatively stable, with low inflation and its external economy in balance, though the average annual growth rate in the period 1971–77 was only 2.7 percent. In contrast, prereform Eastern European countries such as Poland and Hungary faced serious inflation, enormous debt burdens, and large fiscal deficits, in addition to sluggish growth.

Although North Korea's inflation rate is unknown, the average annual growth rate of North Korea's GNP in the period 1990–94 was −4.4 percent, and foreign currency shortages prevent North Korea from importing sufficient grain and petroleum. Thus, with regard to macroeconomic conditions, North Korea is worse off than prereform China and perhaps even worse off than prereform Eastern Europe.

Table 3.6   Socioeconomic Indicators of North Korea and
             Prereform Socialist Countries

	Life expectancy at birth (year)	Infant mortality rate per 1,000 live births	Urban population/ total population (%)
North Korea (1986)	67.7 [a]	34.6 [b]	59.6 [a]
China (1970)	—	69	18
China (1987)	69	29 [c]	38
Bulgaria (1989)	72	13	67
Czechoslovakia (1989)	72	12	77
Hungary (1989)	71	17	61
Romania (1989)	71	27	52
Poland (1989)	71	16	61

NOTES:

[a] Estimates by Eberstadt and Banister

[b] Reported by North Korea; definition of urban population unknown

[c] 1989

SOURCES: Nicholas Eberstadt and Judith Banister, *The Population of North Korea* (Berkeley: University of California, Institute of East Asian Studies, 1992); World Bank, *World Development Report*, 1989, 1991.

Political conditions. The Kim Jong Il regime appears stable and seems to have the capacity to control, though by coercion. With regard to political stability, North Korea seems closer to China than to Eastern Europe. There is a crucial difference, however, in leadership succession between North Korea and China. With military support and thanks to successful economic reform, a coalition led by Deng Xiaoping ousted the Gang of Four and Hua Guofeng and reaffirmed the legitimacy of communist rule. In addition, China linked reform and opening to unification policy, using Taiwanese capital for development.

In contrast, Kim Jong Il, son and heir of Kim Il Sung, remains in power in North Korea. The Kim Jong Il regime is, thus, a mere extension of the Kim Il Sung regime. Kim Jong Il's dilemma is that fundamental reform is necessary to prevent the collapse of the economy, but that reform may lead to his downfall and ultimately the collapse of the North Korean communist system itself.

IMPLICATIONS FOR NORTH KOREA

Economic crisis is the necessary condition for reform, and the more serious the crisis, the greater the necessity for reform. North Korea has recorded negative growth rates for six consecutive years. The structural problems of food, energy, and foreign exchange are major bottlenecks in the economy. All in all, the cur-

Table 3.7   Foreign Trade Participation Ratios of North Korea, Prereform
                 Socialist Countries, and Selected Developing Countries (in %)

	Export/GNP	*Import/GNP*	*Total trade/GNP*
North Korea (1990)	8.7	11.4	20.1
North Korea (1994)	4.0	6.0	10.0
China (1978)	4.7	5.2	9.9
China (1990)	17.1	14.2	31.3
Bulgaria (1992)	30.9	30.9	61.8
Czechoslovakia (1989)	26.8	26.5	53.3
Hungary (1989)	35.0	32.1	67.1
Poland (1989)	19.4	14.9	34.3
Romania (1992)	16.7	23.0	39.7
Colombia (1992)	15.6	15.0	30.6
Philippines (1992)	19.8	31.2	51.0
Thailand (1992)	30.4	37.9	68.3

NOTE: GNP = gross national product
SOURCES: Bank of Korea, "Estimation Results of North Korea's GNP," 1900, 1994; *China Statistical Yearbook 1990*; World Bank, *World Development Report*, 1991, 1994.

rent economic conditions in North Korea are much worse than those faced by prereform China and may be even worse than those of prereform Eastern Europe. Therefore, North Korea needs full-scale reform and change.

What lessons can North Korea draw from the comparison of economic structure and macroeconomic conditions between North Korea and prereform socialist countries? In this section, we draw lessons for North Korea from comparative economic analyses without considering political factors, which are examined in the next section.

First, because the role of agriculture in North Korea is relatively small, agricultural reform by itself is unlikely to ignite economic growth. However, because more than 30 percent of the labor force is in agriculture, and because agricultural reform can alleviate the food and foreign exchange shortages, reform in North Korea should start with agriculture, as was done in China and Vietnam.

Second, the most important economic task of the government is to remove foreign exchange constraints by promoting trade and exchange-rate reform. For this purpose, North Korea should make an effort to create an attractive business environment to attract foreign direct investment. In particular, it needs the capital and know-how of the South, just as China used the capital and know-how of the overseas Chinese in Hong Kong and Taiwan. China's approach to trade reform, which was more gradual than that of Eastern Europe, may suit North Korea, as it has worked well for other East Asian economies.

Third, the distribution and service sectors should be liberalized, and, if possible, small-scale privatization should take place; these reforms are likely to have the fastest payoff, as confirmed by the experiences of China and Eastern Europe.

Fourth, price reform is also necessary to disseminate the effects of foreign direct investment and the reforms in agriculture and the service sectors. China's gradual price reform involved a dual-price system that preserved planned allocation while drawing incremental output into a market system. Its dual-price system succeeded because China started reform under stable macroeconomic conditions and was able to keep rent-seeking behavior and corruption within bounds. North Korea, however, does not have the luxury of stable macroeconomic conditions, and thus gradual price reform may not work.

Last, a gradual approach to state enterprise reform would have limited effects in North Korea because the role of state enterprises there is relatively large compared with that in China. However, because many state enterprises in heavy industry have already so deteriorated that they are burdened with large disguised unemployment, any industrial restructuring in North Korea would not cause large declines in output and employment, as happened in Eastern Europe.

Prospects for Reform

The reforms in China and Eastern Europe originated from economic problems that had been piling up for a long time; however, their direct cause was political change. In the case of North Korea, conditions for reform are ripe in the economic area, but reform has not yet begun for political reasons. Whether North Korea undertakes reform and, if so, what kind of reform it will choose, to a large extent depends on political factors, the most important of which is the stability of Kim Jong Il's regime, for the more unstable the regime, the greater the possibility of sustaining limited opening without reform. Kim Jong Il has been favorable toward China's open-door policy but indifferent to or critical of China's domestic reform. He once confessed to Shin Sang-Ok and Choi Eun-Hee, a well-known Korean movie director and actress whom he had ordered abducted to North Korea (they later escaped via Vienna and sought asylum in the United States), that "it is impossible to solve the problem of feeding people without reaching out toward the Western world." Also when Kim Jong Il visited China in 1984 and was advised of the opening of the North Korean economy by Hu Yao-Bang, he answered, "We will open Chongjin city and Kangwon province but (for security reasons) we cannot open the west coast."[15]

Kim Jong Il's past record also shows that he is not likely to be a true reformer. Important internal economic policies that seem to have been led by Kim Jong Il for the last ten years are as follows: expansion of an independent accounting system, full-scale implementation of an associated enterprise system (*yeon-hap-gi-eop*) and the ensuing reorganization of the planning system, the August Third campaign for people's goods, reorganization of collective farms into national farms or agricultural associated enterprises (agro-industrial complex), and decentralization of trade. These are partial reform measures intended to improve the central planning system, not full-scale reforms for the introduction of a market economy.[16] Also—according to Lee Min-Bok, who worked as a breeding researcher at the Agricultural Science Institute in the North before defecting to the South in February 1995—Park Chul, a researcher who had written a paper insisting on the introduction of family-based farming,[17] Agriculture Minister and Vice Premier Kim Hwan, and Central Party agriculture secretary Suh Kwan-Hee, who had agreed on the introduction of family-based farming, were all severely punished by Kim Jong Il in 1986.[18]

Second, papers that have been published in Kim Jong Il's name since the collapse of Eastern Europe's communist system stress "maintaining our style of socialism" and "carrying out Kim Il Sung's teachings."[19] Kim Jong Il also emphasizes that the cause of the breakdown of Eastern Europe's communist system was "impairing first generation revolutionaries and obliterating their accomplishments" and that "later generation revolutionaries must protect, defend, succeed and further develop the thoughts and accomplishments of elder revolutionaries."[20] Therefore, even if Kim Jong Il is aware of the necessity for reform, it would be difficult to undertake because it goes against the economic system and policy of the Kim Il Sung era, especially at a time when the regime is unstable.

If North Korea can attract foreign capital by enhancing its relationship with the United States and Japan, economic conditions may improve even without fundamental reform. But, as seen in the first section, North Korea's economic problems are structural and the economy is already in crisis. Full-scale economic recovery is thus unlikely without fundamental reform, and economic reform is inevitable, whether by Kim Jong Il himself or by a new leadership.

Which economic reform model will North Korea choose? As long as the reform is undertaken by the communist regime, the reform model of North Korea is likely to be closer to the Chinese model than to the East European model. But because the macroeconomic conditions in North Korea are more unstable than they were in prereform China, price liberalization will be effective only when it is undertaken, as in Vietnam, in a comprehensive and drastic manner. In addition, because North Korea is more industrialized than prereform China, industrial restructuring is important, that is, downsizing inefficient and uncompetitive heavy industries and developing competitive light industries. To promote industrial restructuring without privatization, North Korea will need foreign direct investment. Just as China needed overseas Chinese capital and know-how, North Korea needs South Korean capital and technology.

Although the role of agriculture is relatively small in comparison to that in

China, reform in North Korea should start in agriculture because agricultural reform can mitigate food shortages and foreign exchange constraints. All in all, North Korea's reform, to be successful, will be close to but also different from the Chinese model.

North Korea's opposition to South-North economic cooperation and South-North dialogue stems from fears that they could trigger instability in North Korean society and lead to its absorption by the South. Furthermore, the power base of the current leadership does not seem strong enough to pursue fundamental change. But if the current policy of limited opening without reform continues, there will be a growing possibility of a crash, which neither South Korea nor its neighboring countries, geographically or strategically, wants to witness.

Notes

1. Gomulka (1991).

2. Balcerowicz (1990), Gomulka (1991), and Murrel and Olson (1991) discuss reasons for the sudden collapse of growth in centrally planned economies.

3. Minimum average calorie intake required for sustaining normal life is 2,100 kilocalories (kcal) a day (the average calorie intake for adults is 2,700 kcal/day). Assuming that calorie intake from other sources than grain is equal to that of South Korea in the early 1970s, the average North Korean needs 1,735 kcal a day from grain. This amounts to 500 grams a day per person and 182.5 kilograms a year per person.

4. Defectors testified that the food problem had become pronounced since 1994 and that grain trade at the farmers' market had become widespread despite the fact that such activity is prohibited by law (*Joong-Ang Ilbo*, 20 January 1995).

5. According to the FAO/WFP report, the average quantity of fertilizer applied to cereal crops was approximately 1,000 kilograms per hectare (kg/ha) in 1989, a normal year; it dropped to 500 kg/ha in 1994 as a result of the declining economic situation in North Korea.

6. International Energy Agency, *Energy Statistics and Balances of Non-OECD Countries*, 1993.

7. This section on coal draws on Hayes (1993).

8. The Ung-gi Power Plant in Sunbong, North Hamgyung province, the only oil-fired plant in North Korea, has the generation capacity of 200,000 kilowatts.

9. It will take the Korea Energy Development Organization eight to ten years to complete the construction of light water reactors, which will generate 10 billion kilowatt-hours annually.

10. For a detailed analysis of "shock versus gradualism," see McMillan and Naughton (1992), Gelb, Jefferson, and Singh (1993), Rosati (1994), Sachs and Woo (1994), and Woo (1994).

11. See Rosati (1994) on why output behavior followed an L-shaped pattern instead of a U-shaped pattern during the initial stages of reform in Eastern Europe.

12. Gelb, Jefferson, and Singh (1994).

13. North Korea's labor force distribution by sectors is not known. According to the occupational distribution of the population ages sixteen and over provided by North Korea to Eberstadt, only about one-fourth of the North Korean adult population is classified as farmers. But these data must be used with caution, for they are peculiar in many respects (Eberstadt 1995, 88–91). Consequently, FAO statistics are used for a cross-country comparison. FAO's economically active population in agriculture is obtained by adjusting statistics reported by member countries to eliminate any differences in classification and taxonomy.

14. See Eberstadt and Banister (1992).

15. "Conversation between Kim Jong Il, Shin Sang-Ok and Choi Eun-Hee" (1984. 8. 4); tape recording of Kim Jong Il's voice, *Monthly Chosun*, October 1995.

16. Chun and Park (forthcoming).

17. This system uses the family as a basic work team unit in the collective farm.

18. *Segye Times*, 14 June 1995.

19. "Our Style Socialism with the People at the Center Will Unfailingly Triumph," *Nodong Sinmun* (Worker's daily), 5 May 1991; "Historical Lessons from Building Socialism and Our Party's General Line," *Nodong Sinmun*, 3 January 1992.

20. "Priority to Ideological Work Is an Essential Requisite to the Socialist Cause," *Nodong Sinmun*, 19 June 1995; "Treating Elder Revolutionaries Is the Noble Moral Duty of Revolutionaries," *Nodong Sinmun*, 25 December 1995.

References

Balcerowicz, L. "The Soviet-Type Economic System, Reformed Systems and Innovativeness." *Communist Economies* 2, no. 1 (1990).

Chen, Kang, Garry H. Jefferson, and I. Singh. "Lessons from China's Economic Reform." *Journal of Comparative Economics* 16 (1992).

Chun, Hong-Tack, and Jim Park. "North Korea's Economic Development." In *The Korean Economy 1945–95: Performance and Vision for the 21st Century*, ed. Dong Se Cha, Kwang Suk Kim, and Dwight Perkins. Seoul: Korea Development Institute, forthcoming.

Eberstadt, Nicholas, and Judith Banister. *The Population of North Korea*. Berkeley: University of California, Institute of East Asian Studies, 1992.

Gelb, A., G. Jefferson, and I. Singh. "Can Communist Economies Transform Incrementally? The Experience of China." *Economics of Transition* 1, no. 3 (1993).

Gomulka, Stanislaw. "The Puzzles of Fairly Fast Growth and Rapid Collapse under Socialism." Paper presented at the Twentieth Anniversary Symposium on Economic Growth of Developing Countries: 1940s–1980s, hosted by the Korea Development Institute in Seoul, July 1–3, 1991.

Hayes, Peter. *Cooperation on Energy Sector Issues with the DPRK*. Berkeley, Calif.: Nautilus Institute, 1993.

McMillan, J., and B. Naughton. "How to Reform a Planned Economy: Lessons from China." *Oxford Review of Economic Policy* 8, no. 1 (1992).

Murrel, Peter, and Mancur Olson. "The Devolution of Centrally Planned Economies." *Journal of Comparative Economics* 15, no. 2 (June 1991):239–65.

Noland, Marcus. "The North Korean Economy." Paper presented at the Korea Economic Institute/Korean Institute for International Economic Policy/Asia Foundation round-table on the North Korean economy, 8 July 1995, Seoul, Korea.

Rosati, Dariusz K. "Output Decline during Transition from Plan to Market: A Reconsideration." *Economics of Transition* 2, no. 4 (1994).

Sachs, Jeffrey, and Wing Thye Woo. "Structural Factors in the Economic Reforms of China, Eastern Europe, and the Former Soviet Union." *Economic Policy* 18 (April 1994).

Woo, Wing Thye. "The Art of Reforming Centrally Planned Economies: Comparing China, Poland and Russia." *Journal of Comparative Economics* 18 (1994).

.... 4 ....

Prospects for a North Korean External Economic Opening

MARCUS NOLAND

Introduction

North Korea seeks to be the world's most autarkic economy. The data, however, show that imports have consistently exceeded exports and that, after peaking in the late 1980s, trade has fallen substantially in the 1990s (see figure 4.1).[1]

North Korea's largest export sectors are apparel, iron and steel, and natural resource–based products such as zinc and edible crustaceans.[2] North Korea's largest import sectors are petroleum, grain, textiles, and capital goods. North Korea also exports arms, with net exports at times exceeding half a billion dollars during the 1980s (figure 4.2). Reduced demand, new competitors, and obsolete designs have all hurt sales, and the most recent estimate of North Korea's net exports of weaponry is much lower, on the order of $30 million.[3]

North Korea's trade partner orientation has varied tremendously over time in response to changing political (as distinct from market) circumstances. Initially North Korean economic relations were heavily oriented toward the USSR and its allies.[4] During the 1970s there was a shift toward the industrial countries. After North Korea's debt defaults this trade more or less dried up, and there was a shift back toward the USSR. With the collapse of the USSR and the implosion of the Russian economy, China has emerged as North Korea's main trade partner, though Eberstadt et al. (1995) argue that even China has limited its exposure to

Figure 4.1   International Exports and Imports, 1985–1993

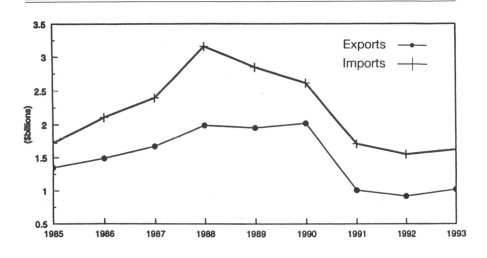

North Korea in official trade relations. (Smuggling of unknown magnitude also occurs across the China–North Korea border.) After China, Japan and South Korea are North Korea's main trade partners. Most of the trade between North and South Korea consists of apparel manufactured on consignment that is trans-shipped through China. Noticeably absent is the United States, which in effect continues to maintain an embargo against North Korea.

Constructing a Balance of Payments

According to the reported trade statistics displayed in figure 4.1, North Korea has been running a trade deficit on the order of half a billion dollars, adjusting for transportation costs. In the absence of nonrecorded exports, service exports, remittances, or other sources of revenue, this would have to be covered by external borrowing.[5]

North Korea's debt is modest in absolute terms ($7.9 billion in 1993), and the vast majority of this figure ($6.2 billion) is long-term debt owed to former centrally planned economies (CPEs). Much of this debt is denominated in rubles, and it is questionable how much if any of this ruble-denominated debt will ever be repaid. Another $649 million of long-term debt is owed to Organization for Economic Cooperation and Development (OECD) countries, a figure that has been relatively constant, reflecting Western banks, governments, and

Figure 4.2   North Korean Arms Trade, 1983–1993 (in US$millions)

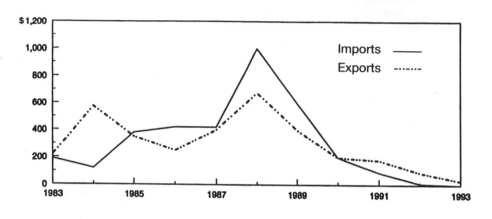

SOURCE: U.S. Arms Control and Disarmament Agency, 1995.

multilateral institutions' unwillingness to increase their long-run exposure in
North Korea. The remainder ($1 billion) consists of short-term loans that are
generally rolled over. Given that, in reality, North Korea has defaulted on most
of its long-term debt, its reservice payments are modest ($70 million), except for
a spike in repayments during the period 1990–91. Compared with other CPEs,
North Korea's ratio of debt to exports (including the ruble-denominated debt) is
quite high (770.6 percent), though the debt service–to-exports ratio is low (6.9
percent) because North Korea has essentially stopped paying its debt and no
longer has access to long-term capital markets.[6] What long-term capital inflows
North Korea obtains apparently come from China.

IMPLICIT SUBSIDIES

Determining North Korea's true terms of trade is no easy task. First the
Soviets, and later the Chinese, reportedly supplied North Korea with oil and
possibly other commodities at below market prices. After the collapse of the
USSR, the Chinese began supplying the North Koreans with oil on an apparently
significantly concessional basis, reportedly "half the world price" (Patrick 1991,
34). In 1992, however, the Chinese announced that they too would no longer
continue this practice and that in 1993 all transactions would be on a cash basis
at the world price (Yeon 1993a). There is some disagreement, however, as to
whether this policy has been implemented; at least one observer believes that
perhaps 35 percent of North Korea's oil imports from China are provided on a
concessional basis.[7] Similarly, North Korea is the only country to which China

has permitted the export of its staple grains, and, again, it is unclear on what terms this trade has occurred, though the consensus appears to be that grain too is being provided on a concessional basis. Recently some have argued that China has halted grain sales owing to its own poor harvest and that some split may be emerging between China and North Korea as a result of the North's growing trade with Taiwan.[8]

NONRECORDED TRADE

A significant amount of illegal movement in goods and people is apparently occurring across the China–North Korea border (though the two governments have recently made moves to halt this), with an unknown number of economic refugees exiting North Korea. Presumably the value of this two-way trade movement roughly balances—it is hard to imagine smugglers accumulating large imbalances. In addition, in the past North Korea has apparently conducted a significant trade in arms (figure 4.2), though net exports for 1993, the most recent year available, were only $30 million.

REMITTANCES

North Korea's trade relations with Japan are dominated by the colonial legacy of approximately 700,000 Koreans residing in Japan, approximately one-third of whom support North Korea through the Chochongryun (Chosensoren in Japanese) (*Nikkei Weekly*, 23 May 1994). The biggest impact of the Chochongryun may be through its organization of remittances to North Korea, which have been estimated at anywhere from $400 million to $2 billion, with the most recent estimates tending toward the lower end of that range.[9] (If the $2 billion figure is accepted, remittances would be twice North Korea's merchandise exports!) It is also thought that these remittances vary considerably from year to year, depending on North Korean pressure on the Chochongryun to raise funds for large political festivals or other events. In any case, these remittances might be important in financing North Korea's chronic trade deficits in light of the North's inability to make use of normal financing channels because of the debt defaults.

The size of these remittances can be estimated as a residual of the balance of payments under a series of assumptions. An accounting identity links remittances to the other trade aggregates:

$$REM = -TB - CAP - NRT,$$

that is, remittances (*REM*) are equal to the negative of the trade balance (*TB*) less net capital inflows (*CAP*) and whatever the balance is on nonrecorded transactions (*NRT*), including nonrecorded trade and reporting errors and omissions.

In the case of North Korea, some uncertainty surrounds each of these magnitudes. In the case of the trade balance, uncertainty exists owing to the difficulties in constructing North Korea's partner country trade as a result of incomplete reporting or misreporting by some partner countries, as previously noted. A second issue arises with respect to trade with other centrally planned economies in that the terms of this trade may deviate significantly from market prices. In response to these uncertainties, three estimates of the North Korean trade balance have been constructed for 1993, the most recent year for which complete data are available. The first is based on the GATT trade data used to construct the previous tables, adjusted for known cases of misreporting (i.e., Mexico) and that imports are reported inclusive of transport costs and exports are not. Moreover, it is assumed that North Korea does not have any outstanding balances in services trade, where data are nonexistent. A second measure of the trade balance is from KOTRA data. A third expunges trade with centrally planned economies, of which the overwhelming share is with China.

Capital flow data come from the OECD, which reports the data in two breakdowns: transactions with OECD countries and transactions with non-OECD countries. Both are used here. The total flow concept would be appropriate if all North Korea's trade were hard-currency denominated and if capital inflows were also in hard currency. The OECD-only formulation would be appropriate if trade with other CPEs was not denominated in hard currencies and was carried out on concessional or nonmarket terms, in which case hard-currency remittances would only be necessary to cover the hard-currency deficit less the hard-currency net capital inflows. In reality the situation may be somewhere between those two extremes, with some, though not all, trade with other CPEs effectively occurring on market terms.

With respect to nonrecorded trade, there is no reason to believe that smuggling, recording errors, or omissions are systematically biased toward a net deficit or surplus; in any event these cannot be observed. There is an estimated $30 million of nonreported arms net exports in 1993. Again, treatment of this aggregate is problematic. It may well be that the $30 million reflects genuinely nonrecorded arms exports that are used to finance imports and thus should be subtracted from the balance-of-payments gap that remittances are necessary to fulfill. It is possible, however, that this trade (allegedly undertaken with Middle Eastern countries that do in fact report trade with North Korea) is simply misreported in other commodity categories and does not represent a net addition to North Korea's balance-of-payments position. A third possibility is that this trade is beyond the control of the central planners and that some or all of it is being accumulated as reserves against future contingencies by either the military or the Korean Workers' Party (KWP). If either of these two hypotheses is correct, then some or all of the arms exports do not represent a genuine independent contribution to the financing gap and should not be used to calculate needed remittances. In response, two values of arms net exports are used: $30 million as a nonrecorded addition to net exports and zero under the assumption that this trade has been counted in other commodity categories or is being accumulated as reserves. Again, reality may lie somewhere in between.

Ten possible combinations of these alternatives are listed in table 4.1. The implicit remittances generated by these calculations exhibit an enormous range, from $633 million to −$325 million. (In the −$325 million case money would actually be flowing *out* of North Korea.) The mean and median values across the ten alternatives are positive (implying capital inflow) though, with the mean value $81 million and the median $71 million. These figures are considerably lower than those that are often conjectured and suggest that the remittances may not be as critical as commonly thought.[10] Alternatively, if remittances are as high as usually reported, either North Korea is running a surplus on its current account, accumulating foreign reserves and exporting capital, or hundreds of millions of dollars in expenditures are unaccounted for.[11]

Recent Reforms

North Korea historically has pursued an autarkic development strategy under the *juche* ideology of Kim Il Sung. The 1970s push for military modernization left the country heavily indebted relative to its meager export earnings, and the 1975 default effectively cut it off from international capital markets. The economy suffered further negative shocks with the withdrawal of Soviet economic support in the mid-1980s and the collapse of the Commonwealth of Independent States (CIS) economies, which had been North Korea's largest trade partner, in the early 1990s.[12] Although increased Chinese support has partly offset the loss of Soviet aid, China too has indicated that there are limits to how far it is willing to go to support the *juche* economy, especially in light of the liberalizing economic reforms undertaken in China. By all appearances North Korea is under significant balance-of-payments pressures with deleterious implications for growth prospects.

In response to this building crisis, the regime has begun some tentative reform measures. In 1984, following visits to China by Kim Il Sung in 1982 and 1983, the North Korean government enacted a joint venture law, apparently modeled on China's (though this is denied by North Korea). Big increases in inward foreign direct investment were not forthcoming, and in 1991, following another visit to China by Kim Il Sung, the government announced the creation of a special economic zone (SEZ) totaling 621 square kilometers in the area of Najin, Chongjin, and Sonbong in the Tumen River delta in the extreme northeast of the country, expanded in March 1993 by 125 square kilometers to 742

Table 4.1   Estimated Remittances, 1993 (in US$millions)

Case	Trade Balance [a]	Trade Balance [b]	Trade Balance [c]	Net Capital Inflow	Net Capital Inflow [d]	Net Arms Sales [e]	Net Arms Sales [f]	Remittance
1	$-498			$933		$30		$-465
2	-498			933			0	-435
3	-498				$5	30		463
4	-498				5		0	493
5		$-638		933		30		-325
6		-638		933			0	-295
7		-638			5	30		603
8		-638			5		0	633
9			$-91		5	30		56
10			-91		5		0	86
Memorandum items:								
Mean								81
Median								71

[a] Noland figures, adjusted for transportation costs.
[b] Korea Trade Association figures.
[c] Korea Trade Association figures, excluding trade with China and Russia.
[d] Net capital inflow from OECD countries.
[e] Arms sales, under assumption proceeds used to finance imports.
[f] Arms sales, under assumption proceeds accumulated as reserves.

square kilometers (Hwang 1993; Yeon 1993a; Suh and Kim 1994). A spate of additional laws followed, establishing the legal framework for foreign firms operating in North Korea (Koo 1992; Yeon 1993a; Suh and Kim 1994; Flake 1995; S. K. Kim 1995). On paper these conditions are better than those in the Chinese or Vietnamese SEZs (D. Lee 1993). Nevertheless, investments have remained relatively small, on the order of $150 million, and more consultative missions have been dispatched to China (Namkoong 1995). The Chochongryun accounts for nearly 90 percent of investment, with most of these investments concentrated in light manufacturing and retailing. Most of the investment has been for processing on consignment, with the North Koreans earning about 27 percent of the value of the exports (Y. S. Lee 1995).

To the extent that the SEZs can contribute to generating foreign exchange, they help relieve this pressure, but whether SEZs alone will be sufficient is another matter entirely. In most other countries that have made use of SEZs, with the aim of importing technology and establishing backward linkages with the rest of the economy, SEZs have been a failure: there has been little integration with the rest of the economy, and the SEZs have amounted to little more than export enclaves to exploit locally cheap labor (Noland 1991a). Ironically, in the case of North Korea, the regime may have little interest in integrating the SEZs with the rest of the economy and indeed may prefer that they remain isolated enclaves. The question then becomes, will they be sufficient for even this limited purpose?

Skepticism would appear warranted for at least two reasons. First, given the highly controlled nature of the rest of the society, it would appear to be a difficult task to make the SEZ work. The successful operation of an SEZ requires freedom of movement and a culture at least of noninterference, if not of efficiency. Everything in the broader North Korean society, where economics is subservient to politics, works against this. The stories of recalcitrant low-level bureaucrats and political interference in staffing are manifestations of this milieu. The second reason is that North Korea is not alone but must compete with China, Vietnam, and other countries throughout Asia and the world for business. High wages, poor infrastructure, and geographic isolation all are potential obstacles.[13]

Prospective Changes

At some point in the future, policy makers may conclude that these changes are inadequate for the problems at hand and that they must confront whether and how to accelerate and deepen the economic reforms. A true reform strategy would have to include price reforms; the introduction of a family responsibility system (or some other scheme) to debureaucratize agriculture; fundamental reforms of the planning mechanism, with the goal of encouraging greater reliance on market signals to inform the decision making of economic agents and competition between domestic enterprises; and the development of functioning capital markets. (This would not necessarily mean a move toward private property. It might be possible to maintain forms of nonprivate ownership, such as the township and village enterprises in China. The critical requirement is that enterprise managers respond to market signals.)[14]

There are economic (and presumably domestic and political) obstacles to reform. Successful gradual reform of a CPE requires resources to cushion adjustment in the heavy manufacturing sector. Propitious initial conditions may have benefited successful and relatively agrarian reformers such as China and Vietnam (see table 4.2): First, in those countries the state-owned heavy industry sector was initially relatively small. Second, China and Vietnam were able to initiate reforms in the agricultural sector, where price liberalization provoked rapid efficiency gains, freeing up low-productivity surplus agricultural labor to be absorbed by the emerging nonstate or semiprivate light manufacturing and service sectors.

Table 4.2   Distribution of Labor Force in
               Selected Centrally Planned Economies (in %)

Country	Agriculture	Sector Industry	Other
USSR (1987)	19 [a]	38 [b]	43
Ukraine (1990)	20	40	40
Belarus (1990)	20	42	38
Romania (1990)	28 [a]	38	34
Bulgaria (1989)	19 [a]	47	34
North Korea (1987)	25 [c]	57 [b]	18
China (1978)	71	15	14
Vietnam (1989)	71	12	17

[a] Agriculture and forestry

[b] Industry and construction

[c] Farmers

SOURCES: USSR, North Korea, and Vietnam, Eberstadt (1995), table 6. Romania and Bulgaria, Commander and Coricelli (1995), tables 5.1 and 6.11. Ukraine and Belarus, Bosworth and Ofer (1995), table 3-1. China, Sachs and Woo (1994), table 2.

These new, expanding sectors were then taxed to provide state revenues to cushion the transition in the heavy industry sector. The initial conditions of China and Vietnam are irreproducible, and such a path does not appear to be viable for more-industrialized CPEs (Riedel 1993; Sachs and Woo 1994).[15] Piecemeal reforms have not been successful in industrialized CPEs facing economic crises: the highly interdependent nature of industrial enterprises means that a whole host of reforms (macroeconomic stabilization, introduction of rational pricing, liberalization of international trade, and introduction of a convertible currency, tax, bankruptcy, and social safety net reforms) are a seamless web and must be done simultaneously for reform to be successful economically and sustainable politically (Lipton and Sachs 1990; Sachs and Woo 1994). Even in China and Vietnam, adjustment in the old state-owned heavy industry sector has proved difficult.[16]

The question arises, what would the North Korean economy look like if it were to undergo successful reform? There would be a reallocation of factors according to comparative advantage, and, were reform accompanied by a reduction of political hostilities with the South, there could be a significant demobilization of the military and a release of productive factors for alternative uses. Based on the experience of other transitional economies, one would expect a significant reorientation of international trade away from socialist allies and toward natural trading partners.

Table 4.3 reports an experiment using a "gravity model" of international trade.[17] According to this experiment, if North Korea traded like a "normal"

Table 4.3   Actual and "Natural" North Korean Trade Shares (in %)

	Actual Trade Share		"Natural" Trade Share
China	26	South Korea	35
Japan	18	Japan	30
Russia	11	China	13
Iran	9	United States	7
Rest of world	36	Rest of world	15

Memorandum:
   Share of Total
   Trade in GDP
	15		71

NOTE: Intra-Korean trade counted as international trade; GDP in current dollars from Bank of Korea.

country, its natural trading partners would be South Korea, Japan, China, and the United States, with South Korea and Japan alone accounting for nearly two-thirds of its trade. Moreover, the share of international trade in national income would roughly quadruple, as indicated in the memorandum item (though the resource reallocation associated with such a large increase in trade would almost certainly boost income significantly as well).

Noland (1996a) reports an analysis of North Korea's prospective comparative advantage on the basis of disaggregated trade and investment data for North Korea, South Korea, and Japan (prospectively North Korea's largest trading partners). This analyis concludes that North Korea's sectors of prospective comparative advantage would largely be in primary-product sectors, including mining; some marine products; niche agriculture, where North Korea's natural resources convey a comparative advantage; and light manufacturing industries, which are declining in Japan and South Korea but could be competitive in lower-wage North Korea.[18] Foreign investment and commissioned production for foreign firms presumably would be the main mechanisms for transforming North Korea's latent production potential into products the rest of the world would want to buy. A general equilibrium modeling exercise suggests that the increases in national income associated with such reforms could be as high as 40–50 percent.[19]

North Korea will not have the luxury of following the Chinese or Vietnamese path of gradual agricultural-led reform owing to its different starting points. Successful reform, if initiated, will require external support, which could come through a variety of channels, the most obvious of which is the Korean diaspora, including industrialists in South Korea, something that other industrialized CPEs have not had going for them in their transition processes (with the exception of East Germany, which is a different matter altogether).[20] Successful implementation of the nuclear deal would mean the provision of energy supplies and a move toward normalization of relations between the United States and North Korea.

The normalization of diplomatic relations between North Korea and Japan and the payment by Japan of postcolonial compensation would be other sources of external support.[21] At the time of normalization of diplomatic relations in 1965, the Japanese government paid the South Korean government $800 million in compensation for colonial and wartime activities.[22] The North Korean government expects similar compensation. Adjusting the South Korean payment for differences in population, accrued interest, changes in the price level, and appreciation of the yen since 1965, one obtains a figure on the order of $12 billion.[23] Such a sum, properly deployed, could go a long way toward restoring North Korean creditworthiness and financing economic modernization.

Under the right circumstances, multilateral development banks could also be tapped. The World Bank has mobilized $1.2 billion over three years for the two million residents of the Occupied Territories in the Middle East, or $200 per person per year. The bank has indicated that this "emergency assistance program" is to "provide tangible benefits to the Palestinian population quickly, equitably, and efficiently" as a foundation for sustainable development and peace (*The Economist*, 1 October 1994). A program of similar magnitude scaled up to the much larger Korean case could mean $4.4 billion annually. Under enlightened North Korean leadership, such capital inflows could go a long way to foster sustained development and peace on the Korean peninsula.

Conclusions

It will largely be the North Korean government, however, which will determine in the end whether these opportunities are seized. Unfortunately, there is little evidence that the North Korean regime is interested in serious reform. One can speculate on several potential obstacles to reform.

First and foremost, the existence of a prosperous democratic South Korea poses an enormous ideological challenge to North Korea. Once North Korea begins reforming, its entire raison d'être will be open to challenge. In Vietnam and China, Marxist ideologues were able to invent tortured rationalizations for market-oriented reforms. This is likely to be much more difficult for the North Koreans.

Second, the sheer scale of change that is likely to accompany significant liberalization is tremendous. North Korea is probably the most distorted economy in the world. Liberalization would mean huge changes in the composition of output and employment. International trade would become far more important, and most of that trade would be with South Korea and Japan, two countries with which North Korea maintains highly problematic relations.

Finally, it is hard to imagine North Korea undertaking significant reform without a more secure external environment. Although it is possible that the military, being the most coherent institution in the society with privileged access to economic assets, could be a prime beneficiary of reform, it may well oppose reform if it believes that this will endanger the nation's military security. And the military may be crucial in determining these outcomes, as suggested by Bueno de Mesquita and Mo (1996). This suggests that economic reform is unlikely to occur before some rapprochement with South Korea.

Consequently, economic reforms, though potentially highly beneficial, may not be undertaken, increasing the likelihood of continued economic decline and growing human misery. Although the regime may maintain its stability in the face of economic decline, such developments raise the specter of a Romanian- or East German–style collapse, accompanied by intervention by external powers.

Notes

1. There are enormous differences in the estimates of 1994 aggregate exports and imports generated by the Korea Trade Association (KOTRA), the National Unification Board (NUB), and the International Monetary Fund (IMF). According to KOTRA, exports were $839 million; according to NUB, $810 million; and according to the IMF, exports were $2.6 billion and imports were $2.2 billion (implying that North Korea was running a trade surplus).

The IMF data appear to have three possible problems. First, in the early 1990s Mexico apparently began misclassifying its South and North Korea bilateral trade, raising imports from North Korea by more than $600 million. Second, the IMF figures indicate an increase of more than $200 million in two-way trade between Austria and North Korea from 1993 to 1994. This, too, may be misclassification.

Third, the IMF figures reveal an enormous increase in trade between China and North Korea. A growing share of North Korean trade consists of processing on consignment, much of which is transshipped through China. It may well be that these inflows and outflows are being double counted by the Chinese, who do not use the same trade accounting procedures as the rest of the world. However, China and North Korea reportedly cracked down on smuggling in 1994, which might tend both to increase legal reported trade and to reduce the true volume of trade inclusive of smuggling.

If one adjusts the IMF figures by taking out the Mexican trade, North Korea still registers an enormous increase in trade but no longer runs a surplus.

2. The commodity and partner composition of North Korean trade has varied significantly over time, largely in response to political factors. These data are subject to considerable uncertainty; the North Korean government regards trade statistics as classified in-

formation and has never published them. The figures reported here are based on partner country reports to the General Agreement on Tariffs and Trade (GATT), supplemented by data from KOTRA in the case of countries such as Iran, which do not report the commodity structure of their trade with North Korea to the GATT.

3. These figures are consistent with Russian trade data as reported by Eberstadt, Rubin, and Tretyakova (1995). The fact that the military maintains its own trading channels outside the central plan is potentially of enormous policy importance: to the extent that the proceeds from arms sales are going directly to the military, the military may have a purely pecuniary incentive to continue selling arms, even if other parts of the government would like to restrict sales for broader foreign policy reasons.

4. The USSR reportedly provided oil to the North Koreans at two-thirds of the world price. At the same time, North Korea was sending products to the USSR, and it is not clear what the terms of trade were. It could be that while the USSR was underpricing its oil, it was also extracting from the North Koreans imports at below world prices, so the net magnitude of the subsidy is unknown. In 1990, Russia announced that it would no longer supply the North Koreans with subsidized oil (although there is disagreement as to how quickly the Russians intended to put this into effect), and the North Koreans responded by suspending repayments. The volume of trade between North Korea and Russia has declined along with worsening political relations and the implosion of the Russian economy, though North Korea continues to supply (under an agreement that officially expired in 1993) 15,000–20,000 laborers to Russia to work in logging camps in the Russian Far Eastern region. For detailed analyses of Russian–North Korean economic relations, see Bazhanova (1992) and Eberstadt, Rubin, and Tretyakova (1995).

5. North Korea may obtain additional revenues from illicit activities including drug trafficking and counterfeiting. See Foster-Carter (1994).

6. See Noland (1996a) for details.

7. Eui-Gak Hwang, personal correspondence, 10 March 1995; Dong-Il Koh, personal correspondence, 13 March 1995; and Ha-cheong Yeon, personal correspondence, 20 March 1995.

8. Additionally, in response to recent floods, North Korea has received grain on a concessional basis from South Korea, Japan, and the United Nations International Children's Emergency Fund (UNICEF).

9. These estimates have been made on the basis of everything from calculating the amount of currency Japanese residents visiting North Korea could take with them, to estimates of profit margins in the pachinko industry in which the Chochongryun has a significant presence. If the money does come in significant part from the profits of the gaming industry, it may well have declined in the wake of the burst of the bubble economy in Japan (Sato 1993; S. K. Kim 1994; Y. S. Lee 1994a; *Nikkei Weekly*, 23 May 1994; *The Economist*, 28 May 1994; Eui-Gak Hwang, personal correspondence, 10 March 1995; Dong-Il Koh, personal correspondence, 13 March 1995; Ha-cheong Yeon, personal correspondence, 20 March 1995; conversations with Japanese government officials, April and May 1995; Cho Myung-Jae interview, 8 July 1995).

10. At the same time, it should be noted that this calculation is for a single year; there

is reason to believe that the remittance flows may exhibit considerable time-series fluctuations.

11. One seminar participant noted that there is a historical precedent for leaders salting away sums on this scale, citing the example of President Mobutu of Zaire.

12. It would be interesting to compare the responses of North Korea and Vietnam to the common shock of the withdrawal of Soviet aid and the collapse of the USSR. My supposition is that the Vietnamese were more effectively able to reform their more agriculturally based economy and boost exports to ease the balance-of-payments constraint; in the absence of greater export orientation, the North Koreans were forced to reduce the level of domestic activity. Unfortunately the extreme uncertainty surrounding the North Korean balance-of-payments position (largely because of the issue of remittances) effectively precludes quantitative inquiry along this line.

13. See Noland (1996a) for analysis of these issues.

14. If the regime were to undertake such reforms, it would face a number of alternatives with respect to its external relations. See Noland (1996a) for discussion of these alternatives.

15. See Oh (1993) and Noland (1996a) for more on the relevance of China's reforms to the North Korean case.

16. Ironically, North Korea's extreme centralization may prove advantageous in at least one regard. Whereas in other CPEs many benefits, most important pensions and housing, are provided through the enterprise (and thus give workers an incentive to oppose enterprise reform), in North Korea these are provided directly by the state. As a consequence, North Korean workers may be more mobile and oppose enterprise less than their counterparts in other CPEs in some future reform situation.

17. The regression model, originally estimated by Frankel and Wei (1995), characterizes the volume of trade as a function of size, income level, proximity, and other factors. North Korean values of these explanatory figures were then substituted into the gravity model regression to generate North Korea's "natural" pattern of trade.

18. Although South Korea was the rice bowl in the past, if trade were opened today, North Korea might end up being a net exporter of agricultural goods to the South. O (1995) asserts that a reformed North Korea could have a comparative advantage in fruits, vegetables, dairy products, and meat (including beef, chicken, and pork).

19. See Noland, Robinson, and Scatasta (1996).

20. See Eberstadt and Bannister (1992), Hwang (1993), S. M. Lee (1993), Yeon (1993b), Chun (1994), H. S. Lee (1994), Y. S. Lee (1994a, 1994b, 1995), Lee and Kim (1994), and Noland (1996b) for analyses of unification issues.

21. Indeed, Japan's decision to consider granting official development assistance to the Palestine Liberation Organization was interpreted in some quarters as easing the way for Japan to provide aid to North Korea before diplomatic relations were established (*Financial Times*, 6 June 1995). More recently Japan provided North Korea with emergency food assistance.

22. The payments took the form of $300 million in grants, $200 million in development assistance loans, and $300 million in commercial credits.

23. This calculation assumes a 5 percent annual real rate of return since 1965 and a yen-dollar rate of 100. Obviously, with different assumptions, one could obtain different figures.

References

Bazhanova, Natalie. 1992. "Between Dead Dogmas and Practical Requirements: External Economic Relations of North Korea, 1945–1990." Manuscript.

Bueno de Mesquita, Bruce, and Jongryn Mo. 1996. "North Korea under Kim Jong Il: Prospects for Economic Reform and Political Stability." This volume.

Chun, Hong-Tack. 1994. "A Gradual Approach toward North and South Korean Economic Integration." KDI Working Paper 9311, Seoul, Korea Development Institute, November.

Eberstadt, Nicholas, and Judith Bannister. 1992. "Divided Korea: Demographic and Socioeconomic Issues for Reunification." *Population and Development Review* 18, no. 3: 505–31.

Eberstadt, Nicholas, Marc Rubin, and Albina Tretyakova. 1995. "The Collapse of Soviet and Russian Trade with the DPRK, 1989–1993." *Korean Journal of National Unification* 4:87–104.

Eberstadt, Nicholas, Christina W. Harbaugh, Marc Rubin, and Lorraine A. West. 1995. "China's Trade with the DPRK, 1990–1994." *Korea and World Affairs* 19, no. 4: 665–85.

Flake, L. Gordon. 1995. "The DPRK External Economy." Paper presented at the Sixth Annual Convention of the Congress of Political Economists (COPE) International, Seoul, 5–10 January.

Foster-Carter, Aidan. 1994. "North Korea after Kim Il-Sung: Controlled Collapse?" *Research Report*, London, Economist Intelligence Unit.

Frankel, Jeffrey A., and Shang-Jin Wei. 1995. "Is a Yen Bloc Emerging?" *Joint U.S.-Korean Academic Studies* 5:145–75.

Hwang, Eui-Gak. 1993. *The Korean Economies*. Oxford, Eng.: Clarendon Press.

Kim, Sang-Kyom. 1994. "Opening North Korea's Economy." In Jang-Hee Yoo and Chang-Jae Lee, eds., *Northeast Asian Economic Cooperation*, Policy Studies 94-08. Seoul: Korea Institute for International Economic Policy.

Kim, Sang-Kyom. 1995. "North Korean Economy: Prospects for Opening and Inter-Korean Cooperation." Seoul, Korea Institute for International Economic Policy. Mimeo.

Kim, Sung Chull. 1994. "Is North Korea Following the Chinese Model of Reform and Opening?" *East Asia Institute Reports*, East Asia Institute, Columbia University, New York, December.

Koo, Bon-Hak. 1992. *Political Economy of Self-Reliance*, Korean Unification Studies series 14. Seoul: Research Center for Peace and Unification in Korea.

Lee, Doowon. 1993. "Assessing North Korean Economic Reform: Historical Trajectory, Opportunities and Constraints." *Pacific Focus* 8, no. 3: 5–29.

Lee, Doowon. 1995. "Inter-Korean Economic Relation: Rivaled Past, Unbalanced Present, and Integrated Future." *Yonsei Economic Studies* 2, no. 1.

Lee, Hy-Sang. 1994. "Economic Factors in Korean Reunification." In Young Whan Kihl, ed., *Korea and the World*. Boulder, Colo.: Westview Press, pp. 189–215.

Lee, Sang Man. 1993. "A Study on Patterns of Economic Integration between South and North Korea." *East Asian Review* 5, no. 3: 91–113.

Lee, Yang, and Joon-Hyung Kim. 1994. "Peace Building on the Korean Peninsula," Washington, D.C., United States Institute for Peace, December.

Lee, Young Sun. 1994a. "The Current Status of the North Korean Economy and Prospects for Reform." *Osteuropa-Wirtschaft* 39, no. 2: 135–45.

Lee, Young Sun. 1994b. "Economic Integration of the Korean Peninsula: A Scenario Approach to the Cost of Unification." In Sung Yeung Kwack, ed., *The Korean Economy at a Crossroad*. Westport, Conn.: Praeger.

Lee, Young Sun. 1995. "Economic Integration in the Korean Peninsula: Effects and Implications." Paper presented at the Second Annual Korea-America 21st Century Council Conference, Washington, D.C., 9–10 February.

Lipton, David, and Jeffrey Sachs. 1990. "Creating a Market Economy in Eastern Europe: The Case of Poland." *Brookings Papers on Economic Activity* 1: 75–148.

Namkoong, Young. 1995. "An Analysis of North Korea's Policy to Attract Foreign Capital." *Korea and World Affairs*, fall, pp. 459–81.

Noland, Marcus. 1996a. "The North Korean Economy." *Joint U.S.-Korean Academic Studies* 6, Washington, D.C., Korea Economic Institute of America.

Noland, Marcus. 1996b. "Prospective Developments on the Korean Peninsula: Lessons from the German Experience." Paper presented at the U.S.-Korea 21st Century Council Conference, Washington, D.C., 8–9 February.

Noland, Marcus, Sherman Robinson, and Monica Scatasta. 1996. "Reforming the North Korean Economy." Washington, D.C., Institute for International Economics.

O, Wonchol. 1995. "A Response to North Korea's Food Crisis," revised and edited English translation of "Ssalboda nonsabop wonjo p'ilyo" *Sin Tong-A*, September, Canberra, Australian National University.

Oh, Seung-yul. 1993. "Economic Reform in North Korea: Is China's Reform Model Relevant to North Korea?" *Korean Journal of National Unification* 2: 127–51.

Patrick, Hugh. 1991. "Peace and Security on the Korean Peninsula: Reflections on the Economic Dimension." Working Paper series no. 56, Center on Japanese Economy and Business, Graduate School of Business, Columbia University.

Riedel, James. 1993. "Vietnam: On the Trail of the Tigers." *World Economy* 16, no. 4: 401–22.

Sachs, Jeffrey, and Wing Thye Woo. 1994. "Structural Factors in the Economic Reforms of China, Eastern Europe, and the Former Soviet Union." *Economic Policy* 18: 101–45.

Sato, Katsumi. 1993. "Japan: Stop Funding KIS!" *Far Eastern Economic Review*, 29 July.

Suh, Jae-Jean, and Byoung-Lo P. Kim. 1994. "Prospects for Change in the Kim Jong-Il Regime." *Series No. 2 Policy Studies Report*, Seoul, Research Institute for National Reunification, December.

Yeon, Ha-Cheong. 1993a. "Practical Means to Improve Intra-Korean Trade and Eco-

nomic Cooperation." KDI Working Paper 9301, Seoul, Korea Development Institute,
    January.

Yeon, Ha-Cheong. 1993b. "Economic Consequences of German Unification and Its
    Policy Implications for Korea." KDI Working Paper 9303, Seoul, Korea Development
    Institute, April.

·············· 5 ··

The North Korean Military Threat under Kim Jong Il

HIDESHI TAKESADA

Historical Setting: Lessons from Wars

The Korean People's Army was founded in 1948, seven months before the birth of the Democratic People's Republic of Korea (DPRK). The fact that the army was established before the state shows that Kim Il Sung thought the military was the foundation of a state. Historically speaking, this is not uncommon in the socialist world, and the DPRK is a typical socialist state.[1]

In 1948 the North Korean army was mainly equipped by the Soviet Union, which wanted to establish a satellite state in the northern half of the Korean peninsula. For his part, Kim Il Sung sought support from the Soviet Union to gain authority. Consequently, he set up cordial relations with the Soviet Union even before the DPRK was established. Thus in December 1948 the Soviet Union dispatched a large military mission composed of generals and intelligence experts to the North, and Kim was invited to Moscow as early as 1949. So we see that North Korea was, from the very first stage, strongly supported by the Soviet Union.

In 1950, the Korean War broke out. During the war, the North was dependent on the Soviet Union and the People's Republic of China (PRC) to fight the U.N. forces. The Soviet Union supported North Korea's cause, and Chinese forces actually participated in the war, making North Korea open to the influence of both countries. Throughout the 1950s the two countries helped North Korea recover from its war damages. Realizing that, North Korea began to emphasize its independent national defense in the early 1960s.

The Korean War and the ensuing reconstruction in the 1950s provide the background for North Korea's independent (*juche*) thought of the 1960s, during which time North Korea also decided to promote an "Independent Defense Policy" and began producing weapons.[2]

In considering the North Korean military, it is important to realize that North Korea has shaped its strategy from the experience of warfare and used it to establish its military capabilities as well.[3] The Korean War was the only one Kim Il Sung fought in after the DPRK was established in 1948; from it he learned three important lessons: First, realizing that it had been defeated by U.S. air supremacy, North Korea became convinced it had to strengthen its air power. Consequently, in the 1950s and 1960s, North Korea did so, with an emphasis on antiaircraft combat capabilities, including purchasing MiG-17, -19, and -21 combat aircraft from the Soviet Union and the PRC. On April 25, 1992, the Korean People's Army (KPA) held a parade on its sixtieth anniversary. On the scene were infantry-combat vehicles, self-propelled artillery, and self-propelled multiple-launch rockets were on the scene, all of which are designed for antiaircraft combat missions.[4]

Second, North Korea's weaknesses as a nonnuclear state were revealed when the United States implied that it would use nuclear weapons in the autumn of 1950. It is reported that it was then that Kim Il Sung began showing an interest in nuclear weapons, including sending North Korean nuclear energy researchers to the Soviet Union. On September 7, 1959, North Korea concluded the Atomic Energy Agreement for Peaceful Use with the Soviet Union. Although the main power resources in North Korea at that time were thermal and hydroelectric power generation, some experts argue that the North Koreans' main concern was nuclear weapons.

Third, North Korea was de facto defeated in the Korean War mainly because the United States intervened, even though it regarded the Korean peninsula as outside its defense line. After its severe defeat, North Korea recognized that unification would not be possible if the United States intervened (though there existed a good chance for a surprise attack). Since the Korean War, the withdrawal of the U.S. forces in Korea (USFK) has been the principal aim of North Korea's unification policy.

North Korea then fixed its eyes upon the Vietnam War, although it did not take part. Once again, it learned three lessons[5]:

First, North Vietnam maintained its supply route to the South and its guerrilla warfare by digging tunnels; North Korea thus realized that tunnels could be useful as a supply route and even as a route to put troops into war.

Second, military capabilities in South Vietnam dropped dramatically because of the discord between the United States and South Vietnam. In addition, the United States lost its hold in Vietnam because of corruption and frictions within the South Vietnamese government. North Korea thus realized that decreasing popular support for the South's government could be effective. Third, North Korea learned that Chinese cooperation and Soviet cooperation were integral to its cause.

Judging from its frequent comments, North Korea also seemed very interested in the gulf war, despite the gulf's distance from the Korean peninsula. This is because, inter alia, Iraq succeeded in its surprise attack at the first stages of the war, U.S. military capabilities were tested, and various kinds of high-tech weapons were used. Again, North Korea learned three lessons from the gulf war: the power of high-tech weapons, the efficiency of a surprise attack, and that U.S. intervention was essential for the positive outcome of any war.

In his New Year's speech immediately after the gulf war in 1993, Kim Il Sung said that "North Korea should rush to introduce high technology." Without a doubt, the gulf war showed North Korea that obsolete weapons, whatever their type, could not match the United States' high-tech weapons. Also, although North Korea probably realized that a surprise attack on the South was still possible, it also realized that the efficiency of such an attack would be offset if and when the United States intervened.

To make a surprise attack effective, and at the same time to prevent U.S. intervention should war break out, North Korea has to arrange for the withdrawal of the USFK. Thus after the gulf war North Korea began putting more emphasis on the improvement of U.S.–North Korean relations and a subsequent peace treaty. North Korean proposals on the armistice agreement also became more flexible and realistic.

In May 1995, North Korea banned U.N. monitors of the armistice agreement from entering its territory at Panmunjom. In February 1996, North Korea proposed signing a temporary accord with the United States, as the first step toward replacing the armistice agreement. The purpose of the proposal seems to be to promote a U.S.-DPRK direct military talks excluding the Republic of Korea (ROK) and to establish a U.S.-DPRK joint military organization at Panmunjom. The North argued that the South should not be a party to this organization because it was not a party to the original armistice agreement. Once U.S.-DPRK direct military talks started, the USFK would be a major item on the agenda.

Kim Jong Il's Nuclear Options

Although it has not yet been confirmed that North Korea is developing nuclear weapons, were it to do so it could ensure its national defense, restore its military supremacy over the ROK, take a tougher line against Japan, and limit U.S. military options should war break out. North Korea started its research on nuclear power generation in the 1950s and successfully developed a nuclear energy sector in the 1960s and 1970s. But in the late 1980s, it was suspected of developing nuclear weapons while the rest of the world focused on nonproliferation. (The world became skeptical about North Korea's attitude toward nonproliferation.)

North Korea's policies include participation in the Non-Proliferation Treaty (NPT) in 1985, ratification of the Safeguards Agreement of the International Atomic Energy Agency (IAEA) in 1992, acceptance of the special inspection by the IAEA, and suspension of its withdrawal from the NPT after the U.S.–North Korean talks. These policies are, in fact, consistent. In other words, North Korea is only willing to show part of its nuclear-related facilities and, while intending to cooperate with the world community on one hand, will not accept the special inspection by the IAEA on the other, a stance that has no doubt strengthened suspicion.

Nuclear weapons and missiles are attractive to North Korea for the following six reasons.

1. North Korea can obtain hard currency by exporting missile technologies and ballistic missiles to the Middle East. Thus, it has maintained intimate relations with Middle East states, including Syria and Iran. North Korea now obtains 500–600 million U.S. dollars a year by selling missiles and guns, which amounts to 7 percent of its foreign debts.[6] If North Korea succeeds in developing nuclear-related technologies and obtaining nuclear materials, it can obtain hard currency more easily.

2. Militarily, North Korea could become independent of the PRC and Russia. The former Soviet Union and Russia have influenced North Korea and its "self-reliance policy" through the supply of weapons since 1945, which has not always been acceptable to North Korea's national pride and independence in defense policy. Self-made weapons of mass destruction may therefore contribute to a policy of independence.

3. North Korea could strengthen its bargaining position vis-à-vis the United States, Japan, and South Korea. Even if nuclear weapons are not used, they may be useful psychologically in certain situations due to the

state of North-South relations. That is, if North Korea says to South Korea, "Make concessions, if you do not want war," sympathy among South Korean people toward the North would decrease. There is a feeling that North Korea would not attack its brothers with nuclear weapons and that only South Korea can persuade the North not to run that risk. In fact, after North Korea announced that "there would be a war if the world exercised sanctions on North Korea," enthusiasm for North-South dialogue grew among South Koreans.

4. As a result of economic stagnation, since the mid-1980s North Korean troops have begun to fall behind the South in the modernization of weapons. North Korea could compete with the modernization of the South Korean troops and maintain its military superiority only with nuclear arms.

5. North Korea could cut its military expenditures. It is believed that North Korea spends more than 20 percent of its national budget on military expenditures. The development cost of nuclear weapons is high, but with nuclear weapons, North Korea could reduce military personnel, as did the PRC, and reduce its financial burden.

6. Kim Jong Il could strengthen his power base. Generally speaking, military organizations tend to prefer conventional weapons to nuclear ones because they are "visible" to the people. But there is no indication that the Korean People's Army (KPA) has opposed the development of weapons of mass destruction, partly because the KPA is the primary power in North Korean politics and thus there is no argument on the distribution of the military budget inside the KPA. Kim Jong Il's credibility would also increase if North Korea succeeded in developing nuclear weapons and missiles.

Personnel Changes under the Kim Jong Il Regime

Some argue that Kim Jong Il does not control the Korean People's Army because of his lack of experience in the military. He could not finish the course at the Air Force School in East Germany. Thus, he remains unpopular in the Korean People's Army after such a poor record in the military. According to the following time line, however, he has held the supreme position in the Korean People's Army for five years.

December 1991 • Kim Jong Il, secretary of the Korean Worker's Party, appointed supreme commander of the Korean People's Army
• Kim Jong Il appointed marshal

December 1992 • Constitution revised; chairman of the National Defense Committee grasps command and control of the military and the right to make personnel appointments of high-ranking officers

April 1993 • Kim Jong Il appointed chairman of the National Defense Committee

July 1993 • Ninety-nine generals or those of equivalent rank promoted by the supreme commander

December 1993 • General Assembly of the Central Committee of the Korean Worker's Party held

Since Kim Il Sung's death on July 8, 1994, Kim Jong Il has been in mourning and has not dealt with personnel affairs. In the meantime, Kim Il Sung's right-hand man, O Jin U, also died, leaving vacant the post of minister of defense. In the autumn of 1995, however, Kim Jong Il announced new personnel appointments; see the following time line:

February 1995 • O Jin U, minister of defense, died

March 1995 • Kim Bong Yul, Kim Guang Jin, and others appointed members of the Central Committee of the Military

October 1995 • New personnel appointments of the Korean People's Army announced
- Choi Gwang, chief of the general staff of the Korean People's Army, promoted to minister of defense
- Kim Young Chun appointed chief of the general staff
- Kim Guang Jin, secretary of defense, promoted to vice minister
- Choi Gwang and Li Ul Sol, chief of the Guard Bureau, promoted to marshal (for a total of three marshals, including Kim Jong Il)
- Cho Myong Nok appointed chief of the Political Bureau of the Military
- Three, including Rhee Ha Il and Kim Young Chun, appointed as deputy marshals
- Three promoted to general, five to major general

From the facts above, we can draw the following conclusions:

- Since 1991, Kim Jong Il has grasped control of all command and personnel affairs in the military.
- Judging from the promotion of the generals of the so-called first genera-

tion of the revolution (who are in their seventies and eighties) after Kim Il Sung's death, relations between Kim Jong Il (born in 1932) and military officers in the first generation are cordial.

- At the same time, however, it is surprising that the former Chief of General Staff O Guk Yul—who resigned that post because of bad relations with the late minister of defense, O Jin U—was not promoted. For when Kim Il Sung realized that Kim Jong Il did not have much ability in the military field, he ordered O Guk Yul to enter the Military School in Moscow in his stead. O Guk Yul, then, was expected to be Kim Jong Il's right-hand man, which means that O's future position is key to the Kim Jong Il regime.

New Policies under Kim Jong Il

Secretary Kim Jong Il has never published his ideas on strategic and military issues. What is in his mind, however, can be guessed at from his writings. In his monograph on *juche* (independent) thought in 1982, he made the following points on national defense.[7]

- A strong self-defense is the prerequisite of an independent nation.
- We do not want war, but we will not be hesitant to wage it. We will never ask imperialists for peace negotiations.
- Imperialists are the root of all evil, and the main root of war and aggression now is American imperialism.
- We should carry out the principle of self-defense against imperialists.
- All army cadres should be tough-minded and be modernized with advanced technology.

Judging from these remarks, Kim Jong Il's strategic thinking—anti-Americanism, polarization of the world (imperialism versus antiimperialism), and an independent defense policy—is similar to Kim Il Sung's.

Compared with his father's, however, Kim Jong Il's publications are rather abstract, partly because Kim Jong Il has not experienced war himself. In addition, Kim Jong Il is interested in the philosophical and cultural field. For example, he established the so-called Three Revolutionary Group in the early 1970s (the three are culture, thought, and technology). Kim Jong Il, however, is deeply attached to thought and culture, and, consequently, his ability in science and technology is still unknown. (Needless to say, the same is true of the field of military technology.) These uncertain elements in Kim Jong Il's regime may lead him to adopt a collective leadership in those fields.

It is of interest to note that Choi Gwang, minister of defense, met with some Pakistani generals in Pakistan on November 20, 1995. Pakistan is suspected of receiving missile technology and nuclear-related parts from China, as well as developing nuclear weapons (see figure 5.1 for possible exchanges of weapons and nuclear-related technology among China, Pakistan, and North Korea).

Despite economic difficulties and the improvement of U.S.-DPRK relations, the North Korean military was strengthened in 1995 under the Kim Jong Il regime as follows:[8]

- Continued its annual military exercises: a combined exercise by the navy and the air force in June 1995 in the Yellow Sea, an air force exercise in June, and an army exercise in July

- Increased the total number of military exercises

- Reinforced the disposition along the DMZ since the end of August 1995

- Increased military personnel from 1,118,000 to 1,128,000

- Increased its armory by seventy 240-mm multiple-launch rockets and 170-mm guns

- Tested a new type of ballistic missile in February

- Worked on developing the Taepodong missile, with a 4,300–9,000-km range, that may be ready to deploy in five years

- Started to mass-produce ballistic missiles with a 1,000-km range

- Increased the number of MiG-29s to forty using an assembly line from the former Soviet Union

- Continued to produce MiG-21s (production began in 1993)[9]

- Considered continuing to export arms to Syria and Iran

From the above, one can conclude that North Korea has reinforced its armory of rockets, guns, and missiles and has made efforts to restore its air superiority and continue regular military exercises despite its economic difficulties. North Korea has successfully introduced technologies for combat aircraft from abroad, as well as assembled and even produced its own.[10]

It is reported that the military industry in North Korea exports weapons worth some 500 to 600 million U.S. dollars a year, which means that the standard of its

Figure 5.1   Possible Exchanges of Weapons and Nuclear Technology
              among China, Pakistan, and North Korea

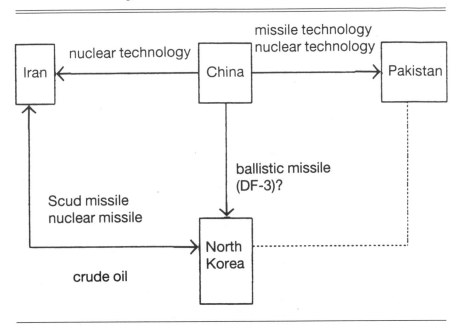

military technology is not low. During the gulf war, Iraq used technology believed to be supplied by North Korea.

The following is a brief overview of the North Korean military (the North
Korean armed forces are detailed in the appendix at the end of this chapter).
North Korea has sixteen corps, including one armed, four mechanical, eight
infantry, two artillery, and one capital defense. One important characteristic of
the North Korean military is its Special Purpose Forces Command with eighty-
eight thousand personnel, ten sniper brigades, fourteen infantry brigades, seventeen reconnaissance aircraft, one airborne battalion, and a Bureau of Reconnaissance. This command, which is transported by a large number of AN-2s, can also
carry out guerrilla warfare.

North Korean surface ships are mainly small naval vessels; twenty-five submarines and about sixty midget submarines are thought to be used for infiltration
by the Special Purpose Forces Command.

Threat to Japan

In August 1995, North Korea stationed its troops and aircraft such as MiG-17s and -19s in the southern part of the country, which worried Japan, the United States, and the Republic of Korea. However, these outdated fighter aircraft, which were used during the Korean War, cannot be a threat to neighboring countries. The most worrisome weapons in North Korea are nuclear warheads and ballistic missiles because of the following five points:

1. The current U.S. policy toward North Korea is to carry out the Agreed Framework of October 21, 1994, maintain communications with North Korea, persuade North Korea to accept special inspections, and discuss such issues as the missile problem and arms exports.

2. The United States estimates that North Korean technology is immature and thus may not regard the nuclear weapons and missiles of North Korea as a threat to the security of the East Asian region in the same way it saw those of the former Soviet Union and the PRC as threats.

3. Compared with the possibility that Russia or the PRC would attack Japan regardless of the damages caused by the ensuing severance of relations, the possibility is much higher that North Korea would attack Japan regardless of the damages caused by the severance of U.S.–North Korean and Japanese–North Korean relations.

In addition, the influence of North Korea's old friends, such as the PRC and Russia who in the past could have persuaded it not to run such a risk, has been decreasing. In fact, neither the PRC nor Russia has succeeded in persuading North Korea to accept special inspection.

4. As to North Korea's being suspected of having nuclear weapons in the past, there are differences in perception between Japan and the ROK on the one hand and the United States on the other. The United States emphasizes solving the "present and future nuclear doubt," but Japan and the ROK emphasize solving it wholly.

Because the United States regards the Agreed Framework as the only way to solve the North Korean nuclear issue, the United States cannot force the North to accept special inspections; if it tries, North Korea will withdraw from the NPT and the IAEA as it did in 1993. Although the United States argues that maintaining its talks with North Korea would lead to stability, Japan and the ROK worry about North Korea's developing ballistic missiles. In this sense, North Korean issues in the future might affect Japan's and the ROK's respective alliances with the United States.[11]

5. The Korean Peninsula Energy Development Organization

(KEDO) project is going well, and the atmosphere between North and South Korea has improved since the general election in South Korea on April 11, 1995. But as the recent North Korean incursions into the DMZ show, there still exists the possibility of a military conflict on the Korean peninsula. In case of war, the U.S. forces in Japan will automatically be involved in a conflict on the Korean peninsula and Japan will be threatened by North Korean ballistic missiles.

In conclusion, one may say that the North Korean military is outdated and lacks modern weapons, electronics capability, and air superiority. In addition, North Korea is suffering from economic difficulties and cannot expect military assistance from the PRC and Russia as it did in the 1980s.

However, as was pointed out earlier, North Korea did succeed in building MiG-21s and assembling MiG-29s and can produce chemical weapons. Thus Kim Jong Il may succeed in maintaining the unity of the state for the time being with his ideology-oriented and military-led policy style.

The characteristics of post–cold war international politics are diversified national interests and changing alliances. The North Korean issue will continue longer than expected, and the differing views of the United States, the ROK, and Japan will not disappear overnight.

The most important things to do now are to implement the light water reactor project, create confidence between North and South Korea, and hold talks among the United States, the ROK, and Japan.

Notes

1. See Katsuichi Tsukamoto, "North Korea: A Heavily Militarized Nation," *Aki Shobo*, 1989, p. 7.

2. Since 1962 North Korea has been seeking independence and strengthening its military forces under a four-point military guideline: all the people should be armed, the country should be fortified, all the soldiers should be trained as cadres, and all the arms should be modernized. "Defense of Japan 1994," Japan Defense Agency, 1994, p. 37.

3. "On North Korean Military," Seoul, Bukkan Institute, 1978, points out that the experience of the partisan struggle in the 1930s is the origin of Kim Il Sung's military thought (pp. 177–80).

Maoist guerrilla warfare was the starting point of the North Korean military doctrine. On this point, see "North Korea: A Country Study," Foreign Area Studies, American University, 1981, pp. 226–28.

4. The North Korean military buildup in the 1950s and 1960s shows the effect of the Korean War on North Korean leaders. Besides air power, North Korea also realized the importance of cross-river combat capabilities. North Korea could not win the Korean War

because its forces could not cross the Nakdong River and push the U.N. forces off the Korean peninsula. Because of this experience, North Korea acquired amphibious vehicles and strengthened its cross-river assault capabilities. See Shigeru Matsui, "Secret Military Power: North Korea," *Kojinsha*, 1994, pp. 100–102.

5. Kim Il Sung's speech on November 2, 1970, at the Central Committee, the Fifth Congress of the Korean Worker's Party. Kim Il Sung, "Monographs of Kim Il Sung," vol. 25, pp. 272–76. In this speech, Kim Il Sung indicated that he was much interested in the Vietnam War.

6. "North Korea Gives Up DMZ Duties," *Korea Times*, April 5, 1996.

7. Kim Jong Il, "Issues on Juche Thought," International Institute for Juche Thought, 1988, p. 102.

8. *Yonap Tonshin*, July 7, 1995; "Monthly Report: North Korean Policy," Radio Press, September and October 1995.

9. Some experts say that North Korean air power is overestimated. And the International Institute for Strategic Studies reassessed the North Korean Air Force in "The Military Balance 1995–96." According to its figures (p. 171), North Korea has fewer aircraft than last year but has thirty more Mi-24 attack helicopters.

10. At the end of the 1980s, North Korea started to produce MiG-21s using a blueprint that had been obtained by a North Korean military attaché to East Germany. After the collapse of the Soviet Union, North Korea purchased parts and technology from Ukraine with which to produce MiG-21s. At the beginning of 1990, North Korea obtained an assembly line for producing MiG-29s from the former Soviet Union. Within less than five years North Korea obtained forty MiG-29s.

11. See Hideshi Takesada, "Korean Peninsula 1995: A Survey," monograph, National Institute for Defense Studies, Japan, 1996, p. 11.

Appendix: Military Power on the Korean Peninsula

	Democratic People's Republic of Korea		Republic of Korea	
Total military	ca. 1,128,000		ca. 633,000	(USFK 37,000)
Army				
Military	ca. 1,000,000		ca. 520,000	
Major units	Motorized infantry divisions ⎱ 26 Infantry divisions ⎰		Mechanized infantry divisions	3
			Infantry divisions	19
	Armored brigades	14	Independent infantry brigades	2
	Motorized infantry brigades ⎱ 23 Mechanized infantry brigades ⎰		Special forces brigades	7
			Air defense artillery brigades	3
	Independent infantry brigades	5	Surface-to-surface	
	Light infantry battalions	22	missile battalions	3
	Heavy artillery brigades	6		
	Independent scud surface-to-surface missile regiment	1		
	Artillery brigades	14		
Surface-to-surface missiles	FROG-3/-5/-7	54		
	Scud-C	30		
	Biological and chemical weapons 1,000 tons			
Navy				
Vessels	ca. 630 ca. 87,000 tons		ca. 220 ca. 139,000 tons	
Major vessels	Frigates	3	Frigates	33
	Submarines	25	Destroyer class	16
	Missile patrol boats	42	Destroyers	7
	Osa class	12	Frigates	9
	Huangfen class	4	Submarines	3+3
	Komar class	10	Missile patrol boats	10
	Sohung class	6		
	Soju class	10		
Marines			Divisions	2
			ca. 25,000 troops	

(*continued*)

	Democratic People's Republic of Korea		Republic of Korea	
Air Force				
Combat aircraft	ca. 509		ca. 461	
Main types of aircraft	H-5 bombers	80	Fighters	
	Fighters		F-16s	60
	MiG-17s	110	F-5A/Es	195
	MiG-19s	130	F-4D/Es	130
	MiG-21s	130	Antiguerrilla aircraft	
	MiG-23s	46	A-37s	23
	MiG-29s	40	Reconnaissance aircraft	
	SU-7s	18	RF-4Cs	18
	SU-25s	35	RF-5As	10
Transport aircraft	An-2s/Y-5s, 6s	282		
Surface-to-air missiles	SA-2s	240	USFK	
	SA-3s	36	F-16s	72
	SA-5s	24		
Helicopter	Armed helicopters	80		
Remarks				
Population	ca. 23,927,000		ca. 44,825,000	
Time spent in military service	Army	5–8 years	Army	26 months
	Navy	5–10 years	Navy, air force	30 months
	Air force	3–4 years		
Reserves	4,700,000		4,500,000	

NOTES: 1. Statistics are based on "Defense of Japan: 1995," Defense Agency, Japan; "Military Balance: 1995–96," International Institute for Strategic Studies, London; and "Korean Defense White Paper: 1996," Ministry of Defense, ROK.

2. Data on U.S. forces in Korea are as of December 31, 1994.

Constraints and Objectives of North Korean Foreign Policy
A *Rational Actor Analysis*

BYEONGGIL AHN

Introduction

The North Korean government recently announced that it does not want to receive any more international food aid with a "political purpose," although North Korea has experienced a serious food shortage for several years. In 1995, following a North Korean request, South Korea, Japan, and other international sources provided food aid for North Korea. From North Korea's brief announcement, we can thus pick up two important hints about North Korean foreign policy.

First, North Korea faces two dimensions of constraints on establishing foreign relations: economic concerns and security concerns. Insufficient domestic resources have forced North Korea to resort to foreign resources to overcome current economic difficulties. However, North Korea does not want foreign input that could potentially disturb its isolated political system. As the last Stalinist country in the world, North Korea has maintained its own peculiar political order based on the former leader's ideology of self-reliance (*juche*). Getting foreign aid obviously contradicts this aspect of its ideology. So it appears that North Korea must weigh its need for foreign resources against the threat of foreign influence that might hurt the North Korean regime's stability.

Second, domestic politics influences the pattern of North Korean foreign policy. It is clear that a hard-line faction in North Korea has rejected the policy of getting more foreign food aid. One report said that the military doubted the positive effect of food aid and was worried about the negative foreign influence on North Korean domestic politics. We might presume that there are at least two political factions in North Korea influencing the direction of foreign policy.

I contend that we need to analyze the above issues to understand North Korean foreign policy. The existing studies on North Korean foreign policy have accumulated descriptions, diagnoses, and predictions without giving enough attention to a theoretical framework of foreign policy. To understand the recent foreign policy behavior of North Korea, I adopt a rational-actor analysis whereby North Korea is assumed to try to maximize the expected benefits of achieving better outcomes through foreign policy under certain constraints.

One traditional approach to North Korean foreign policy has been to focus on the role of the North Korean leaders' idiosyncrasies. Thus many journalists relate Kim Jong Il's personality to the future of the North Korean regime and foreign policy. Portraying him as an irrational or provocative actor—a heavy drinker, a speed-maniac, a womanizer, and so on—makes the future of North Korea seem gloomy. South Korean newspapers have frequently reported that Kim Jong Il is more dangerous than his father and thus more likely to commit an adventuresome attack against South Korea.

We do not know, however, what relationship there is between a political leader's personality and a nation's foreign policy. If a country's foreign policy is determined only by the political leader, without any constraints, the leader's personality could indeed be the most important variable. However, Kim Jong Il is by no means free from domestic or international constraints, including the North Korean economic situation. Any political leader, authoritarian or democratic, must ultimately maintain his or her regime, and thus I do not believe that Kim Jong Il's personality directly affects North Korean foreign policy. Foreign policy is often about a nation's important objectives, and the evidence suggests that North Korean foreign policy has been consistent and goal oriented toward U.S.-North Korean nuclear bargaining and food aid, which will be discussed later.

Another line of inquiry has been to adopt ideology as an important barometer of North Korean foreign policy. Certainly the ideology of communism played an important role in North Korean foreign policy during the cold war era, and its official diplomatic stance against the United States and western "imperialism" is evident in its recent government statements. North Korea has, however, invited foreign capitals to help resolve its domestic economic problems and has established special economic zones to revitalize its economy, both of which contradict the ideologies of the cold war and self-reliance.

Finally, since the end of the cold war, the constraints of international politics have been significantly reduced. It is not a coincidence that North Korea began developing nuclear weapons around the end of the cold war, for it could not have developed nuclear weapons if China and the former Soviet Union had maintained their roles as its patrons. Thus the realist framework of international studies, with its emphasis on the international political system, does not explain current North Korean foreign policy; rather, North Korean domestic politics is becoming more important.

Thus we need no longer see North Korea as basing its foreign policy on its unique ideology and its leader's peculiar personality. More helpful is a line of inquiry that asks what constraints North Korea faces in setting up its foreign policy? and what objectives it wants to accomplish? That is, North Korea will be better understood by considering it as a rational actor.

The "Working Objectives": Economic Revitalization and Regime Survival

The framework of this chapter is to analyze North Korea as a rational actor trying to accomplish its foreign policy objectives under certain constraints. First, we need to clarify these objectives. Article 9 of the North Korean constitution says that "the Democratic People's Republic of Korea strengthens the people's government and brings about the complete victory of socialism in the northern half through the execution of the three revolutions of ideology, technology and culture, while struggling for the realization of unification of the fatherland on the principle of independence, peaceful unification and grand national unity" (Yang 1995, 872). Therefore, North Korea regards reunification as the superior concept in its foreign policy but perhaps not one of the immediate "working objectives"—objectives pursued consistently in major foreign negotiations to fulfill the national objective. Because I am interested in the *actual* and *practical* objectives of North Korean foreign policy, it seems apparent that the "working objectives" should be economic revitalization and regime survival (see table 6.1).

The economic gap between North and South Korea has been deepening for the past five years, with North Korea recording negative growth rates and South Korea showing more than a 7 percent average growth rate for the same period. South Korean GNP (total trade volume) was almost eighteen times as large as North Korea's in 1994. Moreover, floods in 1995 worsened the economic hardship in North Korea (*New York Times*, August 31, 1995). When asking for international food aid at an international conference in Macao, North Korea officially estimated flood damage of $15 billion. Hwang Si Chon, international director of the North Korean Protestants Coalition, said that the floods were more horrifying than war and that North Korea needed 2.3 million tons of grain out of the total demand of 7.84 million tons (*Joongang Ilbo*, February 2, 1996). Thus it is doubt-

Table 6.1   Major Economic Indicators of North and South Korea
             (1991–1994)

		GNP *(in billion $)*	GNP/Capita *($)*	Growth Rate *(%)*	Total Trade *(in billion $)*
1991	North Korea (a)	$ 22.9	$1,038	−5.2	$ 2.7
	South Korea (b)	281.7	6,518	8.4	153.4
	b/a	12.3	6.3		56.4
1992	North Korea (a)	21.1	943	−7.6	2.7
	South Korea (b)	305.7	7,007	5.0	158.4
	b/a	14.5	7.4		59.6
1993	North Korea (a)	20.5	904	−4.3	2.6
	South Korea (b)	330.8	7,513	8.2	166.0
	b/a	16.1	8.3		62.9
1994	North Korea (a)	21.2	923	−1.7	2.1
	South Korea (b)	376.9	8,483	8.2	198.4
	b/a	17.8	9.2		94

SOURCE: "Estimation Results of North Korean GNP" (press release), 1991–1994, the Bank of Korea.

ful that North Korea has the capability to achieve its national objective, a reunification favoring North Korea. The negative growth rates in successive years
imply that the North Korean government must revitalize its economy by any
means available, including foreign policy.

We also understand that the survival of the current North Korean regime
depends on the success of its economic revitalization. Foreign policy, by supplying foreign resources to the retarded domestic economy, might be the last resort
of North Korean economic revitalization. Many defectors from North Korea have
testified that the bad economy and food shortages could provoke regime instability in the near future.[1] Therefore, I delineate economic revitalization and regime
survival as the "working objectives" of North Korean governmental activities.
North Korean political leaders trying to maintain their political leadership thus
need an economic breakthrough, possibly promoted by foreign policy.

Those working objectives were revealed in the nuclear negotiations between
North Korea and the United States. When International Atomic Energy Agency
(IAEA) director Hans Blix visited North Korea to discuss the nuclear issue in
1992, North Korean premier Yon Hyung Muk showed an interest in using foreign aid to replace North Korea's outmoded nuclear reactors with more-advanced
light water reactors (*Washington Post*, June 20, 1992), an outcome achieved in
the 1994 agreement with the United States. This indicates that North Korea has

been pursuing economic revitalization through its foreign policy since the early stages of the nuclear impasse.

Economic hardships (including a lack of hard currency, according to diplomats who have defected) have forced North Korea to close twenty-six foreign offices during the past five years. North Korea now has fewer than 60 permanent embassies out of the 132 countries with which it has official diplomatic relationships. North Korea has also tried to normalize diplomatic relations with its former "capitalist enemies," the United States and Japan. Thus, in July 1995, Kim Yong Soon, the North Korean Workers' Party secretary for international relations, visited Japan to meet with Japanese political leaders to discuss, among other things, diplomatic normalization between North Korea and Japan from which the North would benefit. Financially, North Korea has also continuously requested normalization with the United States throughout the nuclear negotiations. It appears that North Korea wants to gather all available foreign resources for its economic revitalization.

Security Concerns and Economic Concerns

The aforementioned objectives shed light on the constraints of North Korea's foreign policy, with the worsening economy as the driving force behind its incessant pursuit of foreign economic resources. Another indication of North Korea's economic concerns was its establishment of the Rajin-Sunbong special economic zone in 1992. Kim Soo Yong, a professor at Kim Il Sung University, stated in an interview in Japan that North Korea will guarantee secure foreign investments in the special economic zone. He also mentioned that Kim Il Sung University had been educating administrative staff to manage the area (*Hanguk Ilbo*, November 5, 1995). Because the plan of attracting $4 billion in foreign investment by 1995 has not been realized, North Korea has tried to build up an international tourism complex in the same area (*Joongang Ilbo*, January 26, 1996). North Korea also wants South Korea to invest $15 billion to develop the area (*Chosun Ilbo*, February 1, 1996). North Korea even allowed Western businesspeople to enter the area without a visa (*Hanguk Ilbo*, October 17, 1995). North Korea's arduous efforts to attract foreign capital for development of the special economic zone again indicate that North Korean foreign relations revolve around its economic concerns.

Those concerns are so prevalent that North Korea recently signaled a position change in security matters for the sake of the economy. According to Selig Harrison, Lieutenant General Lee Chan Bok, the representative of the North Korean army at Panmunjom, proposed a "new peace mechanism" for the Korean peninsula that includes the presence of the U.S. forces in South Korea. Although this cannot yet be verified as the official line of the North Korean government, it is a significant easing of the North Korean stance. Remarks by Foreign Minister Kim Young Nam and his first deputy, Kang Sok Ju, on U.S. support for the nuclear reactor construction (*Joongang Ilbo*, September 27, 1995; *Washington Post*, September 28, 1995), give us some motives for the sea change. Kim and Kang acknowledged North Korean economic difficulties and possible food crises in the winter of 1995. In another sign of seeking economic benefits from the United States, it was reported that North Korea declared that it would cease terrorist activities completely (*Chosun Ilbo*, February 3, 1996). North Korea is thus more interested in economic and financial matters and is under increasing pressure to attract foreign resources.

The worsening economy also moved North Korea to explicitly reveal its foreign policy position. When North Korean deputy premier Kim Tai Hyun visited the South to discuss the pending North-South agenda in 1992, he expressed North Korean intentions of economic cooperation with the South. The deputy minister of the Board of Finance and Economy, Yi Sok Chae, the South Korean representative at the third South-North talks on the rice issue, reported that North Korea requested additional support for flood victims without discussing the captured South Korean sailors of the *Woosung* (*Joongang Ilbo*, September 30, 1995). (North Korea asked for more rice aid just as the initial aid was in the process of being shipped.)[2] Such an economy-oriented position could be witnessed also in efforts to encourage South Korean investment in North Korea.

We cannot presume, however, that North Korean foreign policy has only economic objectives, for inviting foreign resources could generate regime instability. Although the survival of the current regime depends on economic revitalization, the nearly fifty-year strategy of isolation is still working well for North Korean security. The North Korean government continues to maintain strict control of the border areas to avoid the spread of the "capitalist wind" among its people. For example, North Korea allowed South Korean enterprises to participate in the International Industrial Exhibitions (April and October 1996) only if they met three conditions: that applications be made through third countries, that merchandise not specify the production site as South Korea, and that visiting staffs carry foreign passports (*Joongang Ilbo*, January 29, 1996).

North Korean security concerns frequently blocked enforcement of the Agreement on Reconciliation, Non-Aggression and Exchange and Cooperation in 1991. North Korean attitudes toward implementing the North–South Korean Denuclearization Agreement in 1992 also showed that resolving security issues on the Korean peninsula will never be easy.[3] North Korea wanted access to U.S. military bases in the South to verify that nuclear weapons had been removed. This request was not welcomed by either South Korea or the United States. The North also requested that the Team Spirit Exercises be ended permanently.

Domestic Politics:
"Authoritarian Double-Edged Diplomacy"

Throughout the negotiations with the South and the United States, North Korea has managed the difficult job of balancing security concerns with economic concerns to pursue the objectives of economic revitalization and regime survival. For a deeper evaluation of North Korean diplomatic maneuvers, let us look at politics inside North Korea using the theory of two-level games to understand the linkage between domestic politics and foreign policy. Although Putnam's (1988) original idea of the strategy of reducing the "win set" was designed to be applied to democratic negotiators, a further development of the theory (Evans et al. 1993; Fearon 1994; Mo 1995a) shows that it could be applied to various negotiation situations.

I suggest here a rough model of a two-level game for understanding North Korean foreign policy. North Korean foreign policy is not influenced by such democratic institutions as competitive party politics, parliament, or public opinion. The paucity of such democratic institutions, however, does not necessarily negate North Korean domestic politics affecting its foreign policy. Theoretically, I suggest an authoritarian linkage between domestic politics and foreign policy if there is a domestic division over the issues of foreign policy, which might be entitled "authoritarian double-edged diplomacy."

For convenience of analysis let us suppose that there are two major domestic factions affecting North Korean foreign policy: the hard-liners and the reformists, according to their propensities for making demands against negotiation opponents (South Korea or the United States) and their placing relative weights on security or economic concerns. Such a factional division is mentioned directly in an article by Kim Jong Il in which he harshly criticized economic reformists and ideological revisionists (see *Rodong Shinmun*, December 25, 1995). He went on to argue that "traitors negate the revolutionary philosophy of the proletariat by pretending to accomplish reforms and to construct democracy and a welfare state."

The existence of hard-liners can be verified by North Korean propaganda, which continuously criticizes the South. Harsh attitudes toward the South were also revealed when North Korea forced a South Korean rice transport ship to raise the North Korean flag upon entering a North Korean port. In contrast, the North's flexibility in the nuclear reactor negotiations reveals that the North has been exercising delicate diplomatic skills complicated by a mixture of hard-liners and reformists.

The security-minded hard-liners are assumed to have a higher demand threshold against an opponent than the reformists because the hard-liners usually bear more of the political costs of a possible agreement, such as giving up military strategies and opening up the border areas to outsiders. The hard-liners, therefore, request more benefits from and impose more conditions on negotiations to cover or suppress possible costs. The economically oriented reformists are more eager than the hard-liners to conclude an agreement with an opponent because the reformists want to exploit the possible economic benefits of negotiation. Thus, they have a lower demand threshold than the hard-liners because lower demand tends to increase the possibility of agreement with the opponent. The more North Korea demands or the less the opponent values the agreement, the lower the likelihood of an agreement.

At the domestic level, these two factions coordinate or compete to set up conditions for negotiation with an opponent. It can be derived that North Korean demand would go up (down) if the hard-liners (the reformists, respectively) prevail in the domestic arrangement. If there is no agreement in the negotiation (if the opponent rejects the North Korean demand), they either proceed to the next round or there is a complete breakdown of negotiations.

For a negotiation opponent, two indicators are important for deciding a negotiation outcome: the amount of demand by North Korea and the value of agreement for its own sake, which is usually related to the opponent's domestic politics.[4] The United States and South Korea also have their own economic and security concerns. They put more weight on security (national or regional) concerns, however, because they do not have the working objectives of economic revitalization and regime survival; their objectives are to increase national or regional security levels.

The model gives us useful insight into North Korea's position in nuclear negotiations with the United States. Throughout the negotiation process, North Korea adopted a hard-line stance while demanding economic benefits from the United States and other countries. Because North Korea knew that the United States had a large stake in nuclear nonproliferation, it deliberately prolonged the negotiation process, applying its "authoritarian double-edged diplomacy" to achieve better terms. North Korea dragged the nuclear issue to a satisfactory demand threshold by pretending to be very hawkish.

North Korea never acceded to the IAEA's request for a special inspection of suspected nuclear sites at Yongbyon in 1993 and thus retained the bargaining power of its nuclear card. Although North Korea faced strong criticism worldwide, it had no reason to give up its hard-line position without some economic benefits. When the U.S.–South Korean Team Spirit military exercises were scheduled to resume, North Korea strengthened its tough posture even further by evoking the possibility of war on the peninsula.[5] In March 1993, North Korea's hard-line mobilization climaxed when it announced it was abandoning the nonproliferation treaty, stunning the world. North Korea's hard-liners, led by Kim

Jong Il, were dissatisfied with the previous nuclear negotiations, which they felt provided no practical benefits, and wanted to push the United States to deal with North Korea directly. Kang Sok Ju, North Korea's first deputy foreign minister, and U.S. assistant secretary of state Robert L. Gallucci held high-level talks in New York in June 1993 and agreed to continue the dialogue between the two parties, enabling North Korea to call for a "package deal" on nuclear issues in November (Kim 1995, 532).

Although there was some back and forth exchanges between North Korea and the United States over economic sanctions, the negotiation process, until the Geneva Agreed Framework of 1994, showed North Korea consistently pursuing high benefits behind the mask of the hard-liners. The agreement reads as follows:

> The DPRK is prepared to replace its graphite-moderated reactors and related facilities with light water reactor (LWR) power plants, and the U.S. is prepared to make arrangements for the provision of LWRs of approximately 2,000 MW(e) [megawatts electric] to the DPRK as early as possible . . . . Upon receipt of U.S. assurances for the provision of LWRs and for arrangements for interim energy alternatives, the DPRK will freeze construction of the 50 MW(e) and 200 MW(e) reactors, forgo reprocessing, and seal the Radiochemical Laboratory, to be monitored by the IAEA. (Mazaar 1995, 168)

Three points should be made here. First, North Korea expertly exploited the negotiation mechanism. Making use of the protracted negotiations, North Korea successfully obtained economic benefits with the support of domestic hard-liners and continued to use this strategy after the Agreed Framework was signed. At the first KEDO–North Korea meeting, North Korea representative Ho Jong requested that the United States be responsible for constructing light water reactors, including all the related facilities, and that KEDO not adopt light water reactors of the South Korean type. Because of these North Korean efforts to get more economic benefits and better terms, it took more than a year for the two parties to sign the final agreement (*Joongang Ilbo*, December 17, 1995).

Second, North Korea made some concessions in security (nuclear weapons) by giving up reprocessing facilities and old-style reactors. The working objective of economic revitalization appears to put economic concerns at the heart of North Korean foreign policy (Ahn 1995). In this respect, the reformists' influence cannot be ignored, which hints at North Korea's future pursuit of foreign relations: economy-oriented diplomacy.

Third, the opponent's stake in the agreement played an important role in the negotiation. North Korea's accurate estimates of U.S. interest in nuclear nonproliferation helped it achieve its goals during the negotiations.

The same was true in the case of rice diplomacy between the North and the South. North Korean ambassador Park Kil Yeon said recently that military personnel understand world affairs better than foreign affairs bureaucrats, which leads us to believe that the military hard-liners influence foreign policy making. He revealed that the military opposed international aid after the 1995 floods (*Chosun Ilbo*, February 9, 1996). A North Korean foreign affairs official was quoted as saying that the military was worried about the political side effects of international aid, such as the penetration of North Korea by the outside world, which might affect regime stability. Citing the hard-liners seems to make it easier for North Korean reformers to obtain international aid.

Park also stated that North Korea welcomes the $2 million in aid from the United States because it is not from enemy countries such as South Korea and Japan (*Chosun Ilbo*, February 10, 1996), again showing that North Korea continues to seek economic benefits by referring to domestic resistance by hard-liners. The director of the World Food Plan's Pyongyang office confirmed that North Korea still wanted economic aid from international organizations, citing the remarks of Choi Soo Hun, the deputy minister of North Korean foreign affairs, who was said to have asked the representatives of international organizations to fulfill their pledges of $15 million in aid (*Chosun Ilbo*, February 14, 1996).

In negotiations over aid, however, North Korea does not have the same advantage that it did in its nuclear negotiations with the United States. North Korea's hard-line strategy against South Korea has made the South Korean government unwilling to provide additional rice aid. North Korea needs to find another diplomatic card like the nuclear issue with high stakes for the opponent. Until then, if the North Korean government does not move from the position of the hard-liners to that of the reformists, it will be unable to get significant foreign aid, which is necessary for economic revitalization.

North Korean Foreign Policy

My analysis of North Korean foreign policy suggests that it is a rational actor pursuing the working objectives of economic revitalization and regime survival. Ironically, the two objectives are not always completely compatible under the current political leadership. In the long run, economic revitalization is vital for the survival of North Korea, for without economic reforms, it is almost certain that the regime will collapse in the near future, as the East European countries did a few years ago. The hard-liners, nevertheless, seem afraid of the effects of incoming foreign resources that might encroach on their political power, so they have requested more economic benefits and more favorable terms to compensate for the possible negative effects. The discussion of North Korean authoritarian double-edged diplomacy showed that North Korea used the hard-liners to derive more favorable economic benefits from the nuclear negotiations.

The rice case, however, turned out not to generate a similar advantage because South Korea did not want to provide additional food aid to North Korea after giving up its tough stance on security matters.

Therefore, the outlook for North Korean foreign policy depends on the power distribution between the hard-liners and the reformists as well as economic and security concerns, and evidence indicates that economic concerns have been prevailing over security concerns. North Korea thus appears ready to change its position on security issues, especially those relating to the United States, to seek economic benefits. In the nuclear negotiations with the United States, North Korea sacrificed its nuclear policy in part to get economic benefits. North Korea even hinted at acceding to the U.S. presence in South Korea, a huge turnaround if officially announced. North Korea is also considering giving up international terrorism permanently to get closer to the United States. If North Korea pretends to be tough over security in future negotiations but in reality is oriented toward economic concerns, it would enhance North Korea's economic revitalization. If the hard-liners defend their political power by adhering to security concerns (especially against South Korea), however, it might be a disaster for the current regime, which needs foreign resources for economic revitalization.

Two possibilities emerge. Because foreign resources are critical for the North Korean economic revitalization and regime survival in the long run, the reformists might take over the hard-liners. Because of the economic hardship in North Korea, I expect that the reformists *will* rise; if they can then control the direction of foreign policy, North Korea will get a chance to revitalize its economy with foreign contributions.

The other possibility is that the current hard-liners might rise up and suppress the reformists, ensuring a foreign policy that will not work in the direction of regime survival. Therefore, North Korea's future foreign policy heavily depends on North Korean domestic politics, especially the rivalry between hard-liners and reformists.

Notes

1. The increasing number of defectors includes Kim Jong Il's former wife, the North Korean prime minister's former son-in-law, and North Korean diplomats in Zambia.

2. South Korea provided 150,000 tons of rice to the North between June and October 1995.

3. For the application of linkage between security and economic concerns in the case of Korea, refer to Mo (1995b and 1996).

4. I simplify, for the convenience of explanation, the features of an opponent's double-edged diplomacy because the paper has a specific focus on North Korea. The opponent would try to reduce its acceptable demand threshold by making use of its own domestic

politics. The mechanism is assumed to be incorporated into the idea of how much the opponent values an agreement with North Korea.

5. Kim Jong Il ordered the military to switch to a state of readiness for war on March 9, 1993, blaming the resumption of the joint U.S.–South Korea joint military exercise (*Pyongyang Times*, March 13, 1993, cited in Mazarr 1995, 98).

References

Ahn, Byeonggil. 1995. "Domestic Uncertainty and Coordination between North and South Korea." In Heemin Kim and Woosang Kim, eds., *Rationality and Politics in the Korean Peninsula*. Osaka: International Society for Korean Studies.

Bank of Korea. 1991–1994. "Estimation Results of North Korean GNP" (press release).

Evans, P. B., H. K. Jacobson, and R. D. Putnam, eds. 1993. *Double-edged Diplomacy*. Berkeley: University of California Press.

Fearon, J. D. 1994. "Domestic Political Audiences and the Escalation of International Disputes." *American Political Science Review* 88:577–92.

Kim, D. J. 1994. *Foreign Relations of North Korea during Kim Il Sung's Last Days*. Seoul: Sejong Institute.

Mazarr, Michael J. 1995. *North Korea and the Bomb: A Case Study in Nonproliferation*. New York: St. Martin's Press.

Mo, Jongryn. 1995a. "Domestic Institutions and International Bargaining: The Role of Agent Veto in Two-Level Games." *American Political Science Review* 89:914–24.

———. 1995b. "Relative versus Absolute Gains: The Politics of Trade between Divided Countries." Mimeo.

———. 1996. "Security and Economic Linkages in the Inter-Korea Relationship." This volume.

Pukhan Chonggam (North Korea Overview, 1983–1993). 1994. Seoul: Pukhan Yeonguso.

Putnam, R. D. 1988. "Diplomacy and Domestic Politics: The Logic of Two-Level Games." *International Organization* 42:427–60.

Yang, S. 1994. *The North and South Korean Political Systems: A Comparative Analysis*. Boulder, Colo.: Westview Press.

The North Korean Problem and the Role of South Korea

CHUNG-IN MOON

Pacifying the Korean peninsula is one of the major security puzzles in the post-hegemonic international system. Although the Korean conflict originated out of the cold war, the demise of the bipolar confrontation has not brought about its settlement or resolution. As the recent North Korean nuclear fiasco eloquently demonstrated, peninsular security is still trapped in hyperbolic fluctuations of status quo and crisis.

The Geneva Agreed Framework in September 1994 made a significant contribution to preventing a major conflict escalation on the peninsula, but it has not produced any positive effects on inter-Korean relations. The Geneva settlement and several goodwill gestures on the part of South Korea notwithstanding, inter-Korean relations have been virtually frozen since the death of Kim Il Sung in July 1994.

What is ironic is that the Geneva settlement has posed a mixed blessing to the South. On the one hand, it averted a crisis situation on the peninsula by mitigating the North Korean nuclear problem and served as a vehicle for improving relationships between the United States and North Korea, which could be instrumental for fostering the opening of North Korea's society and economy. Such developments will ultimately facilitate the improvement of inter-Korean relations. On the other hand, however, the Geneva settlement is creating a new dilemma for South Koreans because they fear that North Korea could take advantage of newly established channels of communication with the United States to advance its foreign policy objectives and eventually isolate the South. What also worries the South is that North Korea's diplomatic offensive, which is believed to have gained momentum following the Geneva deal, could lead to a peace treaty with the United States, replacing the existing armistice agreement. North Korea has taken several measures to nullify the agreement, ranging from the dissolution of the Neutral States' Supervisory Commission to the negation of the Armistice Military Commission. More recently, North Korea announced that it will not honor the demilitarized zone or engage in its administration and maintenance.[1] Such measures can be seen as deliberate efforts to secure bargaining leverages with the eventual goal of a peace treaty with the United States. A North Korea–U.S. peace treaty would naturally be linked to the withdrawal of U.S. forces from the South, thus endangering its security.

South Korea now seems obssessed with the possibility of such a development,[2] not only because the peace treaty could deal a severe diplomatic blow to Seoul by undercutting its existing policy line of sustaining the armistice treaty regime but also because it can produce a formidable domestic political backlash. More important, a North Korea–U.S. peace treaty, once materialized, could have two negative implications for peninsular and regional security. First, it could easily destabilize peace and security on the peninsula by undermining the Basic Agreement on Reconciliation, Non-aggression, and Exchanges and Cooperation of December 1991 (the Basic Agreement hereafter), which both parties agreed to utilize as the sole and legitimate mechanism to resolve the Korean conflict. Second, the withdrawal of U.S. forces, followed by a peace treaty, could create a major power vacuum in the region, thus jeopardizing overall regional stability.

Against the above backdrop, this chapter is designed to recast the North Korean problem (as South Koreans perceive it) in a broader context, to review existing policy responses, and to suggest a new alternative that can enhance the role of South Korea in resolving the Korean conflict.

Defining the North Korean Problem

Defining the North Korean problem is not easy because it involves diverse perceptual interpretations. What are viewed as problems to outsiders may not be seen as such by North Koreans.[3] Thus, the North Korean problem needs to be approached from at least two angles. One is to derive problematic dimensions of North Korea through static and objective assessments, and the other is to identify the patterns of North Korea's statecraft that can impose problems on other states through interactive processes. In this chapter, then, the North Korean problem is defined as the malign interactive effects of North Korea's statecraft. In a broad sense, three types of problems can be identified: big bang, free riding, and spoiler behavior.

THE BIG BANG

Big bang refers to a sudden internal collapse of North Korea and the ensuing chaos.[4] The big bang theory postulates that the collapse of the Kim Jong Il regime is imminent and that such a collapse will produce catastrophic effects on South Korea. The big bang thesis is not new. Even before the death of Kim Il Sung, North Korea was in trouble. Faltering economic productivity, an acute energy crisis, and a chronic shortage of consumer goods portended the coming collapse of the North Korean economy. Yet Kim Il Sung's legitimacy and power consolidation appeared to prevent its spillover into social and political crises. Kim Jong Il, however, is facing much tougher domestic problems. In addition to worsening economic conditions, he must cope with precarious succession politics as well as newly ensuing social instabilities. Rumors of social and political instabilities in North Korea abound, and although they cannot be fully confirmed, it is conceivable that prolonged economic difficulties would critically undermine Kim Jong Il by eroding his legitimacy and popular support base. In view of the recent floods and the related famine and the rapidly increasing number of defectors and refugees from the North and their testimonials,[5] a sudden collapse of his regime cannot be ruled out.

In the late 1980s, most South Koreans favored the big bang scenario. In the wake of the German unification, they thought that the internal collapse of North Korea would, by absorption, foster national unification. Developments in post-unified Germany, however, have led South Koreans to think that big bang may be a liability rather than an asset, tantamount to opening Pandora's box. South Korea is not prepared to deal with the myriad of social, economic, and political problems that might arise from a big bang process of integration and ultimately unification by absorption. Apart from unbearably high economic costs, a big bang will entail a wide range of problems involving the influx of refugees, social integration, and political adjustment.

It is in this context that the South Korean government began to think that a premature collapse of the Kim Jong Il regime could do more harm than good in managing inter-Korean relations and steering national unification. South Korea seems to have limited options under this scenario, however. Because a big bang will be a result of North Korea's dismal statecraft and domestic political and social dynamics, it is beyond the control of South Korea. All the South Korean government can do is either to alleviate conditions leading to the big bang or to prepare for the contingency.[6]

THE FREE RIDER DILEMMA

The free rider problem, which occurs when North Korea fails to reciprocate benefits received from outside actors or when it undersupplies collective goods in multilateral cooperation, has been most pronounced in the economic domain. Outsiders' offers of economic assistance to, or cooperation with, the North have by and large been predicated on a gradual opening and structural reforms of its economy. North Korea has not reciprocated, however, and its motives for enhancing external economic cooperation have been instrumental rather than consummate. Easing short-term hardships has always been North Korea's top priority, not reviving the national economy through overall restructuring.[7] As the following example of recent shipments of rice to the North illustrates, North Korea lacks reciprocal arrangements. The South Korean government had decided to ship rice to the North for humanitarian reasons and, in so doing, expected that such shipments would pave the way to a breakthrough in inter-Korean relations. But no reciprocal measures were taken by the North, blocking further shipments. North Korea's tactics of differentiating private firms from the South Korean government to enhance economic cooperation can also be seen as free riding behavior, in that North Korea attempts to maximize economic gains through informal economic interactions with private firms, thus reducing its political liability to the South Korean government.

The North's free riding is not limited to a lack of reciprocity but extends to an undersupply of collective goods. A notable example involves the Tumen River Basin project. Under the auspices of the United Nations Development Program, North Korea sought multilateral cooperation to expedite the Tumen River Basin development but expected the regional actors to assume virtually the entire costs of the development including the social and physical infrastructure. Such free riding behavior has hindered multilateral cooperation on development.

North Korea's free riding seems predictable. Economic assistance is vital to the North to revive its dying economy; yet foreign economic ties cannot be allowed to undermine its political and social stability. Such a balancing act has been responsible for North Korea's erratic behavior in dealing with its external sources of economic assistance. As long as the Kim Jong Il regime stays in power, North Korea is unlikely to alter its behavior drastically but will make every effort to minimize the domestic political and social impacts of economic opening, while maximizing the inflow of foreign direct investment and economic assistance.

The contradictory behavior embedded in North Korea's free riding can impose political and diplomatic problems on the South. First, expanding economic ties between North Korea and private firms in the South might cause problems of coordination. Up to now, South Korean firms have complied with government directives. As they increase their investments in the North, however, they could be held hostage by the North, making it difficult for Seoul to regulate and coordinate South Korean firms. Second, the Geneva settlement has opened new venues of economic cooperation between the United States and North Korea, which will in turn facilitate economic cooperation between Pyongyang and To-kyo. Such developments, while inter-Korean economic cooperation remains stalled, could diplomatically isolate the South as well as deprive South Korea of the chance to get involved in North Korea's economic developments. Third, South Korea has often used economic cooperation as an incentive to bring North Korea to the negotiation table on a wide range of inter-Korean concerns. North Korea's failure to reciprocate could deepen mutual distrust and deter the South's use of economic incentives. Finally, Seoul's chronic failure to preempt or prevent Pyongyang's free riding behavior could have negative domestic political consequences.

NORTH KOREA AS SPOILER

From the diplomatic point of view, the worst North Korean problem is its role as spoiler, by which we mean North Korea's erratic behavior aimed at undermining the status quo on the Korean peninsula by deviating from the existing norms, principles, rules, and procedures of inter-Korean interactions. Pyongyang's brinkmanship diplomacy, as evidenced in the nuclear crisis, threatened not only to violate the international regime (i.e., the Nonproliferation Treaty) but also to reshape regional and peninsular security equations through the possession of nuclear weapons. The Geneva settlement has not brought an end to North Korea's role as spoiler.

South Korean elites perceive that North Korea can spoil peace and security on the peninsula in two distinctive ways. One is to isolate South Korea through a diplomatic offensive with the United States, including signing a peace treaty with the United States following diplomatic normalization. Such diplomatic isolation of the South should not be viewed as a far-fetched idea; since the Geneva Agreed Framework, Pyongyang and Washington have become much closer. An exchange of liaison offices is simply a matter of time, and full diplomatic normalization will soon follow. North Korea seems to have two strategic goals in normalizing its ties with the United States. One is to escape U.S. military threats, and the other is to sign a peace treaty with the United States that will replace the armistice agreement. Such a peace treaty could yield several dividends. First, it could establish a legal and institutional framework through which U.S. forces in the South could be reduced and ultimately withdrawn. Second, it could serve as an effective deterrent to South Korea's military attacks on the North. Finally, such a treaty could be a valuable tool for coping with potential domestic political opposition to diplomatic normalization with the United States, which has long been portrayed as the evil power.

Should it be realized, however, its consequences for peninsular and regional security could be serious, for the treaty would be predicated on the withdrawal of U.S. forces from the South, which could compromise regional and inter-Korean security and peace.[8] A treaty would also imply an outright negation of Seoul's traditional policy of maintaining the armistice agreement. Domestic political consequences could be even worse, posing real diplomatic and political problems for the South. Even if those were averted, Pyongyang's diplomatic offensive to Washington could put Seoul in a difficult position. Given the fiscal rigidity and the growing sentiments for isolationism in the United States, such a move could easily politicize the issue of U.S. forces in the South, narrowing the margin of diplomatic maneuverability for Seoul and Washington. Apart from that, Seoul's mass media are likely to portray such talks as a sign of Seoul's diplomatic isolation as well as a major diplomatic setback.

The second way the North can spoil peace and security on the peninsula is by military provocation, which could take place regardless of whether U.S. forces stay. South Korean policy makers believe that reducing or withdrawing U.S. forces will definitely increase the likelihood of military provocation by North Korea. Even if U.S. forces remain in the South, North Korea could stage a major military aggression under the big bang scenario. Or Kim Jong Il could initiate military adventurism in part out of desperation and in part to defuse a domestic political crisis. Although such a move would be suicide, in a society where a personality cult dominates, such an irrational action cannot be totally ruled out. (In the old days, a military provocation by the North was closely related to acute domestic crises in the South and a proliferation of pro–North Korean sympathizers. Since democratic opening and consolidation, however, military invasion has become a distant possibility. A conservative resurgence in the South has further limited the possibility of North Korea's military invasion by invitation.) For whatever reason, should North Korea stage a military campaign against the South, it would produce a major catastrophe, regardless of who wins.

Of the three problems, North Korea as spoiler worries South Koreans the most. As to the problem of big bang, South Korea can either alleviate conditions leading to its outbreak or simply be prepared for it. Economic free riding irritates the South but is not the overwhelming problem, for South Korea can manage its negative repercussions. The most serious task involves managing North Korea as spoiler. Blocking a North Korea–U.S. peace treaty, preventing the outbreak of war, and ultimately bringing a stable peace to the peninsula thus constitute the most pressing concerns for the South Korean government.

Countervailing Strategies—Three Views

How can South Korea block the peace treaty, prevent a North Korean military provocation, and ensure a stable peace on the Korean peninsula? So far, there are three contending views.[9]

ACCOMMODATION STRATEGY

The first perspective[10] explores the possibility of national unification and a peaceful settlement on the Korean peninsula by accommodating the DPRK-U.S. peace treaty, viewing it as the new momentum behind a major breakthrough in inter-Korean relations. Although the peace treaty could lead to the actual or potential withdrawal of U.S. forces from the South, it would not compromise peninsular security for three reasons. First, South Korea would be able to maintain military deterrence against the North even in the absence of U.S. forces, for South Korea's military strength is equal or even superior to the North's. Second, South Korea could still count on the United States to be an honest broker or a constructive mediator; the United States would not stay idle when or if North Korea shows any signs of military aggression. Third, doing something is better than doing nothing. In view of the political uncertainty in the North, stalled inter-Korean relations could erupt into major or minor conflicts at any time. South Korea should make major concessions to prevent the worst-case scenario.

The accommodative perspective is congruent with North Korea's traditional position and, ideally speaking, seems workable. But it is not acceptable to the South. South Koreans still believe that the North has not abandoned its long-held strategy of liberating the South by force. The signing of the peace treaty and the subsequent reduction or withdrawal of U.S. forces could provide a pretext for an invasion by North Korea. Thus, apart from the perceptual fear, the domestic political calculus in the South would not allow an accommodative strategy because it would be interpreted as an unrealistic diplomatic concession, and accepting the peace treaty would be political suicide. Even to the United States, the option will be unattractive because a peace treaty would make the United States a party to the Korean conflict as long as such a treaty were in effect. Nor would the domestic political climate in the United States permit such a policy move.

LINKAGE STRATEGY

The second strategy is framed around the first but in a more constructive manner, linking the peace treaty to inter-Korean conflict management.[11] This perspective starts with the assumption that, given the overall strategic and budget trends in the United States, the reduction or withdrawal of U.S. forces from the South is unavoidable. Although the United States has recently pledged its continuing security commitment to South Korea, securing budgets could be troublesome.[12] To prevent reduction or withdrawal, South Korea might have to increase its share of the defense burden. Democratization and rising demands for welfare spending, however, could make such an increase difficult, thus leading to U.S. disengagement. This being the case, linkage theorists argue, South Korea should preemptively endorse the DPRK-U.S. peace treaty and the reduction/withdrawal of U.S. forces to use as bargaining leverage to foster inter-Korean confidence-building measures.

Such an endorsement should be contingent on the fulfillment of three prerequisites for inter-Korean confidence-building measures. First, the reduction and eventual withdrawal of U.S. forces should be undertaken within the framework of inter-Korean confidence-building measures and arms control. The U.S. disengagement should be linked to redeploying its offensive forces north of Sariwon as well as restructuring or removing its offensive forces (e.g., special command forces). Second, apart from the Geneva Agreed Framework, the North should resume its talks with the South on nuclear issues by honoring the previous North-South agreement on denuclearization of the Korean peninsula. Third, when the above two conditions are met, both Koreas should return to the Basic Agreement through which they can work out details on confidence-bulding measures and arms control. Once these three conditions have been met, the DPRK-U.S. peace treaty can serve to prevent North Korea from acting as a spoiler until the Basic Agreement is able to ensure a stable peace on the peninsula.

The linkage strategy, however, is workable only if the United States reduces and eventually withdraws its forces from the South and if such a move does not undermine peninsular and regional security. Equally important is North Korea's willingness to redeploy and restructure its offensive forces as well as to participate in inter-Korean arms control in return for South Korea's endorsement. Furthermore, South Korea must be able to forge a broad social consensus on the issue. Otherwise, intense domestic political opposition, especially from the conservative camp, could make such moves futile. Although ideal, satisfying these conditions will be difficult. North Korea's efforts to decouple inter-Korean talks from North Korea–U.S. dialogue, South Korea's deep suspicion of the North, technical and procedural difficulties in linking inter-Korean arms control to U.S. withdrawal, and ultimately electoral sensitivity to such concessions in the South are likely to reduce this strategy's feasibility.

MAINTAINING THE STATUS QUO

The third strategy,[13] which is based on the continuation of the armistice treaty regime with U.S. forces remaining in place, has always been favored by

South Korea. The South Korean government argues that inter-Korean relations should be delinked from the issue of U.S. forces in the South and that the settlement of the Korean conflict through inter-Korean confidence-building measures and arms control should come before negotiations over the reduction and withdrawal of U.S. forces. The U.S. forces should stay until a mature milieu conducive to peaceful coexistence is assured. As Article V of the Basic Agreement stipulates, the armistice treaty regime should be retained until an inter-Korean peace regime is established through the implementation of the Basic Agreement. A DPRK-U.S. peace treaty would complicate the structure of the Korean conflict not only by making the United States a direct party to it but also by provoking resentment in the South. Such a treaty could also make the South Korean military unruly because it would be predicated on the dissolution of U.S. operational control and command over the South Korean military.

South Korea's policy makers believe that, given the track record of North Korea, the accommodation and linkage strategies will increase, not decrease, the probability of overt military conflict on the peninsula. Because the North's peace offensives have always been followed by military provocation, a peace treaty between Pyongyang and Washington could provide another pretext for a North Korean military action, all the more so because of the precarious nature of succession politics and acute social and economic crises in the North. National security should not be compromised under any circumstances. As the Reagan administration proved, negotiations from a position of strength, backed by a formidable military deterrence capability and the presence of U.S. troops, are the only viable way to resolve the Korean conflict without endangering national security.

Thus in view of national security and domestic political considerations, South Korea adheres to the status quo strategy: "inter-Korean peace first and reduction/withdrawal of American forces later." North Korea, however, does not see any incentives in this deal, viewing it as nothing but a strangulation or "withering out" strategy. Accommodating such terms would present a major diplomatic defeat to the North, making the domestic political situation even worse.

The three approaches discussed above cannot satisfy both Koreas simultaneously. The accommodation strategy can satisfy the North but is unacceptable to the South. Although the status quo strategy is favored by the South, North Korea is bound to reject it. Even the linkage strategy—a middle-of-the-road alternative—cannot resolve the North Korean problem. South Korea is concerned about domestic political repercussions that could result from the concessions and remains skeptical of North Korea's will and ability to implement the preconditions. This entangled context perpetuates the inter-Korean stalemate. In the long run, South Korea could benefit from the stalemate if its negative consequences (i.e., big bang or military provocation) can be avoided or managed. Yet, in the process, South Korea will also suffer a variety of diplomatic setbacks. A rapprochement between Pyongyang and Washington and its spin-off effects on the Tokyo-Pyongyang relationship, decoupled from inter-Korean improvements, will bring about a sense of loss of control over peninsular affairs as well as a widespread sense of diplomatic isolation in the South. Domestic political costs will be unbearably high.

A Strategic Offensive and a New Role for South Korea

How can South Korea overcome its current dilemma? In what ways can South Korea redefine its diplomatic role in dealing with the North? The idea of a strategic offensive—preemptive efforts on the part of South Korea to condition, influence, and even dictate the nature and direction of inter-Korean relations and DPRK-U.S. relations by taking a radically new sequence of policy initiatives—might be a viable answer.[14]

Blocking North Korea's attempts to sign a peace treaty with the United States constitutes the first component of such a strategic offensive. This does not mean that the South should impede diplomatic normalization and economic cooperation between the two; South Korea should render full support for such bilateral interactions. North Korea's efforts to link the nullification of the armistice agreement and diplomatic normalization to a peace treaty should be carefully monitored and decisively prevented. Such a series of events could trigger intended or unintended chain reactions involving the withdrawal of U.S. forces from the South and the destabilization of peninsular and regional security.

In doing so, South Korea needs to also think about invalidating the armistice agreement regime,[15] a radical departure from the traditional policy line, but congruent with North Korea's position. Such a preemptive measure by Seoul can be justified for several reasons. First, North Korea has already begun to ignore the armistice treaty by terminating the supervisory role of neutral states, refusing to engage in dialogue with South Korean representatives, and seeking a peace treaty with the United States. Thus, insisting on the armistice treaty regime is like beating a dead horse. Second, the armistice treaty has been a primary cause of the stalemate in inter-Korean relations. Taking advantage of the fact that South Korea is not a signatory to the treaty, North Korea has constantly used the "armistice treaty card" to sabotage inter-Korean talks. South Korea can correct such behavior by preemptively invalidating the treaty regime. An abdication of the armistice treaty by the South could lead to a de jure, if not de facto, state of war between North and South because it removes the legal mechanism for a truce on the peninsula. In view of the past, however, the outbreak of war is unlikely because the peninsular status quo has been maintained not because of the armistice treaty but because of military deterrence. Thus, removing the armistice treaty would not immediately endanger peninsular security.

Such an initiative should convince the North that the direct party to the Korean conflict is South Korea, not the United States, and that any discussions or negotiations about peace and security on the Korean peninsula should take place with the South. It should also be made clear to the North that South Korea does not have any legal obligation to honor a DPRK-U.S. peace treaty and that the Basic Agreement is the only viable means to settle inter-Korean differences in the absence of an armistice treaty.

North Korea is likely to resist the above formula because of the presence of U.S. troops in the South. The North could also reject negotiations over inter-Korean confidence-building measures and arms control for the same reason. Thus, retaining U.S. troops while facilitating inter-Korean talks will emerge as a major task for the South and its allies. Three possible options can be considered in this regard.

One possibility is to retain U.S. forces in the South within the framework of regional security arrangements. In this case, the role of U.S. forces would be less as a deterrent against the North and more as a guarantee of regional stability against Japan's remilitarization, China's hegemonic ambitions, and Russia's role as a potential spoiler in the region. Despite rhetorical opposition, North Korea seems increasingly receptive to the idea. A "two plus four" formula or tighter regional security cooperation regimes could assure the North of stabilizing the role of U.S. forces in the South.

Another possibility is to ensure a symmetrical alliance between the two Koreas by promoting DPRK-U.S. bilateral military cooperation. South Korea can facilitate military cooperation between North Korea and the United States through personnel exchanges, the dispatch of military advisers, and even the transfer of nonoffensive military equipment to the North. Such actions will reduce North Korean fears of an American military attack, while allowing inter-Korean confidence-building measures within the framework of a U.S. troop presence in the South.

South Korea can also enlist the United States in a more active mediating role, as in the case of the Arab-Israeli conflict. In other words, the United States can engineer an inter-Korean peace treaty by arranging a North Korea–South Korea summit meeting (the Camp David accord is suggestive in this regard). Initiating a peace treaty is not difficult, but implementing and maintaining it is. Thus, the U.S. forces could become a peacekeeping force for a finite period of time in cooperation with the United Nations or within a regional security cooperation agreement.

Of these, the first option (i.e., forming a regional security regime) seems most feasible, desirable, stable, and cost minimizing. The issue is, however, whether North Korea would trust regional security cooperation regimes, although it has increasingly become receptive to the idea. If North Korea does not accept the first option, the second option, based on increased U.S.–North Korean military cooperation, can be explored. Domestic opposition could be a major hurdle, but it is a sure way to remove North Korea's phobia of U.S. as well as South Korean military threats. The attractive and innovative third option, the Camp David formula, can serve as an effective vehicle for turning the tripartite entanglement into a dyadic negotiation in which the United States is a neutral umpire. Transforming U.S. forces into peacekeeping forces, however, seems questionable, particularly because the Korean conflict does not involve any overt actions. Yet it seems a worthwhile option to be explored by the U.S. leadership.

If and when the above stages are implemented, North and South Korea can return to the letter and spirit of the Basic Agreement. Implementing military and nonmilitary confidence-building measures as well as structural arms control measures can easily lead to a bilateral peace treaty between the two, paving the way for a peaceful settlement of the Korean conflict and ultimately national unification.

Concluding Remarks

The idea of a strategic offensive seems not only feasible but also desirable for the South. It can turn South Korea's defensive diplomatic posture into an offensive one and sever the vicious cycle of protracted conflict and tension on the peninsula. The initiative will fundamentally alter the nature of the Korean conflict system by making "Korea first" the guiding principle for inter-Korean conflict management. North Korea has nothing to lose but a potential peace treaty with the United States. Yet a solid and viable inter-Korean peace treaty will benefit the North more than a DPRK-U.S. peace treaty. More important, such an arrangement implies the institutionalization of a peaceful coexistence between North and South, which is in turn predicated on Seoul's abandonment of unification by absorption. The United States would also benefit from the arrangement by getting out of the Korean entanglement without compromising its security commitment to the peninsula and the region.

The strategic offensive would not be without drawbacks, however. First, South Korea cannot *unilaterally* invalidate the armistice treaty. Close cooperation with the United Nations, the United States, and other allies is essential. Ideally speaking, it can be done by a United Nations Security Council resolution calling for the termination of the armistice treaty on the Korean peninsula. This requires prudent diplomatic efforts on the part of South Korea. In that adopting such a resoluton will be impossible without U.S. consent and support, forming a bond with the United States and mobilizing its domestic support should be carefully undertaken before engaging in a direct lobby on the United Nations.

Second, there are two technical barriers in this initiative. One involves a contradiction between the initiative and the Basic Agreement, and the other relates to the dissolution of the United Nations Command (UNC). Article V of the Basic Agreement stipulates that the armistice treaty should be tentatively maintained until a stable peace regime has been achieved on the Korean peninsula. Preemptively invalidating the armistice agreement would contradict this stipulation. This problem can be resolved by amending the Basic Agreement, which would not be difficult if both Koreas can expedite the crafting of a peace treaty. The dissolution of the UNC would not pose serious problems because it has been symbolic rather than substantive since the mid-1970s. Nevertheless, dissolution may invite opposition from the U.S. military establishment because it touches on invalidating some U.S. bases in Japan whose use was justified in the name of supporting the UNC in South Korea. This problem is not insurmountable; separate bilateral talks with Japan should be able to resolve it within the framework of the Japan-U.S. mutual defense treaty.

Third, North Korea could interpret the initiative as malign and refuse to participate. To demonstrate its good intention and goodwill to the North, the South should fully support the exchange of liasion offices, diplomatic nomalization, and economic cooperation between Pyongyang and Washington even before resuming the letter and spirit of the Basic Agreement. In a similar vein, Seoul should also facilitate improved Pyongyang-Tokyo ties. Inter-Korean economic exchanges should also be reactivated.

Finally, the most formidable barrier lies in the South, where domestic opposition to the idea of a strategic offensive is likely to be enormous. Both conservative and progressive camps will oppose it. To the conservative camp, it is nothing but an outright accommodation of the North Korean proposal and will gravely jeopardize national security. The progressive camp will reject it because it is predicated on the perpetual division of the motherland. More important, because it will not be easy for the South Korean government to alter its traditional policy line, the quality of political leadership will assume new prominence. Public opinion should not dictate the nature and direction of inter-Korean relations, for it can only lead to erratic policy. Thus, the vision and commitment of the political leadership are essential prerequisites for successfully implementing a strategic offensive.

The time is ripe to resolve the Korean conflict, but the resolution should be initiated by the Koreans themselves. The United States can play only a minor role in facilitating the settlement and resolution. Old ways of thinking will continue to sustain the stalemate; new thinking is needed more than ever before. The idea of a strategic offensive can be seen as a preliminary step toward such new thinking.

Notes

I would like to thank Hong Yung Lee, Jongryn Mo, and Wonsoo Kim for their helpful comments.

1. *Donga Ilbo*, April 5, 1996.

2. See National Unification Board, *Report on Major North-South Korean Issues* (Seoul: NUB, July 1995), mimeo in Korean. Also see Jae-ho Lee, "Which Side Would the United States Support if a War Broke Out in Korea?" *News+*, February 1, 1996, pp. 42–43, in Korean.

3. This has been a typical North Korean position. Perhaps the only exception is North Korea's plea for international support through an official admission of its flood damages last summer.

4. Aidan Foster-Carter has been a leading proponent of the catastrophe theory. See his "Korea's Coming Reunification: Another East Asian Superpower?" *Economist Intelligence Unit Special Report* N. M212 (April 1992). For his revised position, see "North Korea after Kim Il-Sung: Controlled Collapse?" *Economist Intelligence Unit, Research Report* (1994). Also see special features on North Korea in "North Korean Danger: Collapse or Provocation?" *Sindonga*, February 1996, pp. 394–428. For an overview of political changes since the death of Kim Il Sung, see B. C. Koh's chapter in this volume and a report by the Research Institute of National Unification, *One Year after the Death of Kim Il Sung: Trends and Prospects of North Korean Situation* (Seoul: RINU, 1995), in Korean.

5. See Steve Glain and Namju Cho, "China Seeks to Halt Flow of North Korean Refugees," *Wall Street Journal*, February 6, 1996, p. A6.

6. President Kim Young Sam has recently instructed government agencies to draft contingency plans to deal with the big bang scenario. The South Korean Red Cross has a plan to turn 270 schools into temporary refugee camps for North Koreans if they defect to the South en masse. *Korea Herald*, February 9, 1996.

7. See Marcus Noland, "The North Korean Economy," in Korea Economic Institute of America, ed., *Economic and Regional Integration in Northeast Asia* (Washington, D.C.: KEIA, 1995), pp. 155–67.

8. Since 1988, North Korea has eased its position on the reduction and withdrawal of U.S. forces from South Korea. Selig Harrison, who made a recent visit to North Korea, indicated that the North is willing to make a compromise on the issue of U.S. forces in the South. On this issue, see Chung-in Moon, *Arms Control on the Korean Peninsula: International Penetrations, Regional Dynamics, and Domestic Structure* (Seoul: Yonsei University Press, 1996), chap. 4.

9. For an overview of these contending views, see Chung-in Moon, *The Structure of the Korean Conflict and the Withdrawal of American Forces* (Seoul: Korea Policy Development Institute, 1991), in Korean.

10. Very few in the South have advocated this perpective. Those who favor this view are mostly from the radical movement circle.

11. This perspective has been favored by some American observers. For details, see Chung-in Moon, *The Structure of the Korean Conflict*.

12. See U.S. Department of Defense (DOD), *United States Security Strategy for the East Asia-Pacific Region* (Washington, D.C.: DOD, 1995). For a dissenting view, see Chalmers Johnson and E. B. Keehn, "The Pentagon's Ossified Strategy," *Foreign Affairs* 74, no. 4 (July/August 1995): 103–14.

13. This view represents the mainstream scholarly thinking in South Korea. For a detailed analysis of this view, see Research Institute of National Unification, *Comprehensive Implementation Measures for North–South Korean Arms Control—with Specific Reference to North Korea–U.S. and North–South Korean Relations* (Seoul: RINU, 1995), in Korean.

14. For an elaboration of this idea, see Chung-in Moon, "Restructuring of International Order and Reassessment of Inter-Korean Relations—Suggestions for Strategic Offensive," *Tongil Gyungje* (Unification economy), August 1995, in Korean.

15. For an opposing view, see Sung-ho Je, "Options for the Construction of a Peace Regime on the Korean Peninsula," *Kukga Junryak* (National strategy) 2, no. 1 (1996): 59–106; Jin-hyun Baek, "A Study of Alternatives to the Armistice Agreement Regime," in National Unification Board, ed., *In Search of the Realization of the Commonwealth Model of National Unification* (Seoul: National Unification Board, 1991), both in Korean.

8

Security and Economic Linkages in the Inter-Korean Relationship

JONGRYN MO

Introduction

Negotiations between North and South Korea to open trade and investment have been complicated by concerns on both sides about the security consequences of economic exchanges. Using a model of two-level games in international bargaining theory,[1] I explain how security concerns affect the outcome of trade negotiations between two adversaries and, in particular, the conditions under which one side can successfully exercise its economic power to extract political concessions from the other. I argue that the prevailing economic and security conditions on the Korean peninsula are favorable for Seoul to make such security-economic linkages with Pyongyang. Successful linkage, however, requires that the South Korean government act strategically to take advantage of the favorable conditions.

The Development of the North and South Korean Economic Relationship

Since the end of the Korean civil war in 1953, the economies of the North and South have developed in radically different ways. Seoul's policy of export-driven economic development along with public-private cooperation gave rise to an economic takeoff in the late sixties. In contrast, Pyongyang's experiment with Stalinist "socialism in one country" had some initial success but brought about stagnation beginning in the middle of the 1960s. Starting in 1984, economic reforms throughout the communist world forced Pyongyang to consider some modest ones of its own. But the biggest shock to the North Korean economy came in 1989 when the Soviet empire collapsed and North Korea lost its largest export market. As a result, North Korea's export earnings disappeared, creating severe foreign exchange shortages. Worse, Russia and China began to demand market prices and hard currency payments for their exports. Because North Korea accumulated enormous debts with virtually all its trading partners, socialist as well as Western,[2] it has not been able to borrow from abroad.

In the face of such economic hardships, North Korean leaders have experimented with some trade and economic reforms. But so far, North Korea has failed to embark on a consistent course. It copied some of the Chinese economic reforms, for example, the creation of special trade zones, but the level of political commitment remains unclear. Fear of capitalist intrusion and outside influence has kept North Korean leaders from taking far-reaching economic reform policies.[3]

Given its inability to attract trade and investment from other countries, it is clear that North Korea would derive large economic benefits from expanding its trade and investment with the South. Because of unfavorable economic conditions (decreasing gross national product, weak creditworthiness, and limited reforms), North Korea is not an attractive market for investment. Since 1988, North Korea has been enjoying a disproportionate amount of benefits from its limited trade liberalization with the South; trade between North and South Korea via China has been basically a one-way flow, with South Korea paying hard currency for North Korean imports (see table 8.1).[4]

In contrast, the gains from inter-Korean trade would be relatively modest for South Korea. Although some sectors of the South Korean economy, such as the declining labor-intensive industries, may benefit from investing in North Korea, the impact would clearly be smaller than on the North Korean economy.

South Korea's interest in expanding its economic relationship lies with the potential security benefits of inter-Korean economic interaction; Seoul wants to use its economic advantage to improve the inter-Korean relationship. South Korea, which has long desired stability, reduced tensions, and more personal and official interactions between the two Koreas, has insisted on an improved political relationship as the primary condition for trade and investment expansion. This linkage strategy by South Korea stems from its perceived security weakness.

Without a war having actually been fought, it is difficult to obtain a precise measure of the relative military strengths of the two countries. I use four measures to evaluate those strengths: aggregate power, geographic proximity, offensive power, and aggressive intentions.[5] In terms of aggregate power, neither South Korea nor North Korea seems to have a clear advantage. Although the North

Table 8.1   Trade between North and South Korea, 1988–1994
               (in thousands of dollars)

Year	N. Korean Exports to S. Korea (in thousands of $)*	Total N. Korean exports (in %)	Total S. Korean imports (in %)	S. Korean exports to N. Korea (in thousands of $)	Turnover (in thousands of $)
1988	1,037	0.0	0.00		1,037
1989	22,235	1.4	0.00	69	22,304
1990	20,354	11.1	0.00	4,731	25,085
1991	165,996	18.7	0.20	26,176	192,172
1992	200,685	23.7	0.24	12,818	213,503
1993	188,528		0.22	10,262	198,790
1994	178,663		0.17	16,243	194,960

* Almost all inter-Korean trade is indirect; in 1994 direct trade represented only 4.5 percent of total trade.
SOURCES: Ministry of Unification, Bank of Korea, and *Direction of Trade Statistics* (Washington, D.C.: International Monetary Fund).

Korean military has a sizable lead in troop strength and conventional weapons, its population and economy are significantly smaller than South Korea's. The other three criteria, however, all favor North Korea. The location of Seoul, the main population and industrial center in the South, near the border is a geographic disadvantage; the troops of South Korea and its ally, the United States, are positioned to defend, not to attack; and North Korea's invasion of South Korea in 1950 and numerous provocations since then show Pyongyang's willingness to use force. These factors have shaped South Korea's perception of its vulnerability and explain why the South Korean government has shown more interest in reducing the tension on the Korean peninsula than its North Korean counterpart.[6]

The actual negotiations over inter-Korean economic exchanges began on October 7, 1988, when Rha Woong Bae, then deputy prime minister of South Korea, announced that private South Korean companies would be allowed to trade with North Korea and that their executives would be able to visit North Korea. North Korean goods would be imported duty-free, and North Korean ships would be allowed to call at South Korean ports. Although the South Korean government did not attach any conditions, the North Korean trade initiative, as an extension of its Nordpolitik, was aimed at easing the tense relationship between the two Koreas.[7]

The South Korean government soon formalized its linkage policy. When Pyongyang insisted that the annual U.S.–South Korean "Team Spirit" military exercises be canceled as a precondition for any talks between North and South in March 1989, South Korean prime minister Kang Young Hoon decided to link trade to an improved relationship by vetoing some of the joint projects that Chung Ju Young, the founder of the Hyundai group, had negotiated with the North Koreans.[8] Despite these difficulties, however, Seoul's trade initiative in 1988 led to growing indirect trade between the two Koreas.

North Korea has pursued a permissive trade strategy. Although Pyongyang has publicly rejected Seoul's calls for trade and investment, it has permitted the inflow of South Korean goods and investment. As a result, indirect trade between the two Koreas has grown rapidly since 1988.

During 1990–1991, it seemed that South Korea's linkage strategy was finally working. After a series of talks, North and South Korea signed the historic Agreement on Reconciliation, Non-Aggression and Exchanges and Cooperation (hereafter, the Basic Agreement) in December 1991. This Basic Agreement, which outlined a set of principles that would guide future North and South Korean relationships including economic exchanges, was to usher in a period of peace and reconciliation between North and South Korea. Although the South Korean government at the time did not make explicit linkages between inter-Korea talks and economic exchanges, such linkages were implicit in that it was inconceivable that the South would have agreed to expand trade and investment without a general improvement in the inter-Korean relationship.

The negotiations to implement the Basic Agreement collapsed in October 1992, however, amid widespread suspicion about the North Korean nuclear program. When Pyongyang announced that it was bolting from the Nuclear Non-proliferation Treaty in March 1993, Seoul prohibited its firms from making contact with North Koreans, thus effectively halting South Korean investment in North Korea and seriously undermining trade between the two countries. Indirect trade fell accordingly. The South Korean government then formally linked trade to a resolution of North Korea's nuclear program.[9] This ban on inter-Korean contact continued until November 1994, when Seoul lifted restrictions on direct trade and investment in response to the October 1994 Framework Agreement between the United States and North Korea aimed at resolving the nuclear issue.

As we have seen, South Korea's linkage strategy was most explicit between March 1993 and November 1994, when it linked trade and investment to the North Korean nuclear issue. Ironically, this is the period when South Korea's linkage strategy began to unravel. Even before the Framework Agreement was signed, the Kim Young Sam government was wavering; under heavy pressure from local business, it considered lifting the ban as early as September 1993.[10] The Geneva Framework Agreement itself can hardly be considered a successful example of linkage; the North rejected all talks with the South during the negotiations. Although one may argue that Pyongyang gave security concessions for economic benefits, it is not clear whether South Korea's security improved because the inter-Korean relationship worsened after the agreement was signed.[11]

After South Korea lifted the ban, its situation deteriorated further. Pyongyang not only rejected Seoul's call for open trade and investment[12] but also adopted a two-track policy of wooing South Korean businesspeople while refusing any trade talks with the South Korean government. Until the Kim Young Sam government hardened its position following a public backlash over its rice aid policy in the summer of 1995, it appeared too eager to give away economic benefits without reciprocal concessions from the North. During this time, the South made the resumption of official talks the only precondition for trade expansion. To North Korea's credit, some South Koreans began to consider formalizing inter-Korean economic exchanges as a costly concession on the part of North Korea.

Because South Korea has a security disadvantage and an economic advantage, some economic/security linkages seem feasible between North and South Korea. Yet efforts to make economic and security linkages have not been successful. To understand the conditions under which such linkages can be made, I turn to a model of trade negotiation in the presence of strong security concerns.

Security Concerns and Trade Negotiations

Trade negotiations between North and South Korea show how economic and security conditions shape each other's strategies.[13] The distribution of trade gains between the two Koreas has been a powerful influence in opening trade and investment. Although trade produces economic gains, those gains can differ between trading partners. Assuming a simple dichotomy, a country's absolute gains from trade can be either large or small. Thus, in terms of absolute gains, there are four possible distributions of the gains from trade between two trading partners: *small, small; small, large; large, small;* and *large, large*. When two countries negotiate to open trade, it is their relative gains that give bargaining power to one side. When the gains from trade are expected to be asymmetric, the side that expects smaller gains from trade has bargaining power because it needs trade less than the other side. When the absolute gains are symmetrically distributed (i.e., *small, small* and *large, large*), neither side derives leverage from economic conditions.

In the case of North and South Korea, there is little question that inter-Korea trade and investment would bring large gains to North Korea. Evidence also indicates that the size of the gains for South Korea would be small. North Korean exports to South Korea represented only 0.24 percent of total South Korean imports, and some officials in Seoul openly admit the economic insignificance of inter-Korean trade.

But there is no consensus on the importance of inter-Korean trade to the South Korean economy. According to supporters of trade expansion (South Korean businesses), South Korea will derive large gains. They argue that the economies of the North and South could complement each other quite well. The South has capital and technology, and the North has raw materials and cheap labor. Low-cost labor is becoming increasingly attractive for South Korean companies, given their rising labor costs. The model presented here predicts the outcome of trade negotiations when large economic gains are expected by South Korea.

The balance of power has been another factor driving trade negotiations between the two Koreas. I examine two cases, one in which military power is distributed roughly equally and one in which the distribution of military power favors North Korea. In the first case both sides face symmetric security constraints; in the second case the (militarily) strong side and the weak side face different trade-offs in balancing their economic and security interests. As I argued previously, a set of objective criteria seems to indicate that North Korea has an advantage in security.

But it is possible that North Korea's security advantage has weakened or is about to decline. During the 1980s, South Korea's Nordpolitik led to diplomatic relations with China, Russia, and other socialist countries. North Korea became more isolated as internal political developments caused Russia to reevaluate its stance in world politics. If these developments have undermined North Korea's security, both sides may now be locked into a symmetric, competitive situation with high levels of insecurity.

In the model the distribution of military power is assumed to be altered as a result of trade negotiations, especially when explicit security/trade linkages are made. A realization of the gains from trade may also affect the balance of power between divided countries. A country can add new economic gains to military expenditures directly or indirectly from a stronger economy. But I assume that when it has a choice, the military would rather see direct security concessions from the enemy, which have immediate benefits, than the economic gains that trade brings, which are uncertain and indirect. Businesses will resist government efforts to tax their trade gains to increase military spending, so there is no obvious mechanism through which large trade gains translate into security benefits. Likewise, the military would rather give up large economic gains than make security concessions, especially when the enemy already has a security advantage.

Combining the distributions of military power and trade benefits, we arrive at four possible combinations of economic and security conditions. Figure 8.1 indicates whether the gains from inter-Korean trade are large or small for South Korea and whether North Korea has a security advantage or whether the distribution of military power is relatively equal.

For each combination of economic and security conditions, I will show the

Figure 8.1   Outcome of Trade Negotiations between North and South Korea

Economic gains for South/ Security advantage for North	*Advantage*	*No advantage*
Small	Trade with linkages	Economic warfare
Large	Permissive trade	Permissive trade

likely outcome of bargaining over trade liberalization. The first step is to describe states' preferences for possible bargaining outcomes. States can choose essentially three trade strategies toward their adversaries: a policy of economic warfare, a permissive strategy, or a linkage strategy. Economic warfare is the strategy of restricting trade as much as possible. A permissive trade policy avoids any explicit security and economic linkage; its objective is simply to remove barriers to trade and investment. A linkage strategy aims for an agreement in which future benefits from trade liberalization are used explicitly as a means to obtain security concessions; in other words, wealth is traded for security. The three trade strategies then allow for three possible outcomes (i.e., economic warfare, permissive trade, and trade with linkages).

In reasoning about the outcome of trade bargaining between North and South Korea, we note that an agreement is only feasible if both sides stand to gain relative to the status quo. In the Korean peninsula the status quo has been economic warfare. If one side favors a policy of economic warfare, there will be no trade liberalization; the side for which the status quo is optimal will refuse any other outcome. If both sides agree on an outcome (their most preferred outcome), that outcome will be chosen. But what if they have conflicts of interest? To predict the outcome in those cases, we introduce a model of bargaining based on the logic of two-level games.

In North and South Korea, the domestic debate over inter-Korean trade focuses inevitably on its security consequences. Different sectors on both sides have varying degrees of interest in security relative to economic gains.[14] Business will be most interested in economic gains and will pressure politicians to seize the economic opportunities of trade liberalization, but other sectors, for example, the military and security forces, will be primarily concerned about security. In a divided country like Korea, we expect that the position of the military and security apparatus carries a large weight in the domestic policy debate and that their ability to prioritize security concerns imposes a domestic constraint on those negotiating to open trade. In the terminology of two-level games, the military acts as the negotiators' main domestic constituent. According to the logic of two-level games, the bargaining outcome favors the side with greater domestic constraints. In others words, the more inflexible or powerful your military is, the more likely you are to win concessions from the other side. Thus, the outcome of trade negotiation critically depends on the position and influence of the military on each side.

AN ECONOMIC ADVANTAGE FOR THE SOUTH AND A SECURITY ADVANTAGE FOR THE NORTH

Because the gains from trade are asymmetric, South Korea with its economic advantage will seek to reduce tension by linking trade with opening dialogue, confidence-building measures, and explicit security concessions like arms control. The South Korean military and security interests will *insist* on such linkages; they strongly object to permissive trade because it brings large gains to the militarily strong North Korea. Security concerns thus make permissive trade unacceptable to South Korea. South Korea's preference ordering is then linkage, economic warfare, permissive trade (i.e., linkage is the best outcome for the weak side, followed by economic warfare and permissive trade).

In contrast, permissive trade is the best outcome for North Korea; between linkage and economic warfare, North Korea favors linkage. Because of its military advantage, North Korea has more leeway to make security and economic trade-offs. Security concessions, as part of linkage, are acceptable to North Korea because it is compensated by the large economic gains from trade. North Korea's preference ordering is thus as follows: permissive trade, linkage, economic warfare.

Given these preference orderings, it is easy to see that the bargaining outcome favors South Korea, which would rather break off negotiations and continue economic warfare than accept permissive trade. North Korea, which finds South Korea's best outcome (linkage) acceptable (i.e., better than the status quo of economic warfare) will give up its most preferred outcome (permissive trade). Trade with linkages will therefore be the outcome of trade bargaining. In terms of the logic of two-level games, the outcome of bargaining favors South Korea because it has greater domestic constraints; the South Korean military with its security disadvantage will be less likely to compromise than the North Korean military.

NO ECONOMIC ADVANTAGE FOR THE SOUTH AND A SECURITY ADVANTAGE FOR THE NORTH

When the expected gains from trade are large and symmetric, neither side derives a bargaining advantage from future trade, but the militarily weak side will still pursue a linkage strategy to alleviate its security concerns. In this situation, South Korea (the weak side) prefers linkage to economic warfare. Because South Korea derives large absolute gains from trade, and because the distribution of gains is symmetric, it also prefers permissive trade to economic warfare. South Korea's choice between linkage and permissive trade is less clear and depends on whether the two sides can agree on a linkage that Pareto-dominates permissive trade.

North Korea, as the militarily strong side, prefers permissive trade to economic warfare; permissive trade will not change the existing security situation, which favors the strong side, because the gains from trade are distributed symmetrically. North Korea also prefers linkage to economic warfare, first, because North Korea, with its military advantage, will be open to some trade/security trade-offs and, second, because the large gains from trade will lead to strong support from business and the military will feel pressured to make some concessions. Like South Korea, North Korea does not necessarily have a clear preference between linkage and permissive trade.

Because linkage and permissive trade are acceptable to both sides, either outcome is possible, but I argue that linkage is less likely than permissive trade. For linkage to be successful, the South Korean business community has to make concessions, diminishing the business support for linkage accordingly. Moreover, the military in the South is aware that North Korea can be compensated for any security concessions by means of additional economic gains. Support for linkage in South Korea will thus be wavering and conditional on the economic price demanded by North Korea. As a result, South Korea may not desire linkage to begin with; if it does pursue a linkage strategy, it will lack the necessary support from its domestic constituents. Therefore, I predict that the outcome of bargaining will be permissive trade. In this scenario, the North Korean government correctly anticipates that the South Korean government will allow firms to establish inter-Korean economic links without an intergovernmental agreement.

AN ECONOMIC ADVANTAGE FOR THE SOUTH AND NO SECURITY ADVANTAGE FOR THE NORTH

The side with small potential gains, South Korea, still derives bargaining power from the possibility of trade and will demand security concessions from the side with large potential gains, North Korea. Permissive trade is unacceptable to the South because it would give larger economic benefits to the North. Thus, the South's preference ordering is linkage, economic warfare, permissive trade.

North Korea, in contrast, would like permissive trade from which it expects to derive large economic gains that it could even use to achieve a military advantage in the long run. Linkage is the least attractive outcome for the North; although Pyongyang would derive large economic gains, it would have to make security concessions, thus altering the distribution of military power in favor of Seoul. Consequently, the North's military will strongly oppose such linkage.

North Korea's preference ordering becomes permissive trade, economic warfare, linkage.

The countries have diametrically opposed preferences in this case. Neither side will accept the outcome that the opponent prefers, and there is no zone of agreement. As a result, the negotiations will reach a deadlock, and the status quo of economic warfare will continue.

NO ECONOMIC ADVANTAGE FOR THE SOUTH AND
NO SECURITY ADVANTAGE FOR THE NORTH

When the gains from trade are large and symmetric, and the distribution of military power is symmetric, neither side gains from the possibility of trade or is insecure enough to attempt security linkages. When neither side strives for linkage, both sides prefer permissive trade to economic warfare so that they can profit from trade. Permissive trade will be the outcome.

SUMMARY

The analysis shows that negotiations between North and South Korea to open (and expand) trade and investment will not necessarily lead to a single outcome. All three possible outcomes—trade with linkages, permissive trade, and economic warfare—can result, depending on the distribution of economic and military powers.[15] The analysis also shows how the outcome of inter-Korean economic negotiations will evolve as economic and security conditions change. In the next section, I examine the implications of the two-level game analysis for South Korean policy where the economic and security conditions themselves or the actors' perception of them can be altered.

The Logic of Two-Level Games
and South Korean Policy

From South Korea's perspective, the best outcome is trade with linkages. South Korea hopes that expanded trade and investment will help end its adversarial relationship with North Korea, paving the way toward eventual reunification. Because a linkage policy can succeed only if the South has the economic advantage and the security disadvantage, Seoul has an incentive to maintain its economic advantage and play up its vulnerable security position.

The government of South Korea must maintain or further its economic advantage, which is the only credible leverage it possesses. Domestically, excessive competition among firms to obtain first-mover advantages in North Korea should be discouraged or at least not allowed to become an open conflict. The South Korean government must also encourage its firms to invest in places like China and Vietnam, independently of the North Korean situation. South Korea needs to demonstrate that it has options outside North Korea. Taiwan's failure to enforce its "go south" policy—wherein it encouraged its firms to invest in Southeast Asia rather than the mainland where they could become vulnerable—should not be repeated by South Korea.

Conversely, South Korea needs to reduce the number of outside options for North Korea by discouraging such allies as the United States and Japan from expanding their economic presence in North Korea. Fortunately for South Korea, the business environment in North Korea is so bad that few countries are interested in investing in North Korea without South Korea leading the way.[16]

To its domestic and international audiences, Seoul should present an accurate picture of its security vulnerability. The North Korean threat is credible not because the North possesses the capability to conquer the South in the event of all-out war but because it can impose severe costs on the South. In pursuing its linkage policy, Seoul should also discount the possibility that an economic opening would threaten regime stability in North Korea, for it is not clear that such an opening would lead to the immediate unraveling of the North Korean regime. In any case, North Korea has taken measures to guard against that contingency (e.g., locating free trade zones in remote areas).

Despite favorable security and economic conditions, South Korea's linkage policy can fail for tactical reasons. The logic of two-level games offers the following strategies for the South to increase the domestic influence of its security interests:

First, the South Korean government should make clear its linkage objectives. Strategically, South Korea may not want to demand explicit political and security concessions as immediate conditions for opening trade and investment, but it should not allow any second-guessing about the importance of an improved overall inter-Korean relationship.

Although West Germany made unilateral trade concessions in 1967–69 to East Germany, inter-German trade became part of the economic/security linkages that West Germany demanded. The extent of East German trade with the West depended on the availability of credits, and the linkage focused on this issue. The interest-free "swing" allowed East Germany to run substantial trade imbalances in its trade with West Germany. Political concessions by the East German government were regularly accompanied by upward adjustments of the swing. West Germany supported East Germany's borrowing in the West through government-guaranteed bank credits. East Germany received further direct economic transfers, ranging from presents to private citizens to transit fees and unofficial payments for the release of political prisoners.

South Korea should not, therefore, compromise on its condition that government-to-government negotiations and agreements must govern the inter-Korea economic relationship in the hope that initial economic exchanges will somehow change North Korea's hard-line position. Despite its large investments there, Taiwan has been able to win few political concessions from mainland China. (Ironically, it is Beijing that is now using Taiwanese investors as a lever to alter the behavior of the Taiwan government.)[17]

Second, South Korea can win political concessions from the North if its negotiators credibly display the domestic constraints (i.e., the military and security interests) imposed by the hard-liners. The key is to show the credibility of their constraints, which can be done in a number of ways. The South Korean government can declare a set of nonnegotiable principles, one of which should be official regulation of inter-Korean economic exchanges, and stick to them. After the controversial rice aid to North Korea, the South Korean government has moved in this direction; the government has steadfastly insisted on resuming inter-Korean governmental dialogue before expanding economic exchanges and has decided to raise the issue of North Korean human rights abuses.

Because South Korea is now a democratic government, it can enhance its leverage by institutionalizing its domestic constraints. South Korean officials can, for example, blame public opinion or an uncooperative National Assembly for rejecting unfavorable North Korean demands or requiring concessions.

Third, South Korea should recognize that the North, too, has a strong incentive to take advantage of its domestic constraints. In private, North Korean negotiators have expressed their frustration about the hard-line position of their military. Some even express worries that the North Korean military may start a war on its own. The South Korean government should also realize that it is to North Korea's advantage to exaggerate such claims.[18]

Lastly, to the extent possible, South Korea should strive to become proactive in taking advantage of the domestic divisions in North Korea. In the same way that North Korea tries to drive a wedge between business and government in the South, South Korea should try to strengthen the position of North Korean moderates. Paradoxically, the best way to help North Korean moderates is to have a consistent linkage policy; North Korean hawks should not be led to believe that South Korea will give in without security concessions from the North.

Notes

I would like to thank Uk Heon Hong, Won-soo Kim, Hong Yung Lee, and Chung-in Moon for their comments.

1. Robert D. Putnam, "Diplomacy and Domestic Politics: The Logic of Two-Level

Games," *International Organization* 42 (summer 1988); Keisuke Iida, "When and How Do Domestic Constraints Matter? Two-Level Games with Uncertainty," *Journal of Conflict Resolution* 37 (September 1993); Jongryn Mo, "The Logic of Two-Level Games with Endogenous Domestic Coalitions," *Journal of Conflict Resolution* 38 (September 1994); Jongryn Mo, "Domestic Institutions and International Bargaining: The Role of Agent Veto in Two-Level Games," *American Political Science Review*, December 1995; Robert Pahre, "Who Is on First, Who Is on Second: Actors and Institutions in Two-Level Games," mimeo., University of Michigan. Critical surveys of the empirical literature are offered by Andrew Moravcsik, "Introduction: Integrating International and Domestic Theories of International Bargaining," in Peter Evans, Harold Jacobson, and Robert Putnam, eds., *Double-Edged Diplomacy* (Berkeley: University of California Press, 1993); Taehyun Kim and Taejoon Han, "Making Your Voice Heard in International Economic Negotiations," in *Korea's Economic Diplomacy* (Seoul, Korea: Sejong Institute, 1995).

2. Aidan Foster-Carter, "Korea's Coming Reunification: Another East Asian Superpower?" The Economist Intelligence Unit, Special Report No. M212, April 1992, presents data that estimate North Korea's total foreign debt at between 4,495 and 4,790 million dollars, about a third of which is with Russia ($1,300–$1,500 million).

3. Ha-Cheong Yeon, "Practical Means to Improve Intra-Korean trade and Economic Cooperation," KDI Working Paper No. 9301, Korea Development Institute, January 1993; Nicholas Eberstadt, "Reform, Muddling through, or Collapse?" in Thomas H. Henriksen and Kyongsoo Lho, eds., *One Korea? Challenges and Prospects for Reunification* (Stanford: Hoover Institution Press, 1994).

4. The definitions of direct and indirect trade are not clear in the literature. Yeon, in "Practical Means," says that North Korea has accepted "direct forms of transaction" since 1991 but does not explain how they are distinguished from the common form of indirect trade and does not give the volume of such transactions. The *Financial Times*, in contrast, reported that Ssangyong's plan to import cement from North Korea was the first direct North-South trade deal (December 12, December 20, 1994).

5. Stephen M. Walt, *The Origins of Alliances*. Ithaca, N.Y.: Cornell University Press, 1987.

6. Based on a statistical study of inter-Korean conflicts since 1950, Chi Huang, Woosang Kim, and Samuel Wu show that South Korea has been more sensitive to hostility from North Korea than the other way around. This supports my view that South Korea feels more vulnerable than North Korea. See Chi Huang, Woosang Kim, and Samuel Wu, "An Expected Utility of Inter-Korean Relations," in HeeMin Kim and Woosang Kim, eds., *Rationality and Politics in the Korean Peninsula* (East Lansing: Michigan State University–International Studies and Programs, 1995).

7. "Reaching Out: South Korea Tries to Forge Economic Links with the North," *Far Eastern Economic Review*, November 3, 1998.

8. "Seoul's Skepticism Is Slowing Attempts to Build Economic Ties with Pyongyang," *Asian Wall Street Journal*, March 27, 1989.

9. It is, however, noteworthy that neither side moved to prohibit indirect trade throughout the crisis.

10. "South Korea, under Corporate Pressure, May Drop Its Ban on Trade with North," *Wall Street Journal*, September 12, 1994.

11. For a similar view of the consequences of the Geneva Agreed Framework on inter-Korean relations, see Chung-in Moon, "The North Korean Problem and the Role of South Korea," in this volume.

12. "South Korea to Lift Curbs on Business Ties to North," *New York Times*, November 8, 1994; "North Korea Dismisses Trade Proposals by South," *New York Times*, November 11, 1994.

13. The discussion in this section is based on Dorrusen, Han, and Jongryn Mo, "Relative versus Absolute Gains: The Politics of Trade between Divided Countries," typescript, Department of Government, University of Texas at Austin, 1996.

14. Byeonggil Ahn, "Constraints and Objectives of North Korean Foreign Policy: A Rational Actor Analysis" (this volume), also sees the conflict between the hard-liners and soft-liners as the primary determinant of North Korean foreign policy.

15. A necessary condition for linkage on the Korean peninsula may be that North Korea's preference ordering shifts from a "military-oriented" type to an "economy-oriented" type. For a game-theoretic analysis that ties the two Koreas' economic and military relationship to their belief systems, see Byeonggil Ahn, "Domestic Uncertainty and Coordination between North and South Korea," in Kim and Kim, eds., *Rationality and Politics in the Korean Peninsula*.

16. "Dream On: North Korea Hopes in Vain for Foreign Capital," *Far Eastern Economic Review*, January 25, 1996.

17. "For Beijing, Taiwanese Money is a Lever," *Wall Street Journal*, September 5, 1995.

18. Kim Kyung-Won, "A Warning against North Korea," *Hankook Ilbo*, December 4, 1995.

9

The Korean Nuclear Understanding
Three Alternative Futures

HENRY SOKOLSKI

Overview

For better or worse, the Geneva Agreed Framework U.S. officials struck with the Democratic People's Republic of Korea (DPRK) October 21, 1994, now defines U.S. relations with the DPRK and will continue to do so until and unless that regime gives way to one truly acceptable to the South. How (and if) the nuclear deal is implemented, though, is hardly fixed. It largely depends on what South Korea and the United States are aiming to achieve regarding the communist regime in Pyongyang. If the aim is to support this regime, one need only proceed with the nuclear deal as it is now being executed. If, however, South Korea and the United States want to keep North Korea in a weakened position, highlighting the nuclear deal's potential legal-political difficulties concerning U.S. nuclear cooperation with North Korea would be useful, as would encouraging greater South Korean participation in the deal's provision for nuclear construction. Finally, if the objective is to accelerate the downfall of the communist government, suspending or terminating the nuclear deal could be accomplished by focusing on the deal's stipulations for denuclearization and North-South dialogue. Properly understood, then, the Agreed Framework is a kind of Rorschach test: Its substance and implementation are dictated less by its specific terms than by South Korea and America's strategic objectives.

A Deal Forever in the Making

As I have argued elsewhere,[1] how well the Agreed Framework is implemented depends as much on how South Korea, the United States, and North Korea interpret it as it does on the deal's specific terms. The reason is simple: As a political understanding, the Agreed Framework is not legally binding and, as such, is no more than what the parties believe it to be.

After months of negotiations the parties to the understanding have agreed on a number of points. They have determined not to supply North Korea with an electrical grid that can distribute the two gigawatts of nuclear power now under construction directly but instead to help North Korea "find a a foreign partner who will start tackling this task." They have agreed, however, that KEDO should supply North Korea with nuclear reactor training, improved roads, buildings to house "foreign experts," and new port facilities ("to minimize the capitalist influence" on North Korean citizens that the overland transit of reactor materials and personnel might otherwise have) and to extend North Korea interest-free loans (due seventeen years after completion of the first plant) to allow it to gain title on a turnkey basis.

All this is now part of the deal. None of it was specified in the Agreed Framework's text.[2] Other ambiguities, such as the precise meaning of the deal's heavy oil clauses, also seem to have been clarified: The United States has insisted that measures be adopted to assure that this oil only be used for "heating and electricity production," not for industrial purposes.

Still, negotiations are likely to continue. Indeed, many of the deal's key operational terms (e.g., "freeze," "dismantle," "completed," "significant portion of the LWR project," "engage in North-South dialogue," etc.) are nowhere defined and could easily become matters of political dispute unless they are clarified.

Then, there are ellipses. The text of the original understanding, for example, is unclear on precisely when North Korea will have to begin dismantling its production reactor and plutonium reprocessing plant (the heart of its known bomb-making capacity). Administration officials, claiming that North Korea must begin dismantling these plants as soon as the first LWR is completed, managed to get North Korea to agree to this in the December 1995 round of negotiations. Yet, the October 21, 1994, text specifies only that dismantlement be finished when the second LWR is operational (sometime after the first reactor is completed). What constitutes "dismantlement" and what milestones, if any (for completing, say, "half" of the dismantlement by a given date, etc.), have not been addressed. North Korean authorities have made it clear, however, that any time they believe that the United States has failed to live up to its end of the deal, North Korea will "automatically" resume nuclear weapons material production.[3]

Potential Sticking Points

What issues are likely to require further negotiation to implement the Agreed Framework? Many are unknown; two are certain. The first is the framework requirement that North Korea "implement the North-South Joint Declaration on the Denuclearization of the Korean Peninsula" and "engage in North-South dialogue."[4] The second is that the United States and North Korea "conclude a bilateral agreement for cooperation in the field of peaceful uses of nuclear energy,"[5] which is necessary if the United States is to supply the DPRK with two reactors "of advanced U.S.-origin design and technology currently under production."[6]

The first of these requirements—that the DPRK engage in talks with the South—has been emphasized by those skeptical of the deal. Last November a joint resolution passed in Congress requiring the U.S. president to report on the progress of inter-Korean dialogue in ninety days and every six months thereafter. Although the resolution's intent was to pressure the DPRK to honor its commitment to North-South talks, the immediate reaction from Pyongyang was negative. "The South Korean authorities are not [a] qualified . . . dialogue partner," insisted a DPRK foreign ministry spokesman, and American efforts to pressure Pyongyang into such talks "may endanger the hard-won [nuclear] agreement itself."[7]

Closely related to this requirement for North-South dialogue is the Agreed Framework's stipulation that the DPRK implement the North-South Joint Declaration on Denuclearization signed in December 1991. This formal agreement called on both North and South Korea not to make nuclear weapons or to possess nuclear reprocessing or enrichment facilities. It also called on each side to conduct mutual inspections of each other's nuclear facilities under procedures that a Joint Nuclear Control Committee would establish. Negotiations to create the Control Committee, however, were suspended in 1992 after the DPRK rejected South Korea's proposals for mutual challenge inspections.

More important, some proliferation experts have questioned whether the DPRK actually froze their nuclear weapons material production activities. There is evidence, for example, suggesting that the DPRK may have undeclared uranium enrichment and small-scale reprocessing facilities still operating.[8] Then there is the question of what the hundreds (if not thousands) of North Korean nuclear workers are now doing who were building and running reactor and reprocessing facilities frozen under the Agreed Framework. Have any of these workers been shifted to undeclared nuclear activities? No one knows.[9]

This brings us to the second potential sticking point: Will the United States reach a nuclear cooperative agreement with the DPRK as called for in the Agreed Framework? Under U.S. law, key nuclear power reactor components listed on the U.S. Nuclear Regulatory Commission's Nuclear Trigger List cannot be exported to nations with which the United States does not have a nuclear cooperative agreement. Given that the two light water reactors that the United States promised to supply to North Korea must be of "advanced U.S.-origin design and technology currently under production," some of the key components for these machines are only available from U.S. nuclear vendors. As such, neither of the reactors can be completed *unless* a U.S. nuclear cooperative agreement with the DPRK is reached.

This is hardly automatic. There are several legal requirements for reaching a nuclear cooperative agreement. First, U.S. nuclear cooperative agreements are treatylike obligations between sovereign governments. They involve presentment to Congress and have only been reached with governments that the United States has formally recognized. The president on his own could decide to recognize the current North Korean government, but any bilateral consular treaty, which would normally follow such recognition, requires congressional approval.[10]

Second, and perhaps just as important, under Section 129 of the U.S. Atomic Energy Act, "No nuclear materials and equipment or sensitive nuclear technology" can be exported to any nonnuclear state that the president has found to have

1. Terminated or abrogated International Atomic Energy Agency (IAEA) safeguards

2. Materially violated an IAEA safeguards agreement

3. Engaged in activities involving source or special nuclear material and having direct significance for the manufacture or acquisition of nuclear explosive devices and has failed to take steps which, in the president's judgment, represent sufficient progress toward terminating such activities

These conditions are relevant in North Korea's case. In fact, U.S. officials have already stated publicly (as has the IAEA) that North Korea violated its IAEA safeguards agreement when it suspended IAEA inspections in 1994. More important, under the framework's terms, North Korea is not required to be in full compliance with its IAEA safeguards obligations until sometime *after* "significant" completion of the first advanced U.S. light water reactor but *before* delivery of "key" nuclear components is made. Thus, the president can reach such an agreement but only by waiving at least the first two of these legal conditions. He can attempt this under the law, but it will not strengthen his case with Congress. In fact, it would be a first.[11]

Because of this, some have suggested having the president skirt Congress by reaching an executive agreement on nuclear cooperation with North Korea. This, however, ignores two important legal requirements. The first is the Case

Act, which requires the president to report all executive agreements to Congress and explain why they are not being submitted as treaties (or in this case, as a nuclear cooperative agreement).[12]

This judgment is not simply a subjective call: The State Department has fairly clear criteria for when an executive agreement is inappropriate.[13] Among these criteria are when the agreement's subject matter and implementation require the substantial exercise of congressional power and when it is desirable to give "utmost formality to the commitment" on both sides in "the interest of long continued respect for its terms."

Given that Congress and the president agreed in the Atomic Energy Act that cooperation involving reactor commerce and construction must be formalized in a nuclear cooperative agreement, Congress is unlikely to let the president do so without such an agreement. Indeed, the last time a president attempted to make such treatylike obligations by executive agreement, Congress objected and forced him to renegotiate the agreement as a treaty.[14]

The second and far more important legal requirement is that the president formally recognize the government of North Korea. Executive agreements, it turns out, are legally binding and, as such, presume formal diplomatic recognition of the agreeing party. This and presentment to Congress, then, are political obstacles the president cannot avoid.

Three Alternative Futures

Given these potential sticking points, is the Agreed Framework in trouble? The answer is both yes and no. No, none of these points necessarily dooms the Agreed Framework's implementation, but, yes, they could be used to stop, slow, or even modify the nuclear deal. What is likely to determine whether the Agreed Framework continues to be executed as it is, however, is not so much any legal technicalities or even how well the parties live up to the stated requirements in the understanding but instead what South Korea and the United States determine to be their overall strategic aims regarding the DPRK.

Three general aims are possible. The first is to support the communist government in North Korea and somehow bring it into the family of nations. The assumption here is that stasis or gradual reform is most likely for the DPRK and that the Agreed Framework is the West's best hope for supporting these options and avoiding either a destabilizing collapse or war.

A second possible objective would be to buy time by not doing anything to help the DPRK but avoiding anything that might precipitate its collapse. The aim here would be to buy time not for the North to adopt the kinds of reform needed for unification, but rather for the South to gird itself for unification.

Finally, a third objective might be to accelerate the DPRK's decline as the only realistic option given the DPRK's disinclination to liberalize and the growing economic disparity between the North and South.

The first objective seems clearly to be the aim of those in North and South Korea and the United States most supportive of the Agreed Framework and its current implementation. As they see it, the deal is the West's best vehicle for normalizing relations with the DPRK or at least keeping it in stasis so as to avoid war. The deal, after all, requires the United States and the DPRK to "reduce barriers to trade and investment, including restrictions on telecommunications services and financial services." More important, each side must open up a liaison office in the other's capital so that progress can be made on issues of concern to both sides—emergency food relief, locating prisoner-of-war remains, developing economic zones in the North, restraining North Korea's missile program (including strategic weapons proliferation to the Middle East), encouraging North-South rapprochement, and so on. Under the Agreed Framework, as progress is made on these issues, relations are to be upgraded to "the Ambassadorial level."[15]

What of North Korea's other possible nuclear activities and its unwillingness to hold talks with the South? Supporters of the Agreed Framework argue that these difficulties are temporary. They allow that we would like to know more about North Korea's nuclear program but argue that we will learn more with the deal than without it. As for rapprochement, they note that the very act of letting South Korean nuclear workers into the North (even if only in compounds behind barbed wire) should be seen as progress, no matter how meager, and, again, is certainly far better than the alternative of having no deal.

Finally, that the nuclear deal requires the United States to reach a nuclear cooperative agreement is something that the deal's proponents see as an advantage, not a liability. It is this feature, they argue, that is likely to force reluctant parties in the U.S. Congress and South Korea to support normalized relations with the DPRK. Indeed, in three to five years the stark alternative will be to risk losing the billions of dollars that will have been invested in the KEDO reactor project (in the form of a noninterest-bearing loan to the DPRK), halt the reactors' construction (just when they were about to be completed), and risk a resumption of North Korea's suspended nuclear weapons material production efforts.

From the proponents' perspective, then, little needs to be changed in the Agreed Framework, current U.S. law, or policy. Waiving the legal conditions for reaching a nuclear cooperative agreement with the North may be politically tough, but it is legally permissible.[16] Beyond this, greater bureaucratic attention to implementing the nuclear deal and lower public expectations concerning the pace of improved relations with the DPRK would be helpful, but they may not be critical to success. Indeed, for those supporting the deal, the logic and likelihood of eventually normalizing relations with the DPRK seem more certain than not.[17]

Others in the United States and South Korea are not so sure. They still see the DPRK as a threat. As long as the Communists are in control of the DPRK, they argue, North Korea will remain a military threat to South Korea and its friends. They also worry that the communist North could collapse precipitously. This might lead to war or to pressures for unification that South Korea is not now able to cope with politically or financially.

For this group, the West's strategic objective should be to neither support nor strengthen the DPRK (much less to make it "normal") but simply to buy time until peaceful unification is possible on terms acceptable to the South. This means avoiding war with the North, on the one hand, and doing nothing that might prompt the DPRK's immediate collapse, on the other, *without* making concessions that would strengthen the Communists' freedom of action. The time thus gained would be used not so much to achieve significant reforms in the North (which are thought to be unlikely) as to achieve the political, legal, and economic liberalizations needed in the South to make unification a process the South and its prosperous liberal democracy could survive.[18]

Trying to buy this kind of time would require limiting the DPRK's ability to manipulate the Agreed Framework to its advantage. Specifically, it would require avoiding anything that might make the provision of U.S. goods—reactor parts, oil, financing, political recognition, and so on (as distinct from those from South Korea)—the pacing factors in the nuclear deal's implementation or the prerequisites to stable relations with the North.

Given these objectives, it would actually be beneficial to emphasize some of the potential legal obstacles to full U.S. nuclear cooperation on the KEDO project. Thus, one might dodge a possible crisis in three to five years regarding congressional consideration of a nuclear cooperative agreement by revisiting the reactor design issue now or in a year or two with the aim of making it possible to complete the two light water reactors *without* having to use U.S. nuclear trigger list components. Here, of course, it would be preferable—again to encourage closer North-South cooperation—if the reactor's design was one that the South Koreans could complete. This would allow the project to be completed without waiting for the U.S. Congress and possibly bring North Korea closer to the date (as required in the Agreed Framework) to open itself up to IAEA special inspections.

Yet other critics of the deal demand immediate action. Rather than support or tolerate the DPRK or await South Korean reforms and increased confidence to unify, these critics would try to eliminate the communist regime as soon as possible by isolating and punishing it. The reasoning here is that delaying unification will only make it more difficult. Certainly, the longer one waits, the greater the economic and political disparity between the North and the South are likely to become. Also, they argue, the DPRK is no Vietnam or China: Unlike the rulers of those countries, the Communists in the North are unlikely to reform themselves.[19]

Associated with this view are Americans who dislike the Agreed Framework and who are more than willing to terminate it the minute North Korea "violates" its terms. For them the possible sticking points noted above are termination triggers. Is North Korea working on nuclear weapons, uranium enrichment, or reprocessing activities in violation of the North-South Joint Declaration on Denuclearization? Will the DPRK live up to its promises to dismantle and open up its sensitive fuel-cycle facilities to international inspection? Has the DPRK continued its refusal to negotiate with the South? Will the DPRK break its specific promises to cooperate with KEDO in the construction of the reactors? If so, the Agreed Framework should be aborted or at least suspended.

Such critics are also likely to oppose efforts to normalize relations with the DPRK. Diplomatic recognition, approving a bilateral consular treaty or a nuclear cooperative agreement, or paying significant sums to help the DPRK dismantle its radioactive reactor and reprocessing plant are all moves that the critics would likely challenge. Beyond this they might also call for suspending implementation of the Agreed Framework if the DPRK were to continue development and export of long-range missiles or take even limited hostile action against U.S. or South Korean troops along the demilitarized zone.

What to Make of It

No one is eager for war, especially on the Korean peninsula, where the price of war is high and all too familiar. Some have insisted that this is what the Agreed Framework was designed to avoid. Yet war is unlikely so long as the DPRK is convinced that the South cannot be defeated without defeating the United States. In fact, the Agreed Framework is not the alternative to war but rather a vehicle for a variety of peaceful outcomes—stasis, gradual reform in the North, reform in the South, and the DPRK's near-term collapse. Implementation of the Agreed Framework will differ depending on what outcome South Korea and the United States choose to pursue. So far South Korea and the United States seem only to have entertained the first two objectives and have implemented the Agreed Framework accordingly. Yet, the two remaining alternative futures—one that would buy time for the South to achieve the liberalizing reforms needed to wage a vigorous, confident effort to unify peacefully with the North and another that would accelerate the the DPRK's collapse—seem no less plausible and, therefore, deserve at least as much attention.

Notes

1. See Henry Sokolski, "The Korean Nuclear Deal: How Might It Challenge the U.S.?" *Comparative Strategy*, fall 1995, pp. 443–51.

2. "Pyongyang Bartered Freedom of Actions for Oil and Reactors," *ITAR-TASS* (Moscow), December 16, 1995, p. A4; "ASEAN Envoys Meet on N.K. Nuke Reactor Project," *Korean Herald* (Seoul), October 29, 1995, p. 2; "NK to Cordon Off Sinpo Reactor Site," *Korean Times* (Seoul), October 29, 1995, p. 2; and "KEDO Likely to Accept N.K. Demands for Appendixes to N-Reactor Project," *Korean Herald* (Seoul), November 1, 1995, p. 2.

3. See Catherine Toups, "N. Korea Signs Accord on Reactors," *Washington Times*, December 16, 1995, p. A8, and "N. Korea Threatens Renewed Activity," *Washington Post*, December 17, 1995, p. A37.

4. See Geneva Agreed Framework between the United States of America and the Democratic People's Republic of Korea, October 21, 1994, Sections II 1. and 2.

5. Ibid., Section I 1.

6. "Joint U.S.-DPRK Press Statement, Kuala Lumpur, June 13, 1995," Section II.

7. See "NK Threatens to Scrap N-Pact with US, *Korea Times*, November 17, 1995.

8. See, e.g., Joseph S. Bermudez Jr., "North Korea's Nuclear Infrastructure," *Jane's Intelligence Review*, February 1994, pp. 74–79.

9. See Victor Gilinsky, "The Nuclear Deal: What the South Koreans Should Be Concerned About," paper presented at the American Enterprise Institute, Washington, D.C., March 17, 1995, to be reprinted in *Fighting Proliferation: New Concerns for the 1990s*, edited by Henry Sokolski (Maxwell Air Force Base, Ala.: Air University Press, forthcoming).

10. See U.S. Congress, Congressional Research Service, "Korea: Procedural and Jurisdictional Questions Regarding Possible Normalization of Relations with North Korea," in *CRS Report for Congress* (Washington, D.C.: Congressional Research Service, November 29, 1994, 94-933 S), pp. 14–16.

11. Nor can the president get around these requirements by shipping key nuclear components to other nations that, in turn, might ship them to KEDO or North Korea. On this the law is clear: Any reexportation of such U.S. items must be approved by the U.S. government and be in accordance with the Atomic Energy Act. The president might try to ask the Nuclear Regulatory Commission to take all of the U.S. reactor components needed to complete the reactors off the commission's nuclear trigger list so that reaching a nuclear cooperative agreement would be unnecessary. But this would require congressional approval.

12. Under the Case Act (1 U.S.C.A. 112(b)), the secretary of state is required to transmit to Congress "as soon as practicable after the agreement has entered into force . . . but in no event later than sixty days thereafter" any international agreements other than treaties that the executive has entered into and believes are legally binding on the United States.

13. See U.S. Department of State, "Standards Followed in Determining Whether an International Agreement Should Be Concluded as a Treaty," memorandum, November 30, 1964, prepared by the Treaty Affairs Staff, Office of the Legal Adviser, MS Department of State, file Pol 4; reprinted in Thomas M. Franck and Michael J. Glennon, *Foreign Relations and National Security Law* (St. Paul, Minn.: West Publishing, 1987), pp. 394–95.

14. Thus, during Nixon's presidency, the Senate objected to a base agreement Nixon had reached with Spain because it contained important mutual security clauses. It was originally submitted as an executive agreement, but after strong Senate objections, President Nixon and, later, President Ford had to renegotiate it and resubmit it as a treaty. See Franck and Glennon, *Foreign Relations and National Security Law*, p. 396.

15. See Agreed Framework, Sections II 1–3.

16. This is not to say that some legal changes might not be desirable. In a recent conversation with the author, one of the American legal advisers to KEDO explained that the organization was examining how a U.S. nuclear cooperative agreement might be reached with the DPRK without formally recognizing the government.

17. See, however, Robert A. Manning, "North Korea Low on US Agenda Though Crisis Looms," *Shin Dong-A*, February 1996.

18. Others have explored this point at great length. On the desirability of greater rule of law, more open markets, and more pluralistic democracy in the South to achieve unification, see, for example, Nicholas Eberstadt, "Can the Two Koreas Be One?" *Foreign Affairs*, winter 1992/93.

19. See, for example, David Lipton and Jeffrey Sachs, "Creating a Market Economy in Eastern Europe: The Case of Poland, *Brookings Papers on Economic Activity*, 1990, pp. 75–148; Jeffrey Sachs and Wing Thye Woo, "Structural Factors in the Economic Reforms of China, Eastern Europe, and the Former Soviet Union," *Economic Policy* 18 (1994): 101–45; Aidan Foster-Carter, "North Korea after Kim Il-Sung: Controlled Collapse?" *Research Report* (London) Economist Intelligence Unit, 1994; and James Riedel, "Vietnam: On the Trail of the Tigers," *World Economy* 16, no. 4 (1993): 401–22.

10

Political and Economic Human Rights Violations in North Korea

KRISTIN R. GUSTAVSON and
JINMIN LEE-RUDOLPH

Introduction

The Democratic People's Republic of Korea (DPRK) has been recognized as one of the world's primary violators of human rights for the past four decades. Indeed, in a report issued by Freedom House in 1995, North Korea was listed as one of three countries rated as "the worst of the worst" in terms of political rights and civil liberties. The full extent of human rights violations in North Korea has been difficult to assess because the regime closely guards data regarding the living conditions of its people. In recent years, however, South Korean scholars and international human rights activists have completed several human rights studies that have been made possible largely through the assistance of North Korean defectors.

This chapter addresses the continuing human rights violations perpetrated by the North Korean government. It begins by laying out a theoretical framework that defines human rights as those rights necessary to realize human dignity. This framework is applied to the United Nations Universal Declaration of Human Rights to explain the international standard for human rights as it is understood in the modern world. We will then look specifically at North Korea's attempt to address human rights. By interpreting the applicable constitutional provisions, we will argue that the government fails to protect the rights that are supposedly guaranteed by law. The North Korean regime treats legal, political, civil, and economic rights as secondary rights that are subordinated to the needs of the community as a whole. Although all human rights violations in North Korea remain a serious issue, this chapter will focus mainly on economic human rights violations because they are currently the greatest threat to people's lives, as well as to the regime.

We will then analyze recent economic developments in North Korea to determine whether economic human rights will continue to be violated under Kim Jong Il's dictatorship. Finally, we will conclude by offering short- and long-term economic policy recommendations for North Korea. In the interim, the rest of the world must provide food aid unconditionally, not only to alleviate North Korean economic human rights violations but also to avoid committing its own violations by letting the North Korean people starve.

Universal Human Rights: Background

According to human rights scholars, human rights are fundamentally related to one's sense of humanity, human nature, and human dignity.[1] Although some scholars argue that human needs establish the boundaries of human rights, others theorize that man's moral nature defines what is needed because human rights are based on the need for a life of dignity. Hence, laws designed to protect human rights should at the very least recognize the worth of human dignity.[2]

If one assumes that human rights are a subset of moral rights, these rights should take precedence over other legal and political claims. In other words, human rights transcend international boundaries and cultures and should be recognized as fundamental rights necessary for any human being to realize the true worth of his existence.

The United Nations Universal Declaration of Human Rights provides a list of internationally recognized human rights ranging from political and civil rights to social and cultural rights. For example, the Universal Declaration provides equal rights under the law, protection against discrimination, prohibition of slavery, and protection against torture. It also provides procedural protection for individuals under the legal and political systems within their respective countries. In terms of economic rights, the Universal Declaration guarantees individuals the right to acquire minimum resources for survival such as food and health care.

Human rights are usually categorized for convenience; however, "to segregate civil and political rights from economic, social, and cultural rights is to distort reality."[3] In actuality, the various categories of rights are interdependent. For instance, violations of political rights also affect social conditions under which individuals live. By prohibiting associations that are not directly or indirectly under government control, the regime violates the individual's right to both freedom of association as well as freedom to socialize with whomever one chooses.

Furthermore, just as the different types of human rights are interrelated, a country's political system directly affects its view of human dignity. "Conceptions of human dignity vary dramatically across societies, and most of these variations are incompatible with the values of equality and autonomy that underlie human rights."[4] In communist states, for example, an individual's worth is secondary to his responsibility toward the state, which means that he is allowed human dignity only to the extent necessary for him to contribute to society. In this type of society, human dignity is measured by loyalty to one's government, not by the amount of freedom one has to choose a course in life.

North Korea's Human Rights Violations: *Juche* and Confucian Ideologies

To understand the concept of human rights as defined by the North Korean government, one must first explain the regime's *juche* ideology, which was derived from the "Ten Principles for Solidifying the [Korean Workers'] Party's Monolithic Ideological System." These principles, allegedly written by Kim Jong Il, were adopted by the Korean Workers' Party (KWP) in 1974 and serve as guidelines for the entire populace. They essentially proclaim that Kim Il Sung has absolute authority and that all North Koreans must show their unconditional devotion and loyalty toward him and his revolutionary ideology.[5]

According to the *juche* ideology, man is master of the world, and, in particular, the working class is the master rather than the bourgeoisie. The working class, however, must follow the *suryŏng*, or "great leader," and only those unified under the party and the *suryŏng* can realize their true independence and self-reliance.[6] The *suryong* is regarded as an infallible god, and those who disobey him will be justly punished. Hence, under the *juche* ideology, North Koreans must idolize both Kim Il Sung, even after his death, and his son Kim Jong Il, who now functions as leader. This all-encompassing ideology often leads to arbitrary rules and treatment that violate North Koreans' fundamental human rights.

In addition, Confucianism, which was originally transmitted to Korea through Chinese influence beginning in the seventh century and is still practiced today, advocates a patrimonial sociopolitical culture. Under Confucianism, people who fail to follow the established moral code may be tortured or executed.[7] Therefore, the North Korean people must revere and obey their leaders and elders not only under *juche* but also under the ancient teachings of Confucius.

Both *juche* and Confucianism contradict the universal notion of human rights. Thus, the North Korean regime cannot avoid violating human rights unless it puts aside *juche* and protects the people's rights as guaranteed in the constitution. But in doing so, the regime would weaken its own power. In other words, human rights can only be protected by putting the fundamental needs of the individual before the needs of the government or its leaders.

Legal Human Rights Violations

The DPRK constitution embodies the fundamental rights of individuals; however, the written laws are not observed. In fact, the boundaries of the law may ultimately be defined by the party rather than by the language of the constitution, as all activities are carried out "under the guidance of the KWP."[8] For example, the KWP oversees most government functions as well as the election process. Moreover, the party controls the judicial system by appointing judges to serve as its representatives.[9]

Because the actions of the *suryŏng* are, by definition, in the people's best interests, Pyongyang argues that there is no human rights problem in the DPRK. In fact, North Korea recognizes human rights not as fundamental rights for every person but as "citizen's rights," which are only for those the state recognizes as citizens. The regime classifies the people into three basic groups: the core class, the wavering class, and the hostile class, which in turn are divided into approximately fifty-one categories that the government does not publicly acknowledge.[10] Classifications are based on several factors: loyalty and potential to work for the state, class or family background, and birthplace. The core class is composed mainly of the relatives and loyal followers of Kim Il Sung and Kim Jong Il. The wavering class consists of those people the regime feels it cannot trust, whereas the hostile class includes those who have demonstrated opposition to the government or have shown discontent by their actions. Members of this class are treated as political prisoners and are often sentenced to hard labor and their possessions confiscated.

North Korea does not recognize the rights of these so-called traitors or anti-revolutionaries. Indeed, political prisoners, opponents of Kim Il Sung and Kim Jong Il, and repatriated defectors have been summarily executed. Defectors claim that the government is currently detaining about 150,000 political prisoners and their families in maximum security camps located in remote areas.[11] Immediate family members as well as distant relatives are also punished as political criminals because they are considered guilty by association.

An individual's category is critical, for it affects one's treatment under the legal system, as well as one's allocation of rations, ability to receive permission to travel, and other essential aspects of life. Educational and job opportunities are also assigned on the basis of political status, regardless of talent, ability, or personal desire, even though the constitution guarantees equal rights to education as well as the freedom to select one's occupation.[12] Letters of introduction are issued to the employer of each person who graduates from school or university or leaves the military, and anyone who does not report to his assigned job will have his rations suspended. Workers in the wavering and hostile classes are often forced to work in places seriously short of labor and are unable to see their families for extended periods of time. By treating each class differently, the regime violates the human right to equal protection for all people.

The penal code has also been criticized by human rights scholars because there is no statute of limitation and because laws have been applied retroactively. Moreover, not-guilty pleas are punished as harshly as guilty pleas, and abettors are given the same punishment as perpetrators.[13] Furthermore, people convicted of crimes against the state are often sentenced to *at least* a specified number of years of hard labor instead of *up to* a maximum number of years in prison, as in most countries.[14]

The most recent revision of the penal code states that criminal cases are to be decided on the basis of scientific and concrete evidence. But the code still does not provide a warrant system for search, investigation of evidence, or arrest. Furthermore, no clearly defined trial procedures or standards exist, and torture of prisoners is still tolerated.[15]

Political and Civil Human Rights Violations

Political and civil violations of human rights are also widespread in North Korea. For example, people cannot vote freely even though Article 66 of the constitution provides that all "citizens" over the age of seventeen and those serving in the People's Army have the right to vote. According to Chang Gee-hong, who defected to the South in November 1991, an unmarked ballot signifies a vote for the only candidate, while a marked ballot is a vote against him. One cannot usually mark a ballot, however, without being caught and punished. Furthermore, those who do not vote are punished because the regime views them as opposing the great leader.[16]

Similarly, even though Article 67 provides that "the citizens have the freedom of association and assembly," only association and assembly approved by the regime are allowed. The U.S. Department of State's *Country Report on Human Rights Practices for 1993* states in its section on North Korea that "no public meetings may be held without government authorization. There are no known organizations other than those created by the government. The state even prohibits apolitical groups such as neighborhood or alumni organizations, and professional associations exist solely as another means for the government to control the members of these organizations."[17] In fact, any independently organized association is regarded as disorderly group action, which is punishable by a sentence of up to five years in prison.[18] Therefore, while in words the North Korean government upholds an individual's universal right to associate freely, in actuality, the regime restricts this right.

Even the most basic political right—freedom of the press—is ignored by the North Korean government. Again, this right is constitutionally protected, as are all other political rights, but in practice the state exercises complete censorship through the KWP. No negative statements regarding the government can be published or broadcast. Private publications are permitted only if they pass the party's inspections. Those who fail to abide by KWP standards are deprived of their personal belongings, sentenced to forced labor, or put to death. Thus the people must suppress their criticisms of the regime. In addition, all radio dials are fixed to the official DPRK broadcasting channels to prevent the people from listening to South Korean or other foreign broadcasting stations.[19] Officials from the Ministry of Public Safety closely monitor censorship compliance by periodically visiting each home. Consequently, the regime strives to keep the people unaware of external events.

Finally, Article 69, which guarantees the right to petition, is just as meaningless as the other constitutional provisions. When a petition or complaint about unsatisfactory administration of affairs (*shinso*) is submitted, the Ministries of State Security and Public Safety seek to identify the perpetrator through handwriting analysis.[20] The suspected individual is thoroughly investigated by the government and punished for committing a crime against the state. Therefore, regardless of the fact that the DPRK constitution recognizes legal, political, and civil human rights, the regime continues to intimidate its people by threatening them with imprisonment or death for exercising their fundamental rights.

Economic Human Rights Violations

Economic human rights are no more recognized in North Korea than are legal, political, or civil human rights. Although Article 24 permits possession of private property for limited purposes such as personal use and consumption, state and cooperative property rights take precedence over personal property rights.[21] In fact, Article 21 of the DPRK constitution states that "there is no limit to the rights of the state possession."[22] In other words, the state is the sole owner of all natural resources, all major factories and enterprises, harbors, banks, transportation, and postal services, as well as the output of individuals' labor. Cooperative groups are second only to the state in terms of ownership rights; they may possess land, livestock, agricultural equipment, fishing boats, buildings, factories, and enterprises. The regime's goal, however, is gradually to nationalize all cooperative property as state property.

The state also sets wages as well as the prices of all goods. Along with the KWP, the state controls the purchase of daily necessities including shoes, clothing, and household appliances. Some textile goods are allocated to cooperative groups, as the supply is inadequate to satisfy individual needs. Those the regime sees as loyal are given preferential treatment in the form of special purchase tickets for luxury items such as watches, television sets, and refrigerators.[23]

All housing also belongs to the state. Most ordinary people live in tenement houses that are designed only for eating and sleeping. Even newly constructed buildings lack modern facilities such as elevators. Moreover, the tenants must use a public toilet system, which creates serious health hazards. A typical tenement house built in 1988 in Sariwon City has two rooms, or twenty-three square meters, for each family, with only one public bathroom for forty families.[24] Furthermore, the water supply in public apartments is restricted because of North Korea's energy shortage. In rural areas, the water is turned on for only one or two hours a day, which means people are not able to bathe daily. Even in Pyongyang, the wealthiest city in the country, the water is on for only five or six hours each day.[25]

The regime also rations clothing. Standard work clothes and undergarments are provided at low prices or free of charge, with a person's class determining the quality and quantity of clothing received. In general, however, North Koreans lack sufficient undergarments, shoes, socks, gloves, overcoats, and other clothing. For example, although "workers are supposed to receive a pair of work shoes every two months and students are to receive sports shoes," they are often given only one pair a year.[26] People may purchase additional clothing if they can afford it but only with a government-approved permit, which cannot be lent or sold to others.

Food rations are also issued based on political status; however, occupation is also taken into account. Military personnel, heavy industry and defense workers, and members of Kim Jong Il's family receive the most food (700–900 grams a day), followed by party and government officials. Pyongyang residents receive larger rations than those living outside the city. By contrast, prisoners and others classified at the lowest level receive around two hundred grams of food a day,[27] which is much less than the five hundred grams a day that are minimally required to sustain life.[28]

Although the regime may deem it appropriate to allocate more rations to those whose occupations are considered useful, it is severe and arbitrary to assign a lower level of rations to the 70 percent of the population perceived as "wavering" or "hostile."[29] This economic human rights violation becomes more egregious when rations are reduced as punishment for infractions such as absence from work without permission.[30] Hence, the regime's tight control over the distribution of goods and services on the basis of political status deprives the people of their economic human rights to exercise personal preferences and to adequately provide for themselves and their families.

Food Shortages and Human Rights in North Korea

Rations have been low in North Korea for the last several years owing to food shortages. The shortages, as well as the general economic downturn, have evolved as a result of the regime's failure to liberalize its economic and military policies appropriately. Pyongyang's continued insistence on its *juche* ideology has led to the huge growth of the North Korean military and the inordinate allocation of economic resources to the military sector. Another product of *juche* is the regime's reluctance to accept foreign-offered food aid, even though the country is currently unable to feed its own people. The fact that *juche* has resulted in Pyongyang's dire economic situation ironically contradicts the concept of self-reliance.

According to a special report issued in December 1995 by the Food and Agriculture Organization/World Food Program (FAO/WFP) Crop and Food Supply Assessment Mission, North Korea's agricultural productivity and overall production have been declining at an increasing rate over the last seven years,[31] largely because of the inefficiency of collectivized agriculture. An ongoing fuel shortage stalls irrigation and paralyzes agricultural machinery, resulting in the return to the use of animals in agriculture, which greatly reduces productivity. Poor crop diversification, the absence of large-scale crop rotation, and a fertilizer shortage have all had a negative effect on soil fertility. The annual output has also been reduced by Pyongyang's use of intensive farming methods in an attempt to maximize production from the currently cultivated land instead of finding ways to expand the planting area.

The withdrawal of support from the former Soviet Union and China compounded North Korea's economic woes. Pyongyang had been propped up by Soviet credits and aid for years until the Soviet Union fell apart in 1991. Ties with China, North Korea's main trading partner, were greatly weakened in 1993 when China began insisting on the use of hard currency in trade. North Korea's hard currency shortage and poor international credit rating due to defaulting on debts made it difficult to replace these trading partners.

Left virtually without economic support, North Korea began to experience considerable grain shortages. Pyongyang compensated for the shortages in 1992 and 1993 by reducing rations and in 1994 and 1995 by dipping into its sizable grain stock to supplement the low rations. These shortages remained, even though 14–15 percent of the total grain demand has been imported annually from Russia, China, and Thailand.[32]

The reduced rations issued for the last several years are now standard.[33] During the 1990s, food conservation slogans have publicly acknowledged the regime's inability to feed its people. The "let's eat 2 meals [a day]" campaign is ongoing throughout the country except in the capital city, and the "patriotic rice" campaign requires most people other than mine workers and the military to conserve 20 percent of their rations and contribute them to the state's food reserves.[34]

The North Korean people have been depending on grain rations for 90 percent of their total diet as a result of additional shortages of vegetables, fruits, livestock, and fish.[35] A lack of protein has stunted physical growth in North Korean young people. According to one study, North Korean boys are 8 percent shorter than South Korean boys on average and North Korean girls are 3 percent shorter than South Korean girls.[36] The regime's "movement to grow taller" attempts to address this problem, but it will have little effect unless rations increase and the overall diet improves.

If a merely temporary problem had left Pyongyang unable to feed its people in the short term, the lapse would be understandable. But the regime's consistent failure to provide adequate nourishment for its people over many years and the lack of any attempt to improve the situation constitute violations of the people's economic human right to minimum resources for survival. Moreover, the regime strictly limits people's movements within the country and prohibits them from leaving it, which in turn prevents them from searching for supplemental food. This policy is both a civil and an economic human rights violation.

Politics of Food Aid

North Korea's food shortages were exacerbated by the July and August 1995 floods, the worst in a hundred years. Those floods left 500,000 people homeless, destroyed North Korea's crops shortly before harvest when it was too late to replant, and dumped sand on a significant portion of the limited arable land, rending it useless for cultivation until it can be cleared. Pyongyang estimated losses of 1.9 million tons of grain,[37] while loss estimates by the United Nations were slightly more conservative, 1.5 million tons.[38] The regime claimed to have a 50 percent grain shortfall after the floods,[39] or about 3.875 million tons, but the United Nations could not confirm this estimate. Donations of rice from Japan and South Korea as well as imports from Thailand still left a 40 percent shortfall as of mid-September.[40]

Unable to cope with this desperate situation, Pyongyang appealed in September to the International Federation of Red Cross and Red Crescent Societies (IFRC) for emergency aid for the first time in history. World Food Program officials had expected South Korea and China to be generous because preventing North Korean instability is in their interest; however, the outside world sent little food aid at first because many countries doubted the seriousness of the shortage and suspected the regime of attempting to stockpile food to avert a potential collapse. L. Gordon Flake, director of research at the Korea Economic Institute, suggested that the regime might blame its structural economic problems on the floods to hide its inability to feed its people. Such a policy could provide an excuse for the regime to continue requesting help in order to avoid the economic overhaul and, by implication, the admission of failure that will be necessary to end the food shortages.[41]

But the December FAO/WFP *Special Report* asserted that the shortages were not exaggerated. In 1990, Pyongyang was supposedly still holding about 4 million tons of food grain stock, but by 1995 the need to maintain ration levels had almost totally depleted the grain stock. The little remaining grain stock, about 626,200 tons according to regime estimates, was destroyed in the floods.[42]

Despite North Korea's food shortages, however, it seemed unlikely that South Korea, Japan, the United States, and other countries would help unless Pyongyang was willing to make political concessions over certain foreign and nuclear policies that had long been a source of frustration and concern. South Korean government spokesman Kim Kyung-woong stated in January 1996 that South Korea would refuse to provide food aid unless the North agreed to engage in direct inter-Korean talks, stop anti-South propaganda, and request aid through official channels. South Korean foreign minister Gong Ro-myung said that South Korea, Japan, and the United States would only provide food aid if Pyongyang guaranteed that the aid would not be diverted to the army.[43] In early February, the United States finally agreed to contribute $2.2 million for the purchase and delivery of food to North Korea through the World Food Program (WFP).[44] This amount was enough to deliver about 12,800 tons of rice, a quantity that, although helpful, could hardly be compared with South Korea's donation in 1995 of 150,000 tons[45] or Japan's of 500,000 tons,[46] let alone the estimated 1995 shortfall of 3.875 million tons.

Pyongyang expressed disappointment at the world's suspicion and lack of magnanimity. Li Jong Hua, a representative of the DPRK Flood Damage and Rehabilitation Committee, clarified the regime's position on humanitarian aid and responded to donors' concerns in communications with Bernard Krisher, a former *Newsweek* correspondent in Asia who has made several trips to North Korea to distribute aid obtained through the Internet. Li stated that purely humanitarian aid would be accepted but not aid tied to any "political or other self-interest conditions" aimed at "blocking donations, causing mistrust of our distribution system and creating a picture of instability of our society." Any nonfood aid not specifically requested and any aid that challenged *juche* would also be rejected.[47] Li denied that any food aid had been diverted to the military. Trevor Page, head of the WFP operations in North Korea, confirmed Li's statement in a conversation with Krisher during his March visit. According to Krisher, Page said that the North Korean distribution system seemed efficient and appeared to be fair and trustworthy, far more so than in other countries where he had worked.[48]

According to Krisher, Li denied the existence of a famine and questioned whether foreign comments about starvation and malnutrition were "intended to . . . undermine an image of stability" in North Korea or were an attempt to insult the nation's dignity,[49] a dignity that prohibits foreign donors from labeling the goods they ship to North Korea. This policy is intended to avoid loss of credibility for the regime by hiding its inability to feed the people, but it creates a great deal of extra work for foreign donors or for the regime if donors do not comply. When a South Korean National Red Cross shipment of 100,000 packages of noodles arrived in January, North Korean Red Cross authorities removed the labels but stated that "they would reject such aid in the future, claiming it required too much time and labor."[50] As an alternative, the North Korean Red Cross requested cash instead of food aid for the next shipment, which would certainly give donors a reason to doubt North Korean claims of fair aid distribution. For although aid distribution is monitored by international organizations, it would be difficult to ensure that cash is translated into food to be distributed instead of being diverted to the military. South Korean National Red Cross officials responded to the North's cash request by hinting that they "might stall further aid."[51]

In January, a North Korean Foreign Ministry spokesman took a step further in expressing the regime's frustration with food donors' attempts to obtain concessions in return for aid: "If hostile elements continue to politicize and attempt to block the humanitarian assistance, we will no longer pin any hope on the so-called 'assistance' and will go our own way."[52] Li explained this policy in his March letter: "We are able to survive even the critical food shortage through *juche*, if necessary."[53] The regime carried out its threat in February by announcing to representatives of international aid agencies that there would be no new or revised appeals for aid. The agencies were asked to leave North Korea once they had finished delivering and distributing aid already pledged.

Enough contributions had been received to cover about 84 percent of the original Red Cross appeal before Pyongyang asked the aid organizations to leave.[54] But the rations the Red Cross was able to provide for distribution to those eligible, or 62 percent of a population of 22 million,[55] were often only 60 percent or less of the already low rations.[56] A March IFRC report stated that the average person was receiving 450 grams of food a day with little supplemental food available. According to a May FAO *Special Alert*, however, rations were substantially reduced in April, down to an average of 300 grams a day and sometimes as low as 250 grams a day,[57] well below minimal needs for consumption. These amounts are a far cry from the 600 grams a day people were receiving in 1995.[58]

The food shortage is especially serious for the three million state farmworkers and their dependents who are eligible to receive rations for only six months out of the year and, most of all, for the five million collective farmworkers and their dependents who receive a portion of each harvest instead of rations.[59] These people are especially in danger of famine because of last year's poor harvest, and the 1996 and 1997 harvests are expected to be disappointing as well.

There have been recurrent but unconfirmed reports of widespread hunger and disease in rural areas in North Korea. U.N. relief officials have described "scenes of hungry residents foraging for roots in plowed paddy fields, and children barely surviving on watered-down corn porridge."[60] Whole-grain maize is difficult to digest, which reduces its available calories. Poor access to any food other than maize is aggravating the already marginal health status of children. Malnutrition, which is already a severe problem in some areas and is likely to remain so until the next harvest unless the food supply improves, is doubly serious because it increases susceptibility to health problems such as respiratory illness and other infectious illnesses, especially in winter. Most at risk are children (2.1 million), pregnant and nursing women (0.45 million), and the farming population.[61]

Fortunately for the North Korean people, the regime finally relented and made its second request for food aid in late March 1996. The IFRC plans to assist 130,000 people from April to October, mostly peasants who do not receive rations.[62] The government estimates that it can meet only 25 percent of normal requirements from May through October, with the lean preharvest months still to come.[63] According to the May FAO *Special Alert*, North Korea needs 978,000 tons of cereals to survive until October, and even under the most optimistic scenario, there will be a structural food deficit of more than two million tons for the next harvest year, 1996–97.[64]

Policy Recommendations for Improving North Korea's Food Situation

North Korea's economic problems are clearly structural and cannot be resolved with simple or cyclic solutions. Economic policy changes must be made in order for the people, as well as the regime, to survive in the long run.

Decreasing the size of the military is one change that could ease the emergency situation in North Korea right away, although it is likely to be a sensitive issue for the regime. The North Korean military budget is said to be around 25 percent of GNP[65] and in 1994 amounted to approximately 11.4 percent of total expenditures.[66] It is difficult to estimate the significance of these figures, however, because actual defense spending may be concealed in other sectors of the economy. The exact number of military personnel is not divulged by the North Korean government. According to the London-based International Institute for Strategic Studies, the North Korean military numbers approximately 1.1 million.[67] It is the fifth-largest army in the world today, behind only those of the four most populous countries. North Korea also has the highest ratio of troops to total population.[68] In addition to the standing military, there is a civilian militia of around five million.[69] Data from 1987 indicate that the military employs 6 percent of the total population. Twenty-one percent of men age sixteen or over and 42 percent of men ages sixteen to twenty-eight serve in the armed forces.[70] The size of the military establishment has become "an insuperable burden" because it is an enormous drain of labor that could be productively used in other sectors of the economy.[71]

Given North Korea's *juche* ideology and hostile view of the United States and South Korea, its military is understandably large. North Korea sees itself as especially vulnerable economically and militarily after the former Soviet Union's staunch support dried up. This perceived vulnerability has led Pyongyang to develop its nuclear program in order to strengthen its bargaining position with respect to the United States, Japan, and South Korea. Finally, the huge military will help the regime maintain its power over the people during the current economic decline.

To end the food shortages, however, Pyongyang must set aside its siege mentality. Decreasing the size of the military will allow a large number of people to be mobilized for infrastructure repair projects such as clearing sand from the covered land so that it can be cultivated for the next harvest. In the longer term, priority must be given to essential construction projects such as power plants to ease the energy shortage and dams for flood control.

A smaller military will not only make more money available for financing food imports but will also leave more fuel for other economic sectors so that hard currency does not have to be used to import it. North Korea heavily depends on fuel, which has been in short supply for a number of years. More fuel will be required for continued transportation of rations and important agricultural operations such as irrigation, operating machinery, and clearing damaged land; rebuilding and restoring critical infrastructure following the floods; and heating buildings in the winter. A great deal of fuel that is being wasted on large military exercises in the winter could be better used in the schools, which were closed for the first time during January 1996 owing to a lack of fuel. The schools reopened in February but without heat, which caused many children to become ill.[72] Hence, the regime's failure to provide minimal amounts of fuel for health and survival constitutes a violation of the people's economic human rights.

Furthermore, a smaller military budget will allow Pyongyang to shift production priorities over the long term from the military and heavy industrial sectors to agriculture, light industry and consumer goods, and foreign trade. This shift in priorities is an important step toward increasing the quality and quantity of manufactured goods that can be sold on the international market for hard currency, which will improve North Korea's foreign trade position and help alleviate the shortages.

In addition, several important agricultural improvements can be made over the long term once the agricultural budget is increased. First, North Korea needs to find ways to cultivate new land not already being used for agriculture. More fertilizer must be developed or imported. Finally, Pyongyang must expand its policy of allowing people to grow their own food.

Such policy changes, however, would have significant ramifications for the regime. Changing policies, not to mention adopting policies advocated by Western countries, would be equivalent to admitting that the old policies were incorrect or inappropriate, which would involve a loss of face for the regime. Therefore, any policy change could threaten the regime's sovereignty, as it would undermine the regime's entire infrastructure and philosophy of *juche*, as well as its justification for existence. It is for this reason that we are recommending only economic changes rather than ideological or political changes.

Despite any ideological obstacles, the North Korean regime and nation should take pride and dignity in rebuilding their country after the floods and building their economic infrastructure for the future. These recommended changes are vital to the survival of the people and the country as a whole; the failure to make such changes would constitute a violation of the people's economic human rights.

International organizations such as Amnesty International, Asia Watch, and the United Nations should continue to monitor and report human rights violations that take place in North Korea. There is little the rest of the world can do to protect the North Koreans' legal, political, and civil human rights, but measures can be taken to stop the current famine.

Although food aid will not help North Korea solve its structural economic problems, it is morally the right policy to adopt because denying emergency food aid to North Korea would mean committing the same economic human rights violations of which the North Korean regime has been accused. The world must not punish the North Korean people for the policy blunders of their aggressive regime.

Many countries have delayed sending food aid because of continued concern that it could be diverted to the military; however, international organizations have monitored the distribution process and reported that the food has been distributed fairly and honestly. Provided the monitoring continues, there is no reason to assume that future distributions will not be carried out in the same manner as long as food aid, not cash, is given and as long as Pyongyang refrains from rejecting acceptable aid or delaying its distribution.

In June 1996, after much deliberation, the United States, Japan, and South Korea formally pledged to give Pyongyang emergency aid in the amounts of $6.2 million, $6 million, and $3 million, respectively, in response to the June 6 U.N. appeal for $43.6 million in aid, including $26 million in food aid.[73] These donations are pledged with no strings attached, although Washington hopes Pyongyang will return the favor by agreeing to at least a preliminary discussion of plans for four-nation talks, which are intended to produce a peace treaty to replace the armistice agreement that ended the Korean War in 1953.

The United States hopes the four-way talks will get the two Koreas speaking to each other again, while China and the United States take a back seat. South Korean analysts, however, do not believe food aid will give the North enough of an incentive to engage in talks that involve the South. Pyongyang, in fact, has long been pressing for bilateral talks with Washington that would exclude South Korea. In anticipation of Pyongyang's reluctance to negotiate, Seoul has stated it will not give further aid until Pyongyang agrees to the four-way talks and has continually encouraged the United States, Japan, and the rest of the world to follow its lead.

South Korea is hoping that holding out until its conditions are met will be an effective diplomatic strategy. It is more likely, however, that Pyongyang will simply accept the aid without agreeing to any further negotiations, unless it is given more enticing incentives to participate. Furthermore, forcing North Korea to agree to negotiations in order to receive further humanitarian aid would be an economic human rights violation rather than an incentive to negotiate. Thus, until better incentives are offered, North Korea will continue to avoid the negotiating table.

Because the North has yet to respond positively to the invitation for the talks, there is still time to involve Japan and Russia in the Korean peace negotiations. Those countries, which have also been important actors in the East Asian region, continue to be affected by security issues on the Korean peninsula and should therefore be included in the Korean peace efforts.

As long as Pyongyang refuses to make fundamental economic changes, North Korea will continue to require outside assistance. The rest of the world will thus be forced to continue sending aid to avoid the consequences that would otherwise result. Without additional food aid, the North Koreans' hunger could lead to a revolt or the collapse of the economy. A less likely but more serious result could be a suicide attack on South Korea. Thus, the world cannot afford to withhold food aid from Pyongyang. To avoid these drastic situations, the world must "put hunger above politics"[74] and practice humanitarian aid along with military deterrence.

Critics may argue that food aid constitutes propping up North Korea's failing economy and rogue military. But the requested aid will not be enough to raise North Korea's living standards, expand its military budget, increase its hard currency supply, or improve its economic infrastructure. Donations will do no more than prevent hungry people from starving. Thus, food aid will not result in an economic or military advantage for North Korea and is thus a politically acceptable policy for the world to follow, although it may seem like giving in to a blackmailing regime.

Food aid is not a zero-sum game that will give Pyongyang an advantage over donor countries. It is merely a stopgap measure that will buy time, both for the regime and for the rest of the world concerned about North Korean stability, until the leadership eventually realizes that the food situation, and the North Korean economy in general, will only continue to deteriorate without fundamental structural solutions over the long term.

Notes

The authors would like to thank Thomas Henriksen and Jongryn Mo for their helpful comments.

1. Jack Donnelly, *Universal Human Rights in Theory and Practice* (Ithaca: Cornell University Press, 1989), pp. 16–27.

2. Ibid., p. 19.

3. Ibid., p. 37.

4. Ibid., p. 67.

5. Ko Young Hwan, "Human Rights Conditions in North Korea," *East Asian Review* 7, no. 4 (winter 1995): 87–89.

6. *White Paper on Human Rights in North Korea* (Seoul, Korea: Research Institute for National Unification, 1996), p. 14.

7. *Human Rights in the Democratic People's Republic of Korea* (Minneapolis, Minn.: Minnesota Lawyers International Human Rights Committee; Washington, D.C.: Asia Watch, 1988), p. 16.

8. *White Paper*, p. 26.

9. Ibid., p. 36.

10. *Human Rights in the DPRK*, p. 34.

11. *Country Reports on Human Rights Practices for 1993* (Washington, D.C.: U.S. Department of State, 1994), p. 662.

12. *White Paper*, p. 85.

13. Ibid., p. 32.

14. Ibid., p. 33.

15. Ibid., pp. 33–34.

16. Ibid., p. 39.

17. *Country Reports on Human Rights Practices for 1993*, p. 664.

18. *White Paper*, p. 40.

19. Ibid., pp. 42–43.

20. Ibid., p. 44.

21. Ibid., p. 55.

22. Ibid., p. 54.

23. Ibid., pp. 55–56.

24. Ibid., p. 64.

25. Ibid.

26. Ibid., pp. 60–61.

27. Ibid., pp. 58–59.

28. See Hong-Tack Chun's chapter in this volume.

29. *Human Rights in the DPRK*, pp. 37–38.

30. *White Paper*, p. 60.

31. FAO/WFP Crop and Food Supply Assessment Mission to the Democratic People's Republic of Korea, *Special Report*, December 22, 1995.

32. "The Recent Food Shortage Situation in North Korea," *Backgrounder* (Seoul), no. 139 (January 29, 1996): 2.

33. Ibid., p. 1. Normal preflood rations issued since 1987 are 10 percent below 1973 levels, which in turn were 12 percent lower than the original ration levels set by the regime.

34. Ibid., p. 7.

35. Ibid., p. 4.

36. Ibid. Source and date of study are unknown.

37. *Assessment of Damage and Immediate Relief Requirements Following Floods: Preliminary Findings of United Nations Assessment Mission*, September 12, 1995.

38. Associated Press, "Politics Squeeze North Korea as Famine Crisis Deepens," December 27, 1995. News articles are obtained from the Internet: newsgroup clari.world.asia.koreas.

39. Associated Press, "South Korea Says No Food Aid Unless North Agrees to Talk," January 4, 1996.

40. *United Nations Assessment*.

41. Associated Press, "Devastating Floods Pry Open Secretive North Korea," September 26, 1995.

42. *United Nations Assessment*.

43. Associated Press, "South Korea Says No Food Aid."

44. WFP *Emergency Report*, no. 6 (February 9, 1996).

45. Associated Press, "South Korea Says No Food Aid."

46. Reuter Information Service, "North Korea Will Soon Run Out of Food—Japan Officials," May 13, 1996.

47. Letter from Li Jong Hua to Bernard Krisher, March 12, 1996, in "Reports from Our Second Donation Trip to North Korea, March 5–12, 1996," published at website http://shrine.cyber.ad.jp/mrosin/flood.

48. Krisher, "Reports from Our Second Donation Trip."

49. Ibid.

50. United Press International, "South Korea Red Cross OKs North Aid," April 29, 1996.

51. Ibid.

52. Reuter Information Service, "North Korea Summons Rare Military View on Famine," January 21, 1996.

53. Krisher, "Reports from Our Second Donation Trip."

54. International Federation of Red Cross and Red Crescent Societies, *Democratic People's Republic of Korea: Flood Relief, March 22, 1996*, appeal no. 12/95, situation report no. 6, covering February 1–March 15, 1996.

55. FAO *Special Alert*, p. 2.

56. IFRC appeal no. 12/95, situation report no. 6.

57. FAO *Special Alert*, p. 3.

58. Ibid.

59. Ibid, p. 2.

60. Associated Press, "U.S. Intelligence Sees Signs of Military Crackdown in Communist North Korea," December 22, 1995.

61. FAO/WFP *Special Report*, December 22, 1995.

62. International Federation of Red Cross and Red Crescent Societies, *Democratic People's Republic of Korea: Flood Relief, March 22, 1996*, appeal no. 06/96.

63. FAO *Special Alert*, p. 2.

64. Ibid., pp. 4–5.

65. *Country Reports on Human Rights Practices for 1995* (Washington, D.C.: U.S. Department of State, March 1996).

66. The Economist Intelligence Unit, *Country Profile: South Korea and North Korea 1995–96* (Dartford: Redhouse Press Ltd., 1996), p. 66.

67. Reuter Information Service, "Main Facts about North Korean Military," May 23, 1996.

68. Nicholas Eberstadt, "North Korea: Reform, Muddling through, or Collapse?" in Thomas H. Henriksen and Kyongsoo Lho, eds., *One Korea? Challenges and Prospects for Reunification* (Stanford: Hoover Institution Press, 1994), p. 15.

69. The Economist Intelligence Unit, *Country Profile: South Korea and North Korea 1994–95* (Dartford: Redhouse Press Ltd., 1995), p. 52.

70. Ibid., p. 63.

71. Eberstadt, "North Korea," p. 19.

72. WFP *Emergency Report*.

73. United Press International, "U.N. Needs Funds for N. Korea's Famine," June 6, 1996.

74. Editorial, "Famine Aid to North Korea," *New York Times*, May 22, 1996.

North Korea's Two Kims and American Foreign Policy

THOMAS H. HENRIKSEN

For more than four decades, American foreign policy overtures toward North Korea have been stymied by Pyongyang's insular recalcitrance and cold war tensions. Washington's efforts to normalize relations have run up against the extreme ideological nature of the Democratic People's Republic of Korea (DPRK). None of the periodic thaws that characterized Washington-Moscow relations carried over to the North Korean regime. Kim Il Sung's rule froze interactions with both the United States and the Republic of Korea (ROK) in a Korean War time capsule. The bitter intrapeninsular war ended in 1953 with an armistice; no peace treaty was ever signed. Fighting stopped but a genuine peace did not ensue. As a result, no closure or healing has taken place between the two Koreas or between the North and the South's principal ally, the United States. Even the basic communications and personal visits between East and West Germany during the cold war have been denied by the North Korean regime. The Orwellian features of North Korea prohibited routine interactions with Washington, except for occasional low-level talks in Beijing and, beginning in 1988, in Geneva and New York City.

Despite the lack of normal state-to-state connections with Pyongyang, the United States has remained fully engaged with the Korean peninsula. Through ten successive American administrations of differing political stripes, Washington has maintained a close and evolving relationship with the Republic of Korea since the closing days of World War II. The United States, in fact, sponsored the birth of the ROK while the Soviet Union supported the rival DPRK north of the thirty-eighth parallel, thereby dividing Korea into two countries and tying the peninsula to the fortunes of the cold war. The Truman administration viewed North Korea's attacks on the South in June 1950 as part of the global communist conspiracy. America's intervention turned back the invasion but thus embroiled the United States in conflict with the People's Republic of China as well as North Korea. This war fixed U.S. attention on Asia to such a degree that America restored Japan to the status of friend from that of foe and signed a mutual security treaty with the ROK on October 1, 1953.

After the war, the United States continued its involvement in Korea. It provided immense economic and military aid to the South, which enabled it to recover industrially and to deter major offenses north of the demilitarized zone. For Washington, the ROK served as an outpost on the Asian mainland in the global struggle with communism. Initially, American presidents viewed South Korea as a dependent state, reliant on U.S. largesse and troops for economic development and military security. Over time, however, the patron-client relationship evolved into a partnership. South Korea's economic growth, democratic reform, and military strength changed the framework of its connection with Washington. Throughout this period, North Korea stood bellicosely apart from the southern section of the Korean peninsula and from the world itself.

The Move Away from Isolation

The collapse of the Soviet Union created a watershed among Asia-Pacific nations as well as in Eastern Europe and Central Asia. First and foremost, the demise of the Soviet system removed Pyongyang's mainstay. Without Moscow's economic and military support, the North Korean client faced a new political landscape. In the changed circumstances, South Korea's adept Nordpolitik (northern policy) undermined Pyongyang's clientage with the USSR and the PRC by expanding trade and diplomatic recognition with North Korea's communist allies.[1]

Even before the passing of his communist regime in 1991, the Gorbachev government established diplomatic relations with Seoul, thereby eliminating the North's exclusive relationship with Moscow. Likewise, China entered into diplomatic contact with South Korea, which weakened the reclusive nature of another of the North's bulwarks. The consequence of these political realignments, in effect, was the diplomatic isolation of the DPRK from its former ideological soul mates and material backers. Compounding the diplomatic estrangement from Beijing and Moscow were the economic and political transformations under way in China and Russia, which lessened their compatibility with the Stalinesque regime in Pyongyang.

Before his death, Kim Il Sung recognized that the emerging correlation of forces demanded a bold initiative to break the North's self-imposed isolation. He looked to the United States as a means to preserve his regime in the altered international environment. With possible American recognition and support, Kim would be able to prop up his contracting economy and save his regime from an implosion similar to that which had taken place east of the Elbe River after 1989. Conditions within North Korea primarily drove this search for a foreign power to rescue a faltering country. Therefore, Kim's foreign policy broke not only with his past alliances with the communist giants but also with his often-stated philosophy of *juche*, or self-reliance.

North Korea's deteriorating economy and dire food shortages placed mounting pressures on Kim's regime. Reports of increasing hardship, indeed, starvation, in the North began to circulate widely in the early 1990s. Rumors followed that the country was near collapse. Scholars, analysts, and commentators speculated on what forms a collapsed society could take. Military officers, relief experts, and politicians offered scenarios on how to deal with a flood of North Korean refugees streaming across the demilitarized zone (DMZ) or with a surprise attack from a suicidal regime making one last desperate bid to destroy its arch enemy and forcibly reunite the peninsula under its own flag. The reunification of East and West Germany only fueled discussion about the dilapidated state of communist economies as compared with free-market systems, which, observing safety and environmental codes, thereby improve the quality of their citizens' lives. The possibility of reunification of the two Koreas seemed less fanciful than in the previous era.[2]

South Korea's economic and political trajectory had ascended during the same period as the North's had plummeted. Building on its increasing economic and social well-being from the 1970s and 1980s, the South came into its own at a point when the Kim Il Sung regime appeared to be the most decrepit and out of step with the world's turn toward democracy and free markets.

The demise of the Soviet Union and its satellites in Eastern Europe initially eclipsed developments in the Asia-Pacific region. But soon these momentous events cast North Korean backwardness into sharper relief. By the early 1990s, the DPRK had grown more and more out of date. As commentators gauged the depth of the so-called third wave of democratic reform washing across the international landscape, North Korea appeared all the more surrealistic. While so many other societies adopted openness, pluralism, and free economies, North Korea seemed a stubborn and evermore dangerous anachronism in a historical sea of change. Isolation and economic decline weighed significantly in Pyongyang's shift in direction toward engagement with the United States.

Just as President Nixon courted China to gain an advantage against the Soviet Union, Kim Il Sung sought to inveigle the United States to play a role in preserving his regime and enhancing its international standing. His high-stakes

gambit worked. The Clinton administration changed American policy from reciprocal hostility to engagement, with the ultimate objective of advancing reform
and openness along the lines of the Nixon-Kissinger démarche toward China.

Background to the Bomb

As North Korea looked for new foreign arrangements to preserve
its out-of-fashion and repressive regime, it turned to unconventional, but not
irrational, means—nuclear weapons. The roots of Pyongyang's search for nuclear
armament date to the mid-1950s and stem, in part, from its perceived vulnerability after the Korean War. A self-declared embattled state, the North embarked on
the development of mass-terror weapons. The Sino-Soviet split in the next decade
added further impetus to attaining nuclear status as Pyongyang sought to sustain
itself in the competition between the two communist giants. But the DPRK's
relations with Moscow and Beijing, in turn, deteriorated as the Soviet Union
opted for "peaceful coexistence" with the West and China underwent the con-
vulsion of its Cultural Revolution. When relations improved with the USSR in
1965, Moscow resumed aid and dispatched a small (two to four megawatts) Soviet
research reactor and a laboratory, which were set up at Yongbyon. The North's
nuclear program has officially centered on this research plant. Pyongyang's nuclear efforts have brought North Korea into the web of international agreements.

In July 1977, a decade after its nuclear inauguration, Pyongyang signed a
"type 66" safeguard agreement with the International Atomic Energy Agency
(IAEA), which opened the Yongbyon research facility to international inspection.
When a U.S. satellite detected a second and larger reactor at Yongbyon around
1984, Washington sought and obtained Soviet assistance in dealing with Moscow's North Korean ally. As a signatory of the nonproliferation treaty (NPT), the
Soviet Union was obliged not to transfer nuclear weapons–related technology to
third countries. Moscow complied with Washington's request, and Pyongyang
was therefore compelled to sign the NPT on December 12, 1985, but delayed
agreeing to the IAEA's inspection until 1992. By this date, North Korea had
aroused international concerns.

By 1989, evidence had surfaced from several sources that the North had
engaged in plutonium reprocessing for weapons-grade material, had possibly
built smaller reprocessing facilities beyond Yongbyon, had established a high-
explosive test range at Yongbyon for the development of explosive casings used
for nuclear weapons, and had begun constructing a larger nuclear reactor at
Yongbyon. Washington and Seoul reacted with concern to the possibility that the
DPRK was attempting to build nuclear weapons, although most analysts thought
that the North was years away from actually possessing a bomb. Nonetheless, the

Bush administration took steps designed to encourage Pyongyang to allow nuclear inspections of its facilities or, better yet, to abandon a nuclear weapons
program.

Washington announced that it would be willing to state categorically in early
1991 that no nuclear weapons existed in South Korea. This meant that existing
nuclear weapons would be withdrawn because their presence had never been
officially acknowledged by the United States. The Bush administration also reaffirmed its security ties with South Korea in the fall of the same year. Because this
announcement took a tough line, Washington and Seoul agreed to lessen tensions by suspending the Team Spirit military maneuvers for one year. In the final
element of Bush's strategy, the United States agreed to hold direct talks with
North Korea for a single session but would allow for further sessions if Pyongyang
cooperated and permitted nuclear inspections. This four-pronged strategy of carrots and sticks achieved some success, as Kim Il Sung's government agreed to
sign IAEA inspection agreements.[3]

Earlier in the fall, a historic by-product of the U.S.-ROK strategy had taken
place with the initiation of contact between North and South Korea. This resulted in the so-called Basic Agreement (Agreement on Reconciliation, Nonaggression, and Exchanges and Cooperation Between the South and the North),
signed in December 1991. This agreement pledged the signatories to nonaggression, an effort long sought by Seoul, and called for a cessation of interference in
each other's internal affairs. The parties also promised to "recognize and respect"
each other. These statements represented profound symbolic measures. Moreover, the Basic Agreement set up a Joint Military Committee, a military hotline,
and a North-South Liaison Office.[4] Although the Basic Agreement later lapsed
because of North Korean noncompliance, it represented a diplomatic breakthrough at the time. Inspections by the International Atomic Energy Agency
began in May 1992, three months after Pyongyang agreed to them. Six inspection
visits took place before Pyongyang halted them early the next year.

This promising improvement in relations with North Korea faltered in late
1992, when Pyongyang demanded access to all U.S. military installations in
South Korea to confirm, so it said, that nuclear weapons had been removed.
South Korea, in contrast, concerned that Pyongyang would have had time to
conceal nuclear weapons before the announced IAEA inspections, wanted to
initiate short-notice inspections (known as challenge inspections) so as to uncover potential violations. The ROK was justly worried about genuine compliance, given both Pyongyang's campaign of terrorism directed against South Koreans and its violation of the NPT. Seoul had ample evidence for skepticism from
the records of both North Korea and the IAEA. Before the Persian Gulf war,
IAEA inspections in Iraq had found no evidence of Baghdad's flagrant violations
of NPT agreements. After the war, an enormous network of nuclear weapons
facilities was discovered, damaging the IAEA's reputation for uncovering violators

of the NPT. Thus, when evidence of the DPRK's cheating by reprocessing plutonium surfaced in the second half of 1992, the IAEA believed its credibility was on the line. Its informal requests for special inspections of two suspected sites at Yongbyon were turned aside. Fearing a North Korean violation, the IAEA demanded a special inspection by February 9, 1993. This represented a precedent in the IAEA's history, as the international agency had never made this demand before. Pyongyang almost immediately rejected the IAEA's order. This reaction virtually confirmed the worst suspicions that North Korea had disregarded its signatory commitment to the NPT by manufacturing weapons-grade nuclear material.

New Administrations in Washington and Seoul

By the time of North Korea's rebuff of the IAEA's request, newly elected governments in South Korea and the United States had taken office. Thus, the task of solving the nuclear imbroglio north of the DMZ passed to Kim Young Sam, head of the ROK's first democratically elected civilian government in decades, and to the Bill Clinton administration in Washington. Both concurred with their predecessors' decision to restart the Team Spirit military exercises in South Korea, despite criticism in the North that the operations were provocative. The previous Roh Tae Woo and Bush governments had argued that the Team Spirit maneuvers should be suspended for only one year, not halted indefinitely. Planning, therefore, proceeded on the joint military training operation scheduled for the first quarter of 1993.

In retaliation, Pyongyang unleashed a vitriolic campaign of words denouncing South Korea and the United States, as well as their combined training preparations. This criticism culminated on March 8, the day before the start of the Team Spirit exercise, with the declaration of "a state of war readiness for the whole country" by Kim Jong Il, commander of the Korean People's Army.[5] Hopes dimmed for a smooth resolution of the North Korean nuclear problem under the auspices of an international agency. But the international community was stunned later in the same month when North Korea announced its intention of withdrawing from the NPT. Pyongyang claimed that the Team Spirit maneuvers undermined the North-South agreement to denuclearize the peninsula. It also argued that the IAEA had become a creature of U.S. policy toward North Korea. Finally, the DPRK asserted that the United States, in fact, had not removed nuclear weapons from South Korea. In its view, these reasons justified abandoning the nonproliferation treaty within three months.

The United States undertook an international campaign to persuade Kim Il Sung not to drop out of the NPT. As Pyongyang's stated deadline for withdrawal approached, the Kim regime dropped its threat and agreed to allow IAEA inspections. Despite this change of heart, a crisis atmosphere persisted in U.S.–North Korean relations because of the fear that Pyongyang had already embarked on a nuclear weapons program.

American efforts at negotiation and the North Korean–generated tension, in fact, served Pyongyang's goals. North Korea's brinkmanship may well have had an internal rationale as well as international objectives: to break out of its self-imposed insularism by gaining concessions in the form of diplomatic recognition and economic assistance. After all, the world would be interested in ensuring stability and avoiding the political collapse of a country in possession of nuclear weapons.

North Korea's succession politics provides another explanation for Pyongyang's bluster. At that time, there was widespread speculation about the transition of power from the aging Kim Il Sung to his son, Kim Jong Il. It was the younger Kim, as head of the North Korean army, who had announced a state of war readiness in reaction to U.S.–South Korean plans to go ahead with the Team Spirit operation. It was this same Kim who, it was rumored, had pushed nuclear weapons development. Such boldness by Kim Jong Il might have been efficacious in shoring up his chances to succeed his father. During the March crisis, Han Sung-Joo, South Korea's respected foreign minister, had been quoted as saying, "This has all been Kim Jong Il's game."[6] In a sense, the status of both Kim the younger and the impoverished and backward country north of the DMZ was elevated as a result of Pyongyang's shrewd use of nuclear blackmail, a gambit whose bluff Washington was unwilling to call or reject.

For its part, Pyongyang stepped up its hostility toward the outside world. It recalled some of its overseas diplomatic delegations, expelled or denied access to foreign officials within North Korea, jammed Japanese and South Korean radio broadcasts, and broke telephone connections with Beijing. Most important, North Korea continued to refute the IAEA's charges and dug in its heels on abandoning the NPT. Although Pyongyang did agree later in the spring to the IAEA's inspection of previously opened nuclear facilities, it would not budge on the IAEA's request to check out the sites where North Korea was suspected of manufacturing weapons-grade plutonium. The North Koreans also made clear their not-so-hidden agenda—they wanted direct talks with Washington, which the Clinton administration granted. By May of Clinton's first year in office, it appeared that the crisis might be resolved with cooperation from the DPRK. Thus, the considerations of using trade sanctions and military action against the North were taken off the table.

Cold water was thrown on these feelings of optimism by the growing realization that North Korea might be secretly moving ahead to build one or more nuclear bombs. Nuclear experts publicly warned that if the North Koreans replaced the spent uranium fuel in their Yongbyon reactor, they would then have

sufficient plutonium for nuclear weapons. This pessimistic assessment resulted
in another downward lurch in the roller-coaster ride driven by Kim Il Sung. His
regime adroitly gave up enough political ground to sustain the belief that a deal
could be worked out with Pyongyang to resolve the crisis. One of these intermit-
tent signs of progress came with the scheduling of joint U.S.-DPRK talks in early
June, but Pyongyang temporarily dashed these hopes by restating its intention to
pull out of the NPT on June 12, as scheduled. Then, the day before the withdrawal date, the North Koreans reversed course and suspended their decision to
abandon the nonproliferation treaty.

The crisis continued, however, because the North Koreans still refused to
allow the IAEA to inspect the two suspect facilities. They had given enough
concessions to avoid sanctions but not enough to end the dispute, thereby continuing to engage the United States. This strategy, furthermore, was beginning to
pay off, for the United States made important concessions that indicated a willingness to strike a bargain favorable to Pyongyang. In July 1993, during talks with
Pyongyang officials, Washington representative Robert Gallucci dangled an inducement to the Kim Il Sung government to accept regular IAEA inspections
and to reenter North-South talks by offering to secure modern light water nuclear
reactors to replace the North's out-of-date graphite reactors. Ultimately, this offer
became the core of the U.S. package, which the DPRK accepted more than a
year later. Proposing it at this early date no doubt convinced Kim Il Sung to hold
out in hopes of winning even more.[7]

The Clinton administration was wedded to continuing dialogue, looking for
a way to make a deal with the North Koreans so as to put off tough policy choices
such as calling for U.N. sanctions or launching air attacks. Many in the administration believed that a trade embargo would be ineffective because of China's
unreliableness. By this time, the administration had publicly ruled out air strikes
to destroy the suspect facilities for fear of spreading airborne nuclear contamination to South Korea, China, and beyond. Moreover, because some of the nuclear
sites were hidden in secret locations, finding and destroying them presented
difficulties. The question remained as to how to end the standoff; Pyongyang's
interests were served by prolonging the crisis in hopes of obtaining a payoff
settlement for its blackmail, while Washington appeared ineffectual.

Working through the Crisis

The Clinton administration had made North Korea an object of
defense planning from its first months in office. During 1993, the Clinton defense team conducted a comprehensive review of U.S. defense requirements.
Known as the Bottom-Up Review (BUR), this reassessment formed the basis of

Clinton's 1995 defense budget and of the administration's overall strategic out-look. North Korea figured prominently in the BUR. Les Aspin, then secretary of defense, set forth in the *Report of the Bottom-Up Review* two primary military scenarios that captured attention. One scenario envisioned aggression "by Iraq against Kuwait and Saudi Arabia" and the other "by North Korea against the Republic of Korea." These two potential crises were labeled as major regional conflicts (MRCs), and the Defense Department declared that it must be prepared to fight two MRCs "nearly simultaneously." Doubts surfaced immediately and continue to this day about the American military's capability to wage two MRCs owing to drastically reduced military forces. In subsequent years, the Clinton administration has made additional cuts in defense spending. If anything, the paring of dollars from national security accounts was to North Korea's advantage. Pyongyang realized that the Clinton administration was more eager to make a deal than engage in expensive military counteractions.

To bolster his own standing in the polls as much as to forestall a war with North Korea, Clinton in mid-1993 visited Seoul, where he appeared resolute in the defense of South Korea. Throughout the fall, the crisis bubbled up with some urgency. The American and Japanese media reported a North Korean military buildup along the DMZ. The North also blocked further IAEA inspections, at first prohibiting the agency from changing film and batteries in its observing cameras within the Yongbyon facility. In yet another clever move, Pyongyang then offered to allow the resupply of film and batteries and subsequently entered into low-level talks with Seoul, as the United States had wanted. Therefore, North Korea maintained the crisis at a boil without allowing it to blow its top. The IAEA stood its ground, calling for full inspections, thereby forcing the Clinton admin-istration to adhere to IAEA standards rather than temporize on the issue of com-plete access for inspections of all sites. The midlevel talks, which began during October in New York City, stalled over the issue of full and routine inspections in the North. The IAEA's report to the United Nations resulted in a 140-to-1 vote (with China abstaining) that urged Pyongyang to cooperate with the international inspection agency.[8] More important, the IAEA verged on declaring a break in its "continuity" of monitoring North Korea. Such a decision would have triggered calls for sanctions in the United Nations and other confrontational decisions that the Clinton administration, along with Tokyo and Seoul, reportedly wanted to avoid.

At the Seattle meeting of the Asian Pacific Economic Cooperation forum, Clinton seemed open to finding a means to work around the North Korean crisis: "It was obvious to me that no one in the region wants North Korea to become a nuclear power . . . so we're going to do everything we can, in close consultation with the countries most affected in the region, to try to find a resolution to this."[9]

Along with this rise in tensions, other American officials sounded a pessimis-tic note. U.S. secretary of defense Les Aspin voiced the opinion that the nuclear issue would not be resolved without the United Nations' involvement and the implementation of sanctions against North Korea. In late 1993, even Clinton spoke somberly of the nuclear problem turning into a full-blown crisis: "I hope we can avoid one, but I am not positive that we can."[10]

Despite firebrand rhetoric emanating from North Korean officials, its spokesmen sought to keep diplomatic channels open with the United States. Administration officials continued to look for clues of a willingness to bargain. A dramatic manifestation of this tendency occurred in mid-November, when a North Korean official issued a statement that the resolution of the problem depended on "how the United States responds to our proposals for a package solution."[11] Fishing for as generous "a package solution" as possible, the North Koreans did not specify what items had to be in the deal, which placed them in the position of rejecting or accepting what was offered in an effort to leverage the package's inducements. The North Koreans' search for a package solution struck a responsive chord in Washington, where some officials sought a comprehensive resolution of the North's nuclear weapons problem. South Korea, for its part, wanted a resumption of North-South talks before the announcement of a package offer, and it wanted adequate consultation with Washington about security matters. Although discord was evident, the United States and the ROK continued to cooperate.

For the United States–ROK alliance, the year 1993 nearly ended on a note of continuing unsettledness with North Korea. Washington needed to respond to Pyongyang's broaching of the "package solution" concept. But a response was far from a simple matter. Washington was gaining a keener sense of the South's predicament. For the Kim Young Sam government, the North Korean nuclear weapons capacity approached the level of a nightmare, not just a foreign policy problem. Thus, American and South Korean reactions to Pyongyang were vastly complicated when news surfaced in U.S. newspapers in late December from a leaked Central Intelligence Agency opinion that North Korea had "probably" assembled one nuclear bomb. No longer could a policy be addressed about the possibility of the North making a nuclear device; policy now had to take into account the distinct likelihood that Pyongyang might already have built at least one nuclear bomb. The fact that North Korea was not just another incoming member to the nuclear weapons club but a paranoid, unpredictable element created a media stir in the United States.[12]

The prospect of a nuclearly armed North Korea brought up short the Clinton administration's handling of the North Korean threat, not only on the Korean peninsula but also to Northeast Asian security. North Korea's missile tests pointed to the DPRK's growing ability to hit Japan and other territories beyond the South. This realization crystallized the real stakes in a settlement of the North Korean challenge in a way that the White House had been unable or unwilling to confront. More important, Washington wanted a yardstick to measure how tough a line it should take against a rogue state bent on acquiring weapons of mass destruction. In consequence, the Clinton administration appeared vacillating, inconsistent, and unengaged in the brewing crisis in Northeast Asia. The beginning of 1994 witnessed continuing vagueness in U.S. policy toward North Korea. At the same time, Pyongyang kept stalling IAEA demands for regular and full-fledged inspections. The North held out for a token one-time inspection designed merely to preserve the "continuity" of adherence to the NPT.

Once again, North Korea stonewalled before the February 1994 meeting of the IAEA's Board of Governors, which pledged to turn the issue over to the U.N. Security Council if Pyongyang continued to block its requests for inspections. In what had become a pattern, the North, after bellicose rhetoric, agreed to limited inspections a few days before the IAEA meeting. Obfuscation soon followed as Pyongyang sent mixed messages. Finally, Washington accepted the North's offer of a one-time inspection so as to continue the NPT and also obtained Pyongyang's concurrence for a resumption of the North-South dialogue. As in the past, however, implementation fell short of initial expectations. While the DPRK negotiated with Washington and Seoul in the resumed North-South talks, the IAEA conducted its inspections in North Korea. When the DPRK failed to win its desired concessions, it walked out of the dialogue and halted this most important IAEA scrutiny. The international agency concluded that Pyongyang had indeed gone forward with nuclear weapons development. Moreover, it concluded that Pyongyang was preparing to change the spent fuel rods in its reactor, thereby gaining enough plutonium for several nuclear bombs. The replacement of the used fuel rods became, in time, the dominating issue between the United States and North Korea. Worse, as they broke off the North-South dialogue, the North Koreans launched a war of words, culminating in one official's often-quoted remark that, in the event of war, "Seoul will turn into a sea of fire."

As it turned out, the collapsed talks and blocked inspections led directly to another nadir in relations with Pyongyang. By the end of March, war on the Korean peninsula appeared imminent. On both sides army units were placed on alert, and Washington publicly reinforced U.S. units in the South with Patriot missiles. Secretly, the Pentagon began deploying additional forces in the western Pacific. Talk of utilizing preemptive military strikes against nuclear targets in North Korea circulated among American columnists and public policy analysts. But many other observers put a damper on such advice by pointing out that bombing not only would be ineffective in hitting the underground targets but also would scatter radioactive materials over a wide region of China, Japan, and South Korea, plus more distant countries.

Madeleine Albright, U.S. ambassador to the United Nations, declared that procedural wheels were in motion to bring sanctions to bear on North Korea unless it permitted routine IAEA inspections. The Clinton administration announced that it was going forward unconditionally with the joint Team Spirit military exercise. Then Washington and Seoul backed away from this concrete stand, stating that Pyongyang's cooperation could still halt the maneuvers. In the end, the Team Spirit exercise was not held. Once again the North Koreans had escalated the tension, and then, when it suited their negotiating position, they backed down. A deadly impasse had been reached and, once more, it dissolved. In this case, Pyongyang agreed to reenter a dialogue with South Korea when Seoul dropped its demand for an exchange of envoys with the North.

Throughout the spring, the IAEA sought inspection of the fuel rod replacement process involving some eight thousand spent fuel rods in Yongbyon's main reactor. Additionally, it wanted to test three hundred of the used rods to ascertain how much plutonium had been produced. Pyongyang acquiesced to inspections but not to the sampling of the used rods. It did permit the IAEA to perform limited inspections in May so as to maintain the continuity aspect of the inspection regimen. The Clinton administration sought to reward North Korea for allowing routine IAEA scrutiny, but North Korea decided to up the ante in the high-stakes nuclear game by carrying on with the defueling process despite demands by Washington, Seoul, and the IAEA for access to the unloading of irradiated fuel rods. Without the required tests of the rods, the IAEA initially argued that it was unable to set benchmarks on which to base future measurements. After other nuclear experts took issue with this view, the IAEA backed off from its totally dire prediction.[13]

To muddy the waters further, Pyongyang offered examination of the rods placed in cooling ponds. By this procedure, the North frustrated efforts to identify past diversion of plutonium for nuclear bombs but left the door open for conciliation in the future. Not knowing whether past violations had occurred or whether the DPRK had produced one or more bombs created doubt in the West about Pyongyang's intentions and capabilities. This doubt had become a negotiable commodity that the North skillfully used in its interactions with the Clinton administration. Pyongyang cunningly played on Washington's uncertainties in the months ahead. Meanwhile, analysts, columnists, and government officials observed frequently that the North's real goal was to build nuclear bombs. All the setbacks to inspections had merely been Pyongyang's delaying tactics until the weapons had been developed.

The month of June witnessed near fever-pitch tensions on the Korean peninsula. North Korea ominously warned that "sanctions mean war, and there is no mercy in war."[14] The IAEA countered by curtailing its technical assistance program, which had been in operation for almost two decades. Then the DPRK declared that it would withdraw from the IAEA and break off the continuity of inspections of its nuclear facilities. Soon afterward, the South Korean government called up army reservists for military maneuvers. South Koreans, particularly in the capital, hoarded food in anticipation of an attack from the North. Meanwhile, Washington had begun to reinforce its forces in South Korea and to forward deploy additional forces in Japan. Media coverage in the United States, especially that of CNN, whipped up the speculation that war could come at any time. These events framed Jimmy Carter's visit to Kim Il Sung.

Former President Carter had made more than one offer to travel to Pyongyang as an unofficial spokesman for the White House. It was reported that Carter was dissatisfied with American policy and the possibility that it might lead to war. Whatever his motives and those of the White House, the Carter mission defused the highly charged atmosphere on the peninsula. Carter not only deflated tensions but also reportedly engaged in deal-making on his own, which had the appearance of undermining the Clinton administration's get-tough approach and its role in developing policy toward North Korea. Carter declared, for example, that the administration's pursuit of U.N. sanctions against the North was over, although the White House had made no such announcement. Despite the reported discord in the media between the administration and the former president, the outcome of Carter's venture to North Korea in mid-June served the objectives of both Clinton and Kim Il Sung. The North Korean leader did not want to negotiate with the IAEA because it had nothing to offer for the DPRK's compliance. By dealing with the Americans, Kim could gain U.S. economic assistance and pressure on Japan, as well as a more helpful stance by South Korea.

The Carter visit cooled the crisis atmosphere surrounding the DPRK's military nuclearization program. His mission also accomplished something that the administration itself felt unable to undertake in the face of strong domestic criticism of its irresoluteness toward a North Korean nuclear menace. A high-level envoy from Washington to Pyongyang satisfied one of North Korea's objectives— direct contact with the United States rather than indirect relations through Seoul. Most important, Carter's so-called personal deal making actually allowed the Clinton administration to put its comprehensive offer to Kim Il Sung without the appearance of caving in to nuclear blackmail. The White House's bundle of incentives to North Korea had largely been worked out during the previous fall but had been withheld because of the refueling crisis. This package solution included replacing the aging graphite reactor with a light water reactor and withdrawing the U.N. sanction threat. In return, Pyongyang promised to "freeze" the processing of plutonium from the spent fuel rods, halt refueling of the nuclear reactor, continue allowing IAEA inspections, and reopen direct talks with South Korea.

Kim Il Sung Exits

Soon after Carter had left Pyongyang, the Clinton administration lost little time in solidifying the former president's diplomatic effort. It first sought to obtain written confirmation of Kim Il Sung's oral response to Carter. An affirmative reply came from Kang Sok Ju, North Korea's first vice foreign minister. Through Robert Gallucci, then U.S. ambassador-at-large, the Clinton administration next moved, despite temporary roadblocks, to clinch the deal that Carter carried to Kim. Both sides agreed to schedule talks for July 8, but on that very day, Kim Il Sung died at the age of eighty-two from a reported heart attack. This development resulted in a temporary delay in the scheduled Geneva talks, which resumed at the end of July. The next month in Geneva saw the acceptance of the "agreed statement" by both negotiating parties. It represented both a breakthrough and a foundation leading to the Agreed Framework two months later.

The Agreed Framework embodied the package carried by Carter to Kim Il Sung. Thus, it codified the bargain that North Korea would replace its graphite reactors with light water reactors, while the United States pledged to secure these new power plants, funding for which ultimately came mainly from South Korea. In return, North Korea promised to suspend the building of two reactors (one, at 200-megawatts electric and the other, 50 megawatts). The Agreed Framework also detailed that North Korea was to receive an alternative fuel once it canceled construction of the two graphite reactors until the new light water reactors were completed. North Korea stipulated that it would forgo reprocessing and allow the IAEA to monitor the closing of the Radiochemical Laboratory.

In a broader political context, the two sides stood prepared to "move toward full normalization of political and economic relations" by first establishing diplomatic representatives in their respective capitals and later reducing trade and investment barriers. Washington also expressed a willingness to pledge nuclear nonaggression. For its part, the Pyongyang government accepted NPT strictures. The major outstanding issue between the two negotiating parties remained the timing of the special inspections of the North's nuclear facilities beyond Yongbyon. The agreed statement broke through much of the impasse between the United States and North Korea over the nuclear issues. Still, there was no clear sailing before the final accord was signed in Geneva.

One major problem developed when sharp criticism of the U.S.-DPRK Agreed Framework was voiced by South Korean president Kim Young Sam. In an interview with the *New York Times*, President Kim lashed out at the Clinton administration for being naive and overly flexible toward Pyongyang's nuclear position. Frustrated by South Korea's exclusion from the U.S.-DPRK talks, Kim said, "The important thing is that the United States should not be led on by the manipulations of North Korea." He argued that "time is on our side" and that "we should not make more concessions in the future."[15] The South Korean president recognized in his verbal assault that the Clinton administration had fundamentally shifted policy toward North Korea. It had changed from isolation (a hands-off approach) to engagement in hopes of reforming North Korea.

But there were discordant views within the South Korean government. Foreign Minister Han Sung-Joo was considered to be a moderate who backed the agreement, but the national security adviser, Chung Chong Wook, was viewed as tough-minded toward the nuclear statement and subsequent negotiations. The National Assembly also lacked cohesion on the proper approach to North Korea. Some South Korean newspapers criticized Kim Young Sam's government of inconsistency and political gamesmanship. Much of the discontent stemmed from a realization that Pyongyang had attained a measure of success in dealing directly with Washington to achieve its goal of partnership with the United States or at least weakening South Korea's exclusive relationship with America. The Clinton administration, for its part, demonstrated impatience with its longtime ally.[16] The White House, nonetheless, pushed on with its negotiations with Pyongyang.

On October 16, 1994, the United States and the DPRK entered into the Agreed Framework in Geneva. Based on the earlier agreed statement, the accord was a complex document with several provisions and a three-phased implementation. North Korea agreed to "freeze" its current nuclear program in exchange for up-to-date nuclear reactors. Specifically, it halted operation of its thirty-megawatt reactor and two five-megawatt Soviet-designed reactors, stopped its reprocessing facility, and refrained from further construction of the two planned graphite reactors and reprocessing centers. It also agreed to store the eight thousand spent fuel rods in special containers and to allow regular IAEA inspections as stipulated under the provisions of the nonproliferation treaty. The IAEA was designated to monitor compliance.

North Korea realized several political objectives by entering into the Agreed Framework. First, the DPRK received a U.S. promise not to employ nuclear weapons against it. To some Americans, this may appear to be a case of misplaced fear because the likelihood of Washington dropping atomic bombs on North Korea seemed remote. But to North Korea it may have loomed large ever since President Eisenhower's secretary of state, John Foster Dulles, had made a threat to use nuclear weapons to end the Korean War. Pyongyang also achieved a major goal of wider and direct trade and political contacts with Washington. The United States and the DPRK agreed to set up liaison offices (diplomatic centers of lesser status than embassies) in each other's capitals. The North agreed to resume an ongoing high-level dialogue with the South, a provision that Pyongyang has failed to honor as of this writing.

To achieve Clinton's stated objective of "a nuclear-free Korean peninsula," the administration pledged to secure the funding for two thousand-megawatt light water reactors, at an estimated cost of more than $4 billion, to replace three planned reactors. This reactor swap benefited the North because the two replacement reactors possessed the capacity to produce more than ten times the energy of the three planned reactors. South Korea, despite the North's strong opposition, became the primary builder and financier of the reactor's construction. In June 1995, the North Koreans finally accepted the fact that the reactors were to be of

South Korean manufacture. But even then, they insisted that a U.S. firm be named program coordinator. In the meantime, the United States, South Korea, and Japan had established the Korean Energy Development Organization (KEDO) as an international consortium to construct and pay for the reactors. KEDO, as expected, was managed by Seoul, just as South Korean companies were to play the central role in construction of the reactors. The United States also pledged to secure fuel oil for North Korea to fulfill its energy needs until the new reactor came on-line. This fuel supply was planned to reach half a million metric tons annually by the second year of the agreement. Since the agreement, Washington has urged Tokyo and Seoul to pay for a greater share of the oil costs.

Pyongyang pledged in the second phase of the agreement to allow the IAEA to undertake its special inspections of the North's two nuclear waste sites when the first light water reactor (LWR) neared completion but before the North received "key nuclear components." Estimates placed this time frame between the years 2000 and 2003. During the third and final phase of the agreement, KEDO would complete construction of the second reactor. Between the completion of the first and second LWRs after 2003, the dismantling of the thirty-megawatt reactor, two graphite reactors, and the reprocessing facility would take place.[17] Two problems arose as a result. First, the North would be allowed to keep possession of the spent fuel rods for about a decade, until after the completion of the second replacement reactor. Thus, it still could have access to the plutonium from the rods. Second, the new LWR would also generate plutonium. Both factors worried those inside and outside the Clinton administration.

Concerns about the Agreed Framework

A North Korea still in possession of a nuclear weapons capability left many experts critical of the Clinton-brokered deal. Critics charged that Pyongyang had violated the NPT by stonewalling IAEA inspections and by possibly producing bombs from nuclear facilities that were obligated, by the treaty, to be used solely as peaceful sources of energy. By the Geneva deal, the United States rewarded a state that had flagrantly breached the NPT provisions by not allowing IAEA inspections and possibly developing fission weapons. Moreover, the critics argued, how could Washington and the international community trust the DPRK? Under the agreed provisions, North Korea would receive aid for five to ten years before it had to comply with its promises. They wondered whether the North could be trusted until the inspections would begin. Other dissenters objected to the suspension of the Team Spirit exercise without a quid pro quo from Pyongyang.

Pundits also questioned the timing of the agreement, which was signed a few weeks before the November 1994 congressional elections in the United States. They argued that Clinton simply wanted to remove the unresolved North Korean issue from the nation's consciousness, lest it become a referendum for the electorate's judgment of his handling of foreign policy. Clinton had often been criticized for determining foreign policy decisions solely on the basis of domestic political considerations. The Somali withdrawal and the Haitian intervention, for example, had resulted from strong internal pressures. Nevertheless, the Geneva bargain spared the United States a potentially expensive involvement on the Korean peninsula through either outright conflict or continued military tension. The distant day of reckoning when Pyongyang would have to comply with the inspection terms of the agreement would come only after President Clinton had left office after a projected second term. Thus, his successor would have to confront any nuclear crisis arising after the deadline had lapsed.

In the meantime, North Korea will receive reactors capable of generating larger quantities of weapons-grade material than the old Soviet models. The agreement also left North Korea free to design, build, and sell ballistic missiles abroad. The sale of North Korean missiles to Middle Eastern states has been a continuing problem for the United States, as well as for Israel and moderate Arab countries threatened by Iran and Iraq.

By renouncing nuclear arms, North Korea avoided the extreme pariah status assumed by Iraq and Libya. It did not escape all U.S. censure, however. The U.S. Department of State continues to list the DPRK among the same seven states around the world that sponsor international terrorism.[18]

Placing North Korea on the "states sponsoring terrorism" list, however, hardly serves as a stick to compensate for the carrots being offered to the DPRK. Nor could it be construed as an inducement to lure the North into the international community or into reopening talks with the South. In addition to being an accurate designation for the North Korean regime, it may help allay Seoul's suspicions that Washington had moved much too fast in approaching the rogue state north of the DMZ.

Among the chief concerns raised by critics was the bad international precedent established by the Geneva agreement. While furnishing a terrorist state with a modern nuclear capacity, could Washington bar other states from selling nuclear components to similar pariah states? Early the following year, Russia's then foreign minister, Andrei V. Kozyrev, publicly stated that the Agreed Framework provided the necessary rationale for Moscow's decision to sell nuclear reactors and equipment for enriching uranium to Iraq.[19] German officials also felt justified in building a nuclear reactor in Iraq. The German firm Siemens proposed to construct a nuclear plant under conditions similar to those that the United States found acceptable in the DPRK. When Washington pressed Berlin to suspend the Siemens plan, the Germans dropped the idea, estimating that the political costs were too high.[20]

The Kim Jong Il Era

Students of history at some future point might speculate on the differing policies of father and son Kim. But the interim judgment is that there is a seamless continuity in the foreign policy of the two regimes. The nuclear agreement begun under Kim Il Sung, in fact, was concluded by Kim Jong Il. Perhaps it would have been of a different nature had Kim senior lived. Or the timing of the conclusion might have been different. Without additional information from North Korean sources, however, an outsider is justified in seeing a continuation of policy between father and son.

More important, the policy of contact initiated by the older Kim has continued under the new regime. The incoming Kim Jong Il government based its credibility on agreement and engagement with the outside world, particularly the United States. These efforts paralleled the nuclear brinkmanship of his father, but Kim Jong Il's maneuvers lacked the deadly magnitude of the prior nuclear blackmail. Instead, they took the form of border provocations. The first such example occurred in late 1994, when a U.S. Army helicopter was shot down and one of the two crewmen was killed.[21] Other incidents entailed repeatedly sending large numbers of heavily armed troops into the DMZ in April 1996, which constituted serious violations of the 1953 armistice agreement. In May, North Korea dispatched troops to fire their weapons in the DMZ, a more flagrant breach of the United Nations–brokered armistice. These incursions presented dramatic evidence of the North's long-held criticism of the armistice, which it wanted to scrap and replace with a peace treaty involving the United States.

Pyongyang announced that it would no longer adhere to the armistice and then dispatched truckloads of soldiers to conduct military exercises in the joint security area at Panmunjom. The North Korean Central News Agency declared that the North would not continue to carry out its duty "concerning maintenance and control" of the area. It added that the North Korean army was undertaking "self-defensive measures." This series of moves took place two years after Pyongyang's withdrawal from the armistice commission that oversees the truce. South Korean president Kim Young Sam called them "intentional, provocative acts according to a willful and long-term conception" and responded by placing ROK forces on an elevated alert status.[22]

The April incursions occurred just days before South Korea's parliamentary elections. As such, observers likened them to the Chinese missile provocations aimed at disrupting Taiwan's first direct democratic elections for the presidency in March. If the DPRK did follow Beijing's heavy-handed saber rattling, then it suffered a similar fate to that of mainland China, as the military provocations backfired in both cases. In Taiwan, Lee Teng-hui, who had been the target of Chinese threats, won the election decisively. In South Korea, President Kim's

New Korea Party lost its majority in the National Assembly but avoided a fall from power by retaining enough seats to form a coalition with independent-minded legislators. Most analysts concluded that the North Korean military maneuvers had convinced enough voters to cast their ballots for stability and for the New Korea Party to preserve its shaky hold on the country.[23]

Yet, during the course of the DMZ incidents, Pyongyang decided to comply with the Agreed Framework by beginning the process of safely storing the eight thousand spent uranium fuel rods. North Korea announced to the IAEA that it had begun to pull the rods out of the cooling pound and place them in secure steel canisters. The North Korean government, however, continued to refuse the IAEA access to the rods. Without samples taken from the rods, the IAEA could not accurately determine whether any material had been used to make bombs.[24]

In the midst of North Korean border provocations, the Clinton administration unveiled an ambitious initiative toward Pyongyang. Meeting on the Cheju Island resort off the South Korean coast, President Bill Clinton and President Kim Young Sam proposed to hold four-party talks to resolve the impasse on the Korean peninsula. After the summit discussion, the two presidents called for representatives from North Korea, China, South Korea, and the United States to hold a joint meeting "as soon as possible and without preconditions." The announcement stated: "The purpose would be to initiate a process aimed at achieving a permanent peace agreement."[25] This reworked initiative represented another effort to replace the forty-three-year-old armistice with a treaty. Similar efforts in 1989 and 1991 had been unsuccessful when the North Koreans failed to respond positively to attempts to engage them.

A few days before the public announcement, Washington and Seoul had communicated their proposal directly to Beijing and indirectly, through Indonesia, to Pyongyang. Although China signaled its openness to the proposal, North Korea remained silent. But U.S. and ROK officials were heartened by the North's willingness to study the proposal and not reject it out of hand. An unattributed statement from Pyongyang's Korean Central News Agency argued that "the outdated armistice agreement should be replaced by a peace agreement."

The American and South Korean optimism about the U.S.-ROK proposal was fueled by reported progress at the U.S.-DPRK talks in Berlin aimed at freezing North Korean missile sales. A few days after the Cheju proposal, the American representatives characterized the beginning of the talks as a "useful start." They disclosed that the United States had evidence of Pyongyang's export of missiles to Iran and Syria. Washington held that the talks were preliminary, but it hoped for eventual DPRK membership in the Missile Technology Control Regime, an arms control agreement.[26]

Washington initiated further contact with Pyongyang by paying the North Koreans $2 million in May 1996 for their help in recovering the remains of U.S. soldiers killed during the Korean War. This first agreement paved the way for a

joint operation in North Korea to uncover additional remains of American ser-
vicemen.[27] The North Koreans, taking advantage of Washington's willingness to
barter, made their own requests to Clinton officials. In July, North Korean officials asked the U.S. State Department for financial aid in return for their entry
into discussions over the American–South Korean initiative toward creating a
permanent peace agreement to replace the 1953 armistice. Kim Jong Il had
learned well the technique his father had employed so artfully during the nuclear
crisis.

The Clinton administration took additional step-by-step efforts to improve
relations with the Kim Jong Il government. Washington showed its willingness to
aid North Korea's hunger plight following the disastrous summer floods along
the Amnuk River during 1995. Representatives from the United States, Japan,
and South Korea met in Hawaii in January 1996 to discuss food aid. Differences
emerged between Washington and Seoul. The South Korean government
wanted more strings attached to food assistance than did the United States, be-
lieving that the food intended for starving civilians would actually be diverted to
the DPRK military. After the meeting, Washington disclosed that it would give
$2 million to the World Food Program, a U.N. agency, to aid flood victims in
North Korea.

These efforts continued the Clinton administration's policies of engagement
through economic inducements. At best, they represented a policy of rewarding
bad behavior and, at worst, a form of appeasement that set precedents carrying
beyond the Korean peninsula. For its part, the Kim Jong Il government continued its policy of alternating between confrontation and conciliation in order to
gain rewards. To date, the strategy has reaped benefits for the embattled regime.
In the short run, North Korea seems to have survived the vicissitudes of the
transition to the post–cold war era. In the long run, however, the regime's survival
is open to question.

Kim Jong Il's foreign policy, whether judged over the long haul as continuous with or changed from that of Kim Il Sung, embraces the state's survival in a
manner substantially different from the foreign policy of most countries. So far,
Kim Jong Il has carried out the international policy changes initiated by his father
to engage the United States. The unconventional means employed by the North
to gain attention reflect its unorthodox nature. As a state with few conventional
assets, such as internationally competitive goods or openness to entrepreneurial
enterprise and foreign investment, it has utilized measures that mirror its inherent domestic characteristics. Its international use of terror, military truculence,
and secrecy derive from the regime's internal repressive policies. Like Mao Zedong, the two Kims have practiced "tension diplomacy" or "limited belligerency"
to win international prestige. But they have also looked increasingly to the outside
world for material support, as a derivative of their rogue behavior. The North
Koreans have every incentive to sell missiles, fissile material, and even nuclear

bombs, thereby cheating on the Agreed Framework. These sales will bring re-turns in the form of hard currency, fuel, or other desperately need commodities, which will prop up the rickety regime along with its international standing.

Few regimes have so calculatedly used military threats in international ne-gotiations for diplomatic and economic gain. The irony of Pyongyang's success is that, if it were expanded into greater gains in international investment, eco-nomic growth, and international exchange, then it would drive an opening wedge of change into North Korea's self-contained society. International success will bring domestic change—something that the North has fiercely resisted. Pyongyang, therefore, must press its skillful foreign policy with care, lest too much success undermine the regime's political elite.

Notes

1. Chae-Jin Lee, "U.S. Policy toward South Korea," in *Korea Briefing*, ed. Donald Clark (Boulder, Colo.: Westview Press, 1993), p. 59.

2. For an illustration of the type of discussion generated by the German reunification, see *One Korea? Challenges and Prospects for Reunification*, ed. Thomas H. Henriksen and Kyongsoo Lho (Stanford: Hoover Institution Press, 1994).

3. Michael J. Mazarr, *North Korea and the Bomb: A Case Study in Nonproliferation* (New York: St. Martin's Press, 1995), p. 43.

4. Chae-Jin Lee, *China and Korea: Dynamic Relations* (Stanford: Hoover Institution Press, 1996), pp. 123 and 170.

5. Mazarr, *North Korea and the Bomb*, p. 98.

6. David E. Sanger, "Son of North Korean Leader May Be Succeeding to Power," *New York Times*, March 25, 1993, p. A10.

7. Robert Gallucci, "U.S.-North Korea Talks on the Nuclear Issue," *U.S. Department of State Dispatch* 4, no. 30 (July 26, 1996): 535–36.

8. Mazarr, *North Korea and the Bomb*, p. 133.

9. Douglas Jehl, "Clinton May Dilute Threats against North Korea: Seoul Is Wor-ried," *New York Times*, November 23, 1993, p. A3.

10. Jeffrey H. Birnbaum, "Clinton 'Not Positive' U.S. Can Avoid Crisis in Showdown with North Korea," *Wall Street Journal*, December 9, 1993, p. A8.

11. David E. Sanger, "U.S. Revises Approach to Disarming North Korea," *New York Times*, November 22, 1995, p. A5.

12. For a typical reaction, see Richard K. Betts, *New York Times*, December 31, 1993, p. A15.

13. Mazarr, *North Korea and the Bomb,* pp. 154–58.

14. Michael R. Gordon, "North Korea Is Said to Have Nuclear Fuel," *New York Times,* June 8, 1994, p. A6, and David E. Sanger, "South Korean Worries Transcend the Bomb," *New York Times,* June 12, 1994, p. A8.

15. James Sterngold, "South Korea President Lashes Out at U.S.," *New York Times,* October 8, 1994, p. A3.

16. Steve Glain and Karen Elliott House, "Kim, Moderating His Earlier Comments, Praises State of South Korea-U.S. Ties," *Wall Street Journal,* October 11, 1994, p. A15, and Andrew Pollack, "Anxious Seoul Reconsiders Its Foe," *New York Times,* November 6, 1994, p. A3.

17. Agreed Framework Between the United States of America and the Democratic People's Republic of Korea, Geneva, October 21, 1994. The agreement is cited in *Foreign Broadcast Information Service—East Asia,* October 24, 1994, pp. 34 and 35, and *Arms Control Today* 24, no. 10 (December 1994): 23–24.

18. "U.S. Accuses 7 Nations of Aiding Terrorists," *New York Times,* May 5, 1996, p. A7.

19. Steven Greenhouse, "Russia to Sell Reactors to Iran Despite U.S. Fears," *New York Times,* February 25, 1995, p. A4, and interview with former Russian minister of foreign affairs Andrei V. Kozyrev, Hoover Institution, May 13, 1996.

20. Charles Lane, "Germany's New Ostpolitik," *Foreign Affairs* 74, no. 6 (November–December 1995): 84.

21. Andrew Pollack, "North Koreans Free U.S. Pilot Held 13 Days," *New York Times,* December 30, 1994, p. A1.

22. Nicholas D. Kristof, "North Korea Sends Troops into DMZ: Seoul Raises Alert," *New York Times,* April 7, 1996, p. A3.

23. Andrew Pollack, "South Korea's Ruling Party Trips but Does Not Fall in Elections," *New York Times,* April 12, 1996, p. A7.

24. "North Korea Said to Store Spent Nuclear Fuel Better," *New York Times,* May 3, 1996, p. A6.

25. "Four-Nation Peace Talks," *Korea Newsreview* 25, no. 16 (April 20, 1996): 6–7.

26. "U.S. Is Optimistic at North Korean Talks," *New York Times,* April 21, 1996, p. A8.

27. "North Korea Is Paid for Aid on M.I.A.'s," *New York Times,* May 2, 1996, p. A7.

Index

Other Asian Studies Titles from Hoover Institution Press

China and Korea: Dynamic Relations
Chae-Jin Lee

One Korea? Challenges and Prospects for Reunification
Thomas H. Henriksen and Kyongso Lho, editors

Shaping a New Economic Relationship:
The Republic of Korea and the United States
Jongryn Mo and Ramon H. Myers, editors

The Effect of Japanese Investment on the World Economy:
A Six-Country Study, 1970–1991
Leon Hollerman and Ramon H. Myers, editors

The Communist Party of China and Marxism,
1921–1985, A Self-Portrait
Laszlo Ladany

Prescriptions for Saving China:
Selected Writings of Sun Yat-sen
Julie Lee Wei, Ramon H. Myers,
and Donald G. Gillin, editors

The Storm Clouds Clear Over China:
The Memoir of Ch'en Li-fu, 1900–1993
Sidney H. Chang and Ramon H. Myers, editors